Balancing Needs of People and Organizations:
The Linking Elements Concept

Balancing Needs of People and Organizations:

The Linking Elements Concept

by Erwin Rausch

The Bureau of National Affairs, Inc. Washington, D.C.

Library of Congress Cataloging in Publication Data

Rausch, Erwin, 1923-
  Balancing needs of people and organizations.

  Includes index.
  1. Management by objectives. 2. Organizational behavior. 3. Management. I. Title.
HD31.R34   658.4   78-62297
ISBN 0-87179-274-5

Printed in the United States of America
International Standard Book Number: 0-87179-274-5

Foreword

BY GORDON L. LIPPITT*

The continual search for compatibility between organization and individual success is being constantly explored by management, behavioral scientists, and practitioners. The kind of organizational system which manifested itself early in history frequently exhibited a high degree of control by managerial coercion that is no longer meeting the needs of today's organized society or the individuals in it. The rapid changes in society have brought with them changes in organizational systems and need for even greater change in management practices. One of the most apparent changes has been that of control through benevolence, persuasion, and other methods. Whether viewed from the paternalism of organizations in the 30s and 40s in the United States or the "sell-the-other-fellow" approach used by sales and pseudo-human relations advocates in the 50s and 60s, such an approach has been very much in evidence in the leadership of industrial, governmental, social, and civic organizations.

There is, however, a third way in which influence can be manifested in organizational life. This has been referred to as the "helping" approach in work relations; it exists where one finds the consultative organizational system at work.

In a sense, the linking of organizational success and individual growth and accomplishment is at the core of the consultative system. Erwin Rausch's *Balancing Needs of People and Organizations: The Linking Elements Concept* is a practical application of the consultative or helping idea and is dedicated to bridging the gap between organizational and individual success.

The need for links between the organization and the individual is expressed in Reinhold Niebuhr's work, *Moral Man and*

*Dr. Gordon L. Lippitt is Professor, School of Government and Business Administration, The George Washington University, and founder and Board Chairman of Organization Renewal, Inc., Project Associates, Inc., and the International Consultants Foundation.

Immoral Society, which points out that we are desirous of qualifying as moral by caring only for persons. If we are to have a
moral society, then we must also care for institutions. We tend
to criticize the bureaucratic and impersonal organization of
today; but my thesis is that it is our attitude and level of caring
about the "system" that needs criticism and improvement. The
essence of *Balancing Needs of People and Organizations* is trying to
contribute to this goal.

The value of the coercive, benevolent, or consultative ways
of influencing others is measured by the degree to which they
contribute to the ability of persons to achieve goals and meet
needs of both the individual and the organization. In an organization, the ability of others to help one meet one's needs and
achieve results is a very important aspect of modern management.

Argyris, in a pioneering work,* points out some significant
incompatabilities between individual personality growth and
the organizational system. As he states it: "If the principles of
formal organization are used as ideally defined, then the employees will tend to work in an environment where (1) they are
provided minimal control over their work-a-day world, (2) they
are expected to be passive, dependent, subordinate, (3) they are
expected to have a short-time perspective, (4) they are induced
to perfect and value the frequent use of a few superficial abilities, and (5) they are expected to produce under conditions
leading to psychological failure." In describing the maturation
of personality, Argyris refers to the fact that as an individual
grows from childhood to adulthood, he or she moves from passivity to a more active social role, from dependence on one's
environment to independence, from specialized functioning to
flexibility, and from a subordinate to a "supraordinate" position in life.

The concept and practices in many organizations are such
as to delimit the opportunity for individual growth. Even organizations with lofty ideals and purposes—such as church,
health, welfare, and educational systems—while giving "lip
service" to the practice of something they refer to as "democratic management," actually execute only the rather obvious,
good-intentioned kind of concern for others that may develop

*Argyris, C., *The Individual and Organization: Some Problems of Mutual Adjustment,*
ADMINISTRATIVE SCIENCE QUARTERLY, VOL. 2, No. 1, 1957.

dependency and warmth but limits the individual's growth to achieve his or her highest needs.

In some approaches we find the control by "systems" that will determine the goals and standardize the process to use in achieving these goals. These approaches do not solve the dilemma of linking individual and organizational needs.

Over the years I have maintained that the consultative system of management is the most promising one. Let me identify some of its characteristics and discuss its relationship to the Linking Elements concept. In the consultative system:

1. *The organization is viewed as an organism, not as a machine.* Implicit in this characteristic is the reality that an organism must adapt to exist. It must change its functioning to meet new needs. In this context, the organization is seen not just as a formal structure, but as a living, flexible, changing, and complex network of relationships among people to achieve both individual and organizational goals. The Linking Elements concept, when applied, appears to facilitate such dynamic behavior of an organization through flexible goal setting and through the processes which bring improved balance of organizational and individual needs. The organization adjusts to the characteristics of its members as much as individuals adapt to their environment.

2. *Provision is made in the organization for widespread decision-making by many members of the organization rather than centralized decision-making by top management.* The process of involving persons in the decisions which they will implement is an important aspect of a consultative process. Obviously, all persons will not be involved in every decision, even though effective communication is one level of involvement. The degree of participation will depend on forces in the situation, forces in the leader, and forces in the subordinate or member. The skills and actions described in *Balancing Needs of People and Organizations* cover these points in a detailed, practical way.

3. *Mutual confidence is the basis for cooperation rather than authority-obedience.* A consultative relationship is built upon the confidence persons have in one another's integrity, goal orientation, and commitment to a problem-solving process. Such confidence does not need to depend upon authority or status in the organization for its success. Managers who follow the Linking Elements concept establish such a relationship without unnecessary reliance on authority.

4. *Persons are seen as members of groups rather than as individuals in assigned "boxes" in the organization*. Recent research has given a great deal of recognition to the importance of the group as the key functional unit in the organization. This has been made particularly evident from productivity and morale studies in numerous types of organizations. These studies clearly indicate that if an organization is to make the maximum use of its human resources and meet both the organizational and individual needs, it will best come to fruition in situations where the individual relates effectively in well-knit and tight face-to-face work units which provide the consultative relationship between leader and members.

Such emphasis on the group is an aid to individual growth and development as well as effective work output. To develop such teamwork relations is one of the goals of the consultative organizational process. A unit manager who follows the Linking Elements concept develops such an effective small group, and the larger organization, which is composed of many such groups, gains in the process.

5. *Development-centered leadership is emphasized over task-centered concerns*. Many factors in the traditional organizational pattern cause the persons in an organization to be seen as the "doers of work." The task is the important concern of the manager. In the consultative approach, the leader sees the major responsibility as the development in others of adult patterns of self-control, the development of effective work-group functioning, and focusing on "person-centered" accountability to "release" the potential of others to achieve. Fortunately, this kind of supervision fits the job to the person rather than the person to the job description. Here again, the Linking Elements concept is completely in step with the consultative approach, especially through the solid and somewhat revolutionary approach to performance evaluation which it proposes.

In the area of performance improvement, the supervisor will make possible opportunities for the person to set "targets" for good achievement, work standards, and personal growth. Through the "target-setting" type of experience individuals meet their task goals in terms of their own drives, standards, and needs.

6. *There is a two-way flow of communication with appropriate "feedback" opportunities rather than a one-way pattern of communication*. Among the assumptions underlying the consultative sys-

tem is the importance of the two-way process of communication which is found in both the formal and informal aspect of organization life. Opportunities to see oneself and the effect of one's work are a prime necessity for effectively achieving organizational goals. The need for a "feedback" communication system is essential. In the practical application of the Linking Elements concept many requirements for two-way communications exist in goals reviews, in rule setting and the resolution of coordination problems, in establishing personal development plans, and in the strategies which lead to an improved climate for satisfying psychological needs.

Each individual and each group needs a feedback process. Individuals need accurate information about the difference between what they are trying to do and how well they are doing it. They need this information to correct or change their actions. Then, basically, they are steering themselves. An organization, through its policies, its philosophy, and the practices of its management, can develop the climate of acceptance of the appropriate skills to permit this level of interpersonal communication.

IMPLICATIONS FOR THE ORGANIZATION

The goals of the consultative system are as follows:

1. *To develop clearly the objectives of the organization so that standards of work relations can be relevant to these objectives.* A number of organizational theorists and practitioners have written about "management by objectives." As discussed in *Balancing Needs of People and Organizations*, when managing with goals becomes a way of life for an organization, then supervisor-subordinate relationships develop in such a way that the goals of individuals are given the same weight as the organizational goals.

2. *To focus training of management at all levels on the ability of leaders to develop a collaborative relationship with their superiors, peers, and subordinates.* The supervisor should be seen by subordinates as a helper, trainer, consultant, and coordinator. To help supervisors satisfy all these roles in a sensitive, insightful, and diagnostic manner, the necessary skills should be at the heart of an ongoing supervisory development program in which each manager assumes the responsibility of helping subordinates achieve their potential. The Linking Element concept can suggest specific techniques—for example, in aligning technical competence, in goals reviews, and in performance evalua-

tion—which supervisors and managers can use to fulfill their responsibilities.

3. *To develop a performance-improvement process along with appraisal and manpower inventory procedures that are consistent with the organization's philosophy, goals, rewards, and training/development program.* Continued growth by the individual on the job is the responsibility of each individual, work unit, and supervisor. If a consultative organization system is to work, there must be present opportunities for individuals in the organization to set their performance standards and, together with their supervisors, to try to achieve, revise, and secure "feedback" on the objectives so set. This jointly fostered growth is separate from the process of appraisal by superiors and the need for organizational management to have an inventory of persons to fill positions from within the organization. The goals of an organization, the personnel (rewards system) policy, and training programs of the organization must be understood by all, and there must be a commitment to the consultative organizational process if the process is to work effectively and influence the direction in which an organization is developing.

SUMMARY

Balancing Needs of People and Organizations: The Linking Elements Concept outlines the ways in which an organization can integrate management science, the management cycle, and MBO in a helpful way to achieve the goals of the consultative system. The consultative system applies when a combination of self-control, member responsibility, accountability, and scientific method are ingredients of problem solving. Where these do not exist, the authority structure has to be brought into action, at least partially, until sound policies bring conditions which allow full use of potentially more promising management styles.

In a society where we have reached the highest standard of living in history, it seems appropriate that higher levels of organizational functioning are realistic and possible. The strength of democracy is directly proportioned to the practice of it by its citizen leaders. So we must work to achieve those kinds of leadership behavior and organizational climate that can provide for optimum individual growth while attaining the objectives of the organization. In the pages that follow the readers will find realistic and helpful concepts and tools to achieve this goal.

GORDON L. LIPPITT

Acknowledgments

Many people have contributed to the preparation of this book and to the development of the Linking Elements concept.

First of all, I must acknowledge the contributions of the many management scientists and behavioral scientists on whose work the Linking Elements concept is built. There are very few thoughts in the entire book that are entirely new. Its value, I hope, will come from the new perspective it provides on the important work which others have done.

An almost equally important contribution to the development of the Linking Elements concept was made by over two thousand working managers at all organizational levels who participated in seminars in which the entire concept or portions of it were presented. The thoughtful questions, suggestions, and criticisms of these men and women helped to sharpen the ideas so that they can be applied more readily to the problems and opportunities which managers face daily.

I am indebted to the training and development managers in client organizations whose confidence in the concept made the seminars possible. They include: Chester Babcock, Richard Babeu, William Berendsen, Jules Borshadel, Joseph Burrell, Edward Callahan, Jay Canna, Ellie Goodwin, Ben Grage, Sister Antonia Grondin, Burton Helgeson, Hillary Hemans, Ronald Hermone, Dennis Hubbard, Betty Jones, Charles Markey, Robert McGrath, Kenneth Michel, Richard Mischke, Boyd Murray, Toni O'Connell, George Oliver, Bruce Rovinsky, John Sisson, Joseph Toomey, and Arthur Weren. Ron Hermone, furthermore, contributed segments of Chapter 9.

Eli Levine contributed many valuable thoughts to the segments on recognition and the satisfaction of psychological needs.

The concept and the book would not exist today if it were not for the help I have received from my associates at Didactic Systems: Harvey Lieberman, whose work with the concept from its inception has added many important points; my wife Grace, whose support was so crucial especially during the early days; and the other staff members, who contributed ideas and edited and typed the manuscript. They include: Maryann Burke, Donna Dzury, Pat Forbes, Helen Gmitro, Lois Nemeth, Maria Menna Perper, Charlotte Peterson, Pearl Ricklis, Cindy Schmitt, Sonya Stelmasky, Rob Wederich, and Joyce Wanca.

These acknowledgments would be incomplete if I did not give full credit to Dr. Leonard Nadler, whose contributions to the science and art of human resource development are well known, for his many detailed and incisive suggestions and concepts on the manuscript, and to Paul Amidei and Don Farwell of the Bureau of National Affairs, the publisher. Of course, any shortcomings in reasoning or elucidation as well as any errors of omission or commission are solely mine.

ERWIN RAUSCH

Table of Contents

List of Illustrations

Figures

Tables

Chapter 1

The Linking Elements Concept:
Introduction and Overview

This is a book for managers* about effectiveness on the job. It is not necessarily for all managers but only those, at all levels, who are willing to devote considerable effort to the pursuit of greater competence. If you are such a manager, you will undoubtedly find many useful ideas as you read on. They will require serious study, however, because the model that will be presented in the following pages is complex.

This book offers a thorough and comprehensive framework—not a simplistic picture. It does not suggest easy solutions to problems. It does provide a roadway through the complex issues which face managers who wish to improve the performance of their organizational units.

THE LINKING ELEMENTS CONCEPT DEFINED

The Linking Elements concept, which is the core of the book, is an attempt to synthesize theory and practical experience into a workable, though difficult, guide to action. It combines the thinking of behavioral scientists and management theorists with the viewpoint of the operating manager. Thus, it offers a systematic, practical approach for managerial problem analysis in the search for greater effectiveness.

The Linking Elements concept starts with a truism—that the level of performance of an organizational unit, to the extent to which it can be influenced by the unit manager, depends on the skills with which the manager can balance the needs and characteristics of the people in the unit with the needs and characteristics of the unit itself. These skills are the Linking Elements. From this definition the book proceeds to analyze,

---

*The title, manager, is used here in its broadest sense and thus includes all persons with supervisory responsibilities. See the section entitled Supervisor or Manager, page 14, for a definition.

1

Linking Element by Linking Element, what managers should know, and do, to improve their skills and, thus, achieve a better balance.

The Linking Elements concept works. It is a pragmatic, realistic system which helps managers develop their human resources and creates a climate in which people can find motivation for achievement. Linking Elements ensure that the roles of managers and employees are defined clearly so that credit for contributions to the organization is given fairly, based on competence and effort, not luck or other extraneous matters.

You probably will not immediately agree with everything that is said here. Some of the ideas may seem, at first, to be in conflict with what you have come to believe; but if you keep reading with an open mind, a comprehensive picture will most likely appear. It will answer some of your objections and explain some of the contradictions between theories, or between theory and what you might consider to be practical guides to action.

When theorists ask that we adopt a participative leadership style, for instance, it often seems as though they are talking only to top management. The idea is great—as an ideal—but how practical is it for the average manager who must meet quotas or performance standards, many of which are dictated from above?

Similarly, if you have had management responsibilities for some time, you have read about Management by Objectives (MBO)* or Management by Results. You may have attended a seminar or two where MBO was discussed at length, or you may be working for an organization which has a goals program of some sort. In any case, you know that it holds great promise to help your organization achieve greater control over its future and, at the same time, to bring greater job satisfaction to employees and managers. But you also know or probably have found that MBO very often can degenerate into a great deal of paper work or into just another attempt by high-level manage-

---

*The abbreviation MBO will be used to designate all goal programs. This book concerns itself primarily with fundamental issues; no attempt will be made to distinguish between Management by Objectives, Managing with Goals, or Managing by Results. Those who have originated these various concepts use them to describe essentially similar management techniques. Apparently, different names are used to avoid any negative connotations that may have built up in the minds of people who have worked on unsuccessful programs and are therefore disenchanted with the program name.

ment to gain tighter control over the actions of people at lower echelons.

You have probably also become acquainted with Maslow's Hierarchy of Needs (see below, p. 146), which seems to provide a blueprint for motivating people. Yet, if you have thought about how you can actually apply it, you have probably come to wonder whether you can really "motivate" anybody to become more achievement oriented. You may also have questioned whether real people actually fit into Maslow's framework. You may have tried to determine how money fits into the scheme or what self-realization (or self-actualization) really means for your secretary or for the other people who report directly to you. If you asked some of these questions, you undoubtedly found answers difficult to come by. Your people are probably like most of us; they do not know where they can find self-realization. It is no accident that "finding one's self" is such a frustrating experience and leads many people on a futile odyssey or to a psychiatrist. The theory is tantalizing—but where is the practical end? How can you help others achieve so elusive a goal?

In theory it is clear that planning is highly desirable and that people should be rewarded for planning their work and working their plans. What happens, though, when you reward those people who achieve the goals in their plans and fail to reward those who fall short? Do people strive harder to stay within budget or reach sales targets? Or do they, instead, devote considerably greater effort to gamesmanship so their budgets or sales targets will be more comfortable the next time around?

It is not only with theories that you have undoubtedly often felt uncomfortable. Have you thought from time to time that you should have handled a situation differently? That you should have made a better decision? That you could have established a better environment for some people so that they would have been more willing to accept the responsibilities which you expected them to assume?

The Linking Elements concept will answer some of these questions. It will *not*, however, provide easy or simple approaches to resolving practical problems. Nor, for that matter, does it claim that any can be resolved in their entirety. In their enthusiasm over their findings, theorists often do not emphasize sufficiently that there are many influences on the behavior of people, from body chemistry to the environment. Obviously, not all of these are under the control of the manager. A person who lacks motivation or dislikes the work cannot be turned into a zealous achiever, no matter how knowledgeable or competent the manager.

The lack of balance in theories has led to the assumption, which underlies most management development programs, that it is within a manager's power to motivate most, if not all, people and that people will get to enjoy tasks they dislike just because the manager treats them "properly." Linking Elements are not based on such an assumption. The concept, in fact suggests that it may be best not to be too concerned with the reaction of specific individuals and, instead, to concentrate on the "climate" in the organizational unit—so that it will become one in which most people can find higher levels of satisfaction from working. In such a climate some people will respond immediately with higher levels of achievement, while others will be reached more slowly; still others may never respond. The effective manager is not overly concerned if one or two people in the unit cannot find true motivation. If others around them have positive attitudes, they too will become better producers than they would be in a less positive climate.

Bridging the Gap Between Comprehension and Application

The Linking Elements concept is a practical theory with many points which can be applied directly—and immediately— to help improve performance of an organizational unit. But it is a complex concept with a deceptively simple facade. It therefore requires a certain amount of effort for complete understanding, and only when it is completely understood can it fulfill its promise. Shallow understanding leads to partial implementation and frequently to disappointments.

If you know anything about cars, you can undoubtedly diagnose the trouble and repair the fanbelt when it breaks. But to improve the car's efficiency and performance, a much deeper level of understanding is required. Similarly, when you first attend a management seminar, many of the thoughts which are expressed have only limited meaning. Gradually, as you gain greater experience, some of them begin to reveal deeper insights.

Good theory is that way. Limited contact usually brings some benefits and deeper study brings many. Greater confidence in the theory's applicability, when many veils hide the fundamental issues, can come only after thorough understanding has been achieved. One of the problems with your work as manager is that you never know whether you are achieving the best that can be achieved, somewhat less, or a great deal less. Fortunate environment or circumstances may bring good results when competence is low. Conversely, even the most competent manager can barely avoid serious problems in highly unfavorable situations. If you are lucky to work in an industry that is rapidly growing, there is no doubt that, if you are at all competent, you will rise quickly. If you are in business for yourself, you will make a very handsome profit. Another manager, far less competent than yourself, can possibly do almost as well. The old, spuriously modest adage "we must be doing something right" is a treacherous guide when conditions change.

As a very competent supervisor in a machine shop used to say to his people, anyone can be a good mechanic on an excellent machine. What separates the men from the boys, or the women from the girls, are the machines that are old but are still good enough to keep. The same is true for almost anything. The differences are minute between a fine operating car and another one, of the same model, that causes constant problems. These differences certainly cannot be detected easily. Yet they are there and their effect on performance can be substantial. Only those who really have a thorough command of the workings of the machine can probably find them. Less competent mechanics must be content to fix one breakdown after the other before the fundamental cause of the trouble becomes clear.

If the new concepts have not been thoroughly integrated into a manager's personal style, awkward situations can sometimes occur as the manager tries to use unaccustomed approaches. There is a tongue-in-cheek story about a large organization that needed to expand suddenly and sharply. It hired many new supervisors, some of them straight out of college. While it was customary for that company to send new supervisors to a one week management development course before they were assigned their duties, at this particular time, the need was so great and the course so crowded that it was decided to put some of them to work directly. Among them was a young man named Jim. On his first day in the shop he was walking down the aisle when he saw one of the employees sitting on a skid having a cup of coffee and smoking a cigarette. He walked over to him and asked "What are you doing?" The employee replied, "Can't you see? I am having a cup of coffee and I'm smoking a cigarette." The young new supervisor, recognizing an infraction of rules, responded, "This is no time to take a break. These are working hours. Please go back to your job or else I will have to discipline you." The employee, knowing better than to argue with the supervisor, doused his cigarette, put down his cup of coffee and went back to his work.

This conversation was observed by Jim's manager and, before the day was out, Jim and he were having a discussion about good management. The upshot of it was that Jim was sent to the supervisory course after all.

A week later he returned to the same position. At about the same time, on his first day, he was walking down the same aisle. There was the same employee sitting on a skid, having a cup of coffee and smoking a cigarette. Jim walked over to him and said, "What is that you are doing, may I ask?" The employee replied, "Just having a cup of coffee and smoking a cigarette, as you can see." To which Jim replied, "Now? These are working hours. Please return to your station or else I will have to discipline you." No sooner were the words out of his mouth, though, when he remembered some of the things he had learned in the course. He walked over to the man who was preparing to return to work, put his arm on his shoulder and said to him, "How was your weekend?"

This is of course an exaggerated example, but it may not be as far from what sometimes happens in real shops and offices as it may seem. Employees can recognize when a manager is not fully sincere with them, even when he or she is not as blatantly manipulative.

One of the errors many managers make after returning from a seminar or a course on some aspect of management or leadership style or some facet of the behavioral sciences is to quickly put some of their new "insights" to work. Such efforts are often self-defeating because they are not thoroughly integrated into the manager's style. They are therefore likely to be in contradiction with the image that other people have of the manager. More than intellectual comprehension is needed for effective implementation of a change in style. A way has to be found to make the change compatible with one's total personality and with the expectations of the people being supervised.

How the Book Is Structured

Besides this introductory chapter, there are ten other chapters in this book. The second chapter traces the history of management as a discipline, a science, and an art from its informal and formal beginnings to the twentieth century. It starts by discussing the four foundations of modern management theory (management science, behavioral science, the management cycle, and management by objectives or results) and by examining the work of some of the leading theorists of the last 75 years.

Chapter 3 provides a very brief overview of the entire Linking Elements concept, which combines management science, Management by Objectives (MBO), and the behavioral sciences into one all-encompassing framework. Chapter 4 discusses MBO or management with goals—a major segment of the Linking Elements concept. Chapters 5 and 6 discuss six of the eight major problem areas which prevent MBO from achieving its promise by showing how planning, performance evaluation, and development of subordinates can be improved. Chapter 7 covers the remaining two problem areas.

Chapter 8 deals with both the tangible and psychological needs of people at work and the skills and strategies a manager can apply to best satisfy them. It attempts to answer some of the questions which Maslow's Hierarchy of Needs has left unanswered, and it explores three practical though difficult strategies for creating an environment in which people can find the highest level of achievement motivation of which they are capable.

Chapter 9 identifies the skills managers need to determine the knowledge and skill requirements of the various positions in their units and to diagnose the strengths and weaknesses of the various incumbents with respect to their present positions and their future career plans. It also discusses strategies for helping people in the organizational unit develop themselves to higher levels of competence and greater personal fulfillment.

Chapter 10 discusses how managers can align the coordination requirements of the organizational unit with the cooperation that its members are willing to contribute. It also explores the role of managers with respect to the rules of the organizational unit and how these can be brought into the greatest possible alignment with the personal behavior code of employees.

The final chapter attempts to show how to apply the concepts discussed as Linking Elements so that each reinforces the others. This section is intended to help the reader plan the application of the Linking Elements concept to his own organizational unit.

ASSUMPTIONS UNDERLYING THE LINKING ELEMENTS CONCEPT

Five assumptions are central to the Linking Elements concept. These are:

1. A manager's actions are shaped by three primary influences—the environment, the people who report to him or her, and the manager's personal characteristics.
2. A person cannot "motivate" other people, but can only create an environment in which the others can find motivation.
3. Decision-making and communications skills are required for all managerial activities; as these skills are improved, it is likely that other skills will improve as well.
4. A major determinant of success for an organizational unit is the extent to which unit needs are aligned with employee needs and characteristics.
5. There is some measure of validity to the findings of all serious, prominent researchers and theorists, and a comprehensive concept must take these findings into consideration.

The Primary Influences on Managerial Action

The first assumption underlying the Linking Elements concept is that three primary influences shape your behavior as a manager:

a. The *ENVIRONMENT* in which you manage, including the changing situation of the moment. This means that what may be a correct action right now may be far from the best action a half hour later if changes have taken place that significantly affect the situation.
b. The *PEOPLE WHO ARE AFFECTED* by your actions. These people influence your decisions. Whether dealing with individuals or groups of people, you need to consider their relationship to you, their level of knowledge, their capabilities and emotional maturity, and their access to information.

c. *YOU*—Your capabilities, including your knowledge, skill, aptitudes—and the way you are perceived by others are the third influence.

Of these three, you have immediately direct control only over the third one—and you can, if you work, bring about significant change. To suddenly make extensive changes is, however, neither easy nor desirable.

Even minor changes sometimes come across as forced or unreal. In your role as manager, as well as in your other roles in life, you are most effective when you are yourself. At the same time, if you seek increasing control over your environment and your destiny, you must gain increasing awareness of yourself, of the various characteristics of your personality, and of your strengths and of your weaknesses, as well as of your impact on the people around you. That can help you cushion and reduce the effect of any undesirable aspects of your decisions and actions while you strengthen and gain increasingly greater advantages from those that are beneficial.

Motivating People

A second fundamental assumption of the Linking Elements concept is that people cannot motivate other people. You certainly do not want someone to "motivate" you. Managers, however, can establish an environment, a psychological climate in which people can develop a desire to achieve and which will encourage them to strive to improve their performance. In short, a manager who tries to "motivate" an employee is likely to fail—though the employee may be induced, cajoled, or forced to the desired actions. But managers *can* help their people find greater motivation in their work.

Decision Making and Communications

The third assumption involves the role of communications and of decision making. Both these skills overlap all other managerial skills and are enormously broad subjects. While some general principles can be isolated that are universally applicable, these principles, by themselves, are not sufficient to help managers improve their performance significantly. (See Appendix A for an overview of these topics.)

If you want to become a better communicator or a better decision maker, your best bet is to study and to practice communications for specific purposes such as selection interviewing or on-the-job training. After one application has been mastered, you can proceed to the next one. This is not meant to deny that there are fundamental principles such as those concerned with listening, speaking, questioning, etc., which need to be understood before one can study, practice, and master a specific type of communications. But communications is no different from other comprehensive subjects. For instance, only very few highly talented people can learn several musical instruments from the study of the fundamentals of music and from practicing on one instrument. Neither have there been many mathematicians who have become skilled in the various fields of mathematics without extensive experience in each one. Yet, when it comes to decision making and communications, there appears to be a lingering belief or a strong hope that managers have the innate capability of transferring knowledge of principles and skill in one area to all the others.

Better communications in interviews comes from detailed study of interviewing and practice of interviewing technique. Good decision making in a specific field, whether it concerns scheduling or some facet of personnel management, requires the application of some general principles. What is more important, though, is that good decision making is usually the result of considerable experience with, or careful study of, the factors that are important to decisions in a particular field of work.

Various aspects of decision making and communications are covered in many places in this book and a brief overview of major fundamental principles is provided in Appendix A.

The Foundation for Success

The fourth assumption concerns the truism that an organizational unit will be as successful as it can possibly be if its manager can achieve a high degree of alignment between its needs on the one hand and the characteristics and needs of its members on the other hand.* This is not meant to imply that it is the manager's task to mold everyone to fit the organization's needs or that the organization must conform to the characteristics of its members. On the contrary, it refers to the dynamic process

---

*"Success" is defined here as the ability to cope with the environment and to achieve growth and/or excellence to the extent to which either is desired or possible; to survive where survival is the best that can be achieved or to dissolve in ways most beneficial to the mission and the future of the people involved; to gain maximum control over the changing environment; or to seek out and adapt to a new, more favorable environment.

of continuous adjustment and mutual accommodation (not compromise) that somehow achieves a total far greater than the sum of its parts.

The Linking Elements and the Findings of Research

One more assumption completes the foundation for the Linking Elements concept—and it is an obvious one. It concerns the findings of theorists and researchers in the management and behavioral sciences. The Linking Elements concept builds on these findings because it assumes that important insights stem from every serious piece of work. It attempts to resolve existing contradictions and important objections that have been raised. As a result, in a few instances the models originally suggested by the researchers have been significantly modified. In general, however, these changes are primarily along the lines of further explanation.

COMMON MISCONCEPTIONS

There are some common misconceptions which have to be discussed briefly in an introductory chapter to a comprehensive management text because they exert considerable influence on attitudes about continuing management development. The following sections consider these misconceptions.

The Starting Point for Good Management

Many managers believe that good management must start from the top because they feel that at their levels it is virtually impossible to practice leadership styles that are not in keeping with those of their superiors. That this is not always the case, however, is obvious from the fact that some managers achieve better results than others in the same environment and in the same situation. Clearly, these managers are either better leaders or better managers or both. Intuitively—or because they have acquired greater knowledge about good management techniques and approaches—they lead their units to higher levels of achievement.

The ideas which are suggested in this book can be used at any organizational level. Admittedly, they have wider application at higher levels; and, when practiced there, it is easier for lower level managers to use them. But they are *not* restricted to top management. They can benefit the smallest organizational unit if its manager commits himself or herself to their use.

Influencing One's Boss

Another common belief that many managers hold is that the upper levels of management are not receptive to their ideas and suggestions. Here, too, there is some truth to the belief. Usually, little can be achieved unless the boss is in a receptive mood. However, if receptivity were all that is involved, how might it be explained that some people exert greater influence than others upon those to whom they report?

The Applicability of General Principles

Many managers believe that principles applicable in one environment may not be equally applicable in another. Managers, no matter what industry they are in, seem to believe that there are environments where certain management concepts apply better than in their own. Many managers believe that their situation is so unique that general principles do not apply at all and they therefore make little or no effort to find ways of obtaining benefits from them. To some extent, of course, they are correct. General principles need interpretation and translation to be effective in a unique environment. Nevertheless, the same principles that provide guidance for managing one's personal life probably apply with similar force to managing a grocery store, a bank, a manufacturing concern, a government agency, or a nonprofit organization.

In every environment, management is concerned with the establishment and accomplishment of goals through the efforts of people. Managers, particularly at high levels, have always been aware of the great similarities in managing different organizations. They know that the required technical skill and knowledge exist among the people in the organization and that they can draw on that expertise in order to accomplish what they would like to achieve. At lower levels of management, on the other hand, managers usually must possess some of that technical expertise themselves. Direct supervision of work requires that the manager understand the intricacies of the work at least sufficiently to recognize what is right and what is wrong. Those who advance through the management ranks must supervise more and more different types of functions and, naturally, can no longer be personally knowledgeable in each one of them. This is why, for instance, the higher levels of government can and do draw their managers from all walks of life: industry, labor, and other governmental agencies and institutions. A competent manager who gains experience in one industry will often do well in a high-level position in another industry or in government, and a manager from a high government position may do well in private industry or in an institution. This interchange of managers between different professions and occupations is evidence that because fundamental management principles exist it is usually possible for competent managers to adapt quickly to new environments.

Management and Common Sense

A fourth widely held belief is that common sense is an adequate guide for most management decisions. People tend to believe that they will do the "right thing" intuitively when the need arises. Intuitive reactions may seem right because they come about naturally, but very often they can be deceptive and thus lead to poor results. Examples of erroneous intuitive reactions are easy to find. We need only to step suddenly on the brake when driving a car and watch the reactions of the passengers. Inevitably, they will brace themselves by stiffening their arms against the dashboard or the seat in front of them and, with both feet, will push hard on an imaginary brake as though an accident were about to happen. This is an intuitive natural reaction, yet it is wrong. Nothing is potentially more dangerous than an attempt to prevent the impact of a high-speed collision with arms and legs that are too weak to resist. If an accident were to occur, such stiffening of the limbs would only lead to more severe injuries. Once the arms and legs give way, the body is thrown into the windshield with additional force. The correct position is exactly opposite the position just described—that is, lean forward loosely and brace the head and body against the dashboard or the seat in front.

Similar intuitive yet incorrect decisions are made by salespeople who charge ahead when a prospect or customer voices an easily refutable objection. Rather than attempting to find the concern that prompted the objection in the first place, such salespeople address the words that may be only a weak reflection of the prospect's actual feelings. The same is true of a supervisor who, when faced with pressure from higher levels of management, immediately passes that pressure along. The supervisor also acts intuitively, and sometimes wrongly, as does the business manager who cuts advertising when business slows down or the teacher who chides students for asking "silly" questions. The examples are legion, yet the conclusion is obvious: Intuitive reactions are often not the best. A few moments of thought between impulse and action can often bring about better actions—and better results.

For good management decisions, managers need a conceptual framework that provides logical consistency while making it possible to act quickly. That framework is usually based on a theory. To quote the words of the English economist John Maynard Keynes: *Practical men who believe themselves to be exempt from theoretical influences are usually the slaves of some defunct theorist.*

SUPERVISOR OR MANAGER?

In most organizations the title of supervisor is used for those who supervise the work itself. Higher level supervisors are generally referred to as managers. In some organizations the distinction is less clear, and higher level managers may be referred to as department supervisors.

In either case, it is important to clearly see that it is possible to *manage* an activity without *supervising* anyone. Supervision refers to directing the work of other people, an activity which is not necessarily a management function. If someone supervises the work of other people, however, that person automatically manages because supervision of others requires specific planning and goal setting and the organizing, directing, and evaluating that is so essential to the management task.

It would therefore appear to be more appropriate to speak of first-line supervision, mid-level supervision, and top-level supervision and to reserve the title of manager for those who manage some function but supervise no one. Thus, a "manager" could be in charge of planning or legal matters or, in small organizations, such functions as personnel, training, or inventory control.

This book is intended for supervisors at all levels and for those preparing themselves for supervision as well. All are managers under the definition used here, regardless of the title their organization has bestowed on them. The term "manager" is employed throughout this book merely for the sake of simplicity and to comply with general use of the titles which gives broader range to the word "manager."

PROCESS AND CONTENT

Finally, one distinction that managers sometimes fail to see clearly is that between "process" and "content." Although the distinction is simple, it is sometimes difficult to keep in mind. For example, if an instructor is teaching about pump operation, then the topic, pump operation, is the "content" of the activity. At the same time, there is a "process" going on: the acquisition of information by the learners, i.e., the learning process. The inadequate or inexperienced instructor may concentrate solely on explaining the topic ("content"). Such an instructor is likely to lecture and possibly not be aware that some of the learners have fallen asleep, though their eyes may still be open. The competent instructor, in contrast, while being occupied with discussing "content," would watch the "process" of information transmittal or acquisition of information by the learners. Such an instructor would constantly be asking what else could be done to help students learn more effectively, how students could apply the information so it would be more meaningful to them, and how students could search for the portions of the topic that they still did not understand in order to gain a broader comprehension of the subject.

For most management tasks, the content of an activity concerns the specific job that has to be done and the steps that are necessary to achieve it. The process that the competent manager keeps in mind, though, concerns the effectiveness* with which a team coordinates its activities, how the team responds to the environment, what major problems occur that need to be dealt with in the future, etc. Managers need self-discipline to keep "process" in mind while performing routine daily activities, whether these activities concern the conduct of an interview, chairing a meeting, or planning a project. A constant awareness of "process" helps to provide the foundation for planning for the future. It is in "process" that long-term effectiveness is developed—an effectiveness that constantly improves an individual's or a team's ability to cope with its environment.

---

*"Effectiveness" is not the same as "efficiency" and should not be confused with it. "Efficiency" refers to the ratio of output to input. The higher the rate of output to input, the higher the efficiency. Efficiency can be measured in pieces produced per hour, lower costs, and so forth. *Effectiveness* is a much broader term than efficiency. Effectiveness concerns not only the immediate results, but also the impact of today's actions on the future. For example, an effective manager is one who makes efficient use of personal time, who follows policies and procedures that will bring efficiency in the use of materials and in the use of time of subordinates, but who does not sacrifice actions or expenditures that build for the future in order to have better results today.

Chapter 2

The Four Foundations of Modern Management Thinking: Management Science, the Management Cycle, the Behavioral Sciences, and Management by Objectives

Good practices often exist long before people become aware of the theoretical foundation on which they rest. Bridges were built and ships navigated the seas in the days when there was no science involving strength of materials and when astronomy was more myth than discipline. The pyramids of Egypt, the Great Wall of China, and the magnificent cathedrals of Europe all attest to the competency of the skilled managers of the times. The successful construction of the pyramids—the planning efforts, the methods for moving the huge blocks of stone, the supervision of the thousands of men and women who toiled directly and indirectly in the construction work itself and in the supply of tools, materials, and food—could never have been realized without the efforts of many knowledgeable managers. Unfortunately, there are few records of the techniques these managers used to guide their work forces.*

MANAGEMENT BEFORE MANAGEMENT THEORY

Despite the tremendous size of some of the spectacular projects that required managerial skills, in the early days of civilization most management functions were performed on a small scale.

Then, as now, individuals managed their personal activities by themselves. However, few people thought of this as management. For example, farming was not considered to be management of an enterprise because most of the production

---

*There is, however, in the Holy Scriptures a passage which hints at formal organization: "And Moses chose able men out of all Israel, and made them heads over the people, rulers of thousands, rulers of hundreds, rulers of fifties and rulers of tens. And they judged the people at all seasons; the hard causes they brought unto Moses, but every small matter they judged themselves." EXODUS 18:25 and 26.

went for personal use. It was much less complicated than it is now because there were no complex machines to worry about, no special fertilizers, no pest-control chemicals, and no bank loans or multi-page tax forms.

Although there were some people who might be thought of as managers, real managers were few. Noblemen often employed the services of tax collectors (similar in function to today's credit and collection managers) to collect goods, rent, or taxes from tenants. This, however, can hardly be thought of as management as we know it today. And the type of management that was needed for barter trade with faraway places, while it required planning, organizing, and executing, was hardly complex enough to warrant development of a formal theory. It, too, followed a pattern and was done the way it had always been done.

Nevertheless, supervisors in the large governmental organizations and offices, in the early armies and navies, and on large estates were concerned with obtaining the largest possible output from the workers or slaves. They also were involved with other managerial activities.

1. *The span of control* must have been given serious consideration by not only Moses but also navies and armies and large governmental organizations as well. There is no doubt that managers and military officers were aware of the problems in controlling many people; they knew that a wide span of control (many subordinates reporting directly to each manager) meant that they would be closer to the line and maintain better vertical communications. They were equally aware that a more limited number of direct subordinates meant more levels between themselves and the action and that longer lines of communication made them slower and less reliable.

2. *The extent of delegation* of authority and responsibility always was dependent upon the varying capabilities of subordinate managers. Those who were in charge of large organizations always had to give careful thought to how they delegated, when, and to whom.

3. *Communication systems*, similarly, had to be carefully designed and required thought and constant monitoring, or else they could not possibly maintain cohesion among the many groups which a large organization spanned.

4. *Salary administration* had to be equitable in relation to most of the same principles that guide salary administration today (see pages 239–244).

5. *Financial systems* had to exist to assure that adequate monies (or substitutes) were available when and where needed to meet payrolls as well as demands for payment for supplies and services purchased (or bartered) from outside the organization.

6. *Planning and production* had to be organized just as well then as now in order to place huge armies into the field, to erect large structures, or to conduct large-scale trading operations.

7. *Administrative lines* had to be drawn. Line and staff functions were separated and limits were set to authority, at least to a degree. (However, the tales of intrigue and conspiracies which have been recorded are ample evidence that the checks on authority did not deter the ambitious and unscrupulous.)

THE FOUNDATIONS OF MANAGEMENT THEORY

The limited number of managers in antiquity and down through the Middle Ages did not make management a topic of popular concern. Not until the Industrial Revolution did the increasing complexity of management and the growing number of managers lead to the development of management theory.

Management theory as we know it today has evolved gradually from four major foundations: management science, the behavioral sciences, the management cycle, and management by objectives.

1. *Management science*, whose establishment as a separate discipline is credited to Frederick Winslow Taylor, concentrates on the efficiency of the work processes and the way the individual employee performs tasks.

2. The *behavioral sciences*, which developed considerably later than management science, explore the way people behave in their work environment and the influence their behavior has on the amount and quality of work output.

3. The *management cycle* concerns an entirely different aspect of management. It steps away from analyzing the employee and concentrates on the manager's task—on how to make the manager's work more effective so that

the people who report to the manager will achieve improved results.

4. The *management by objectives* concept—or management
   with goals—is an outgrowth of the management cycle.
   It is a significant refinement of, and in some major ways
   supersedes, the management cycle, although many
   managers today view it as an independent concept.

The Linking Elements concept builds on all four foundations and uses them to create one comprehensive framework
which can provide guidance for managers who want to improve
the performance of their units. Thorough understanding of
the Linking Elements concept requires an appreciation of the
history of management theory. The development of the two
major foundations, management science and the behavioral sciences, is therefore outlined very briefly here and is discussed in somewhat more detail in Appendices B and C respectively. The management cycle is described in this chapter, and
management by objectives is such an integral part of the Linking Elements concept that it is discussed together with the latter
in Chapter 4, and explored in depth in Chapters 5 through 7.

Management Science

The Impact of the Industrial Revolution

With the advent of the Industrial Revolution came many
changes that affected the work patterns of the average person.
Hand looms faded from existence and were replaced by textile
mills. Potters gave up their wheels and went to work in the pot-
tery factories. The small crafts and guilds, the people working
at home in their cottages, and the little shops that previously
turned out cooking utensils, clothing, needles, and other neces-
sities were replaced by something new to civilization—the mills,
plants, and factories that came into being during the Industrial
Revolution.

The transition from cottage to factory changed farm hands
and small entrepreneurs into factory workers. Now the large
mills, plants, and factories needed managers to assure effective
operation. Not too much was recorded at first about the management practices of the day. This was primarily because few
people could read, fewer could write, and the general public
had little or no knowledge of scientific subject areas beyond
rudimentary arithmetic.

Throughout the nineteenth century awareness of management as a distinct discipline grew, but it was not until the end of the century that this awareness was formalized in the work of Frederick Winslow Taylor. Management science or "scientific management," considered to have begun with the work of Taylor, concentrated on the way the work of employees could be organized to obtain greater output. Management science included several topics:

- *Methods study,* which is concerned with the way an operation should be performed and how the workplace should be organized.
- *Work measurement,* which attempts to determine how long various tasks take, and
- *Work standards,* which specify the "normal" or "standard" time it should take to do a task.

Work standards formed the basis of piece rates (payment for production of a unit of work—a piece) and other incentives. These were intended to induce employees to work faster and harder, but also provided an opportunity for higher earnings. It is interesting to note that management science provided the earliest form of performance evaluation, which was based completely on results and linked directly to compensation.

Management science branched out from the basic types of measurement described above into the mathematical techniques that are widely used today to determine the ways of doing things. Operations analysis, inventory-control principles, linear programming, production-line balancing and scheduling techniques all sprang from the broadening search for better work arrangements. Management science led to computers, to today's self-correcting machinery, and to many mechanical devices that perform so much of the monotonous, repetitive, or menial work in modern society.

Methods Study, Time Study, and the Modern Manager

What is the significance of the findings of early management scientists for modern managers? The answer to this question, of course, depends in part on one's point of view. There are those researchers and theorists who feel that setting standards for people is likely to be demotivating, dehumanizing, and therefore self-defeating. People naturally resist the regimentation of standard setting. They are likely to strive for the lowest possible standards because that gives them either the widest freedom of movement or the highest income or both. If they can obtain easy standards, they are often likely to restrict their work output to come close to those standards, even if that can be done in a small part of the workday, to avoid raising questions about validity of the standards.

Researchers opposed to setting standards will concede, of course, that there is value to methods study which simplifies work so that more can be produced with less effort; but they often hold that in most situations formal study by people other than those doing the work is not necessary. They maintain that employees have the inherent intelligence to find the best work method if management will only give them the chance to do so.

Other experts take a somewhat broader view. They see many manufacturing plants and offices where one person is dependent on the output of another, and they feel that it is essential that the work load be divided up fairly and evenly. Specialized skills in time study as well as methods study are essential in order to achieve these results, and only people formally trained in these skills can set high quality standards. Those who hold such views do not consider it practical to train all employees so they can be equally proficient in standard setting.

Summary and Perspective

Management theory was born as management science. Emphasis was on efficiency—on methods, on time study, on piece rates, and on scheduling. The search was for better ways to do things so that society would have more goods and services with the same amount of effort. The concept that more production leads to greater wealth, originally from Adam Smith, was the guiding principle. It was assumed, without question, that higher income was the most important motivator. Better work methods lead to higher revenues and profits. They, in turn, permitted higher wage payments. Various incentive plans were shaped to share the increased income and at the same time, so it was hoped, stimulate maximum motivation in employees. This was all that was considered necessary to bring a better world. There were problems with people, of course, but the causes were believed to be with inadequate precision in methods and time study and in incentive payment systems.

The search for solutions kept management scientists looking for ways to overcome the problems. The result was a focus on *techniques* with little attention to the *psychological needs* of people. Not until, almost by accident, this search led to unexpected results, did the attention of management thinkers shift away from single-minded concentration on financial rewards to the broader needs of people at work.

The Behavioral Sciences

The second major foundation of modern management theory can be found in the behavioral sciences. Though the behavioral sciences became part of management theory almost accidentally, their impact has been very large indeed. As the level of education of employees rose and machines took over more and more of the repetitive and easily measurable tasks, appreciation for the importance of motivation as a prime determinant of output increased by leaps and bounds.

The roots of the behavioral sciences lie in two areas: (1) formal psychology, and (2) the humanistic movements, such as those of the Ricardian socialists and the Utopians of the early nineteenth century, who believed that societies could be formed in which the relationship between work and life could be more harmonious than that which they saw around them. Both roots contributed philosophical considerations as well as a pool of knowledge on which the early behavioral scientists could draw.

The development of behavioral science, which was not so called until after it was well established, started during the first third of the 20th century with attempts to determine how the work environment influenced productivity. The questions to which some of the management scientists wanted answers dealt with the effect of work breaks on productivity, the impact of fatigue, and the impact of lighting and other environmental factors. The most famous of the investigations were conducted at the Western Electric Company's Hawthorne Plant in Chicago between 1927 and 1932.* Western Electric's scientists found that work output did not change, as they had predicted, when they manipulated the physical conditions. They called in Dr. Elton Mayo of Harvard University to conduct further studies. The results of many experiments in the Hawthorne studies were startlingly different from the researcher's original hypothesis. In the most famous of the experiments, six young women were

---

*Henry A. Landsberger, HAWTHORNE REVISITED (Ithaca, N.Y.: New York School of Industrial and Labor Relations, Cornell University, 1958).

detached from a department where hundreds of workers assembled a simple telephone relay component. Working in a separate room under careful observation and friendly attention from the researchers, they were given rest periods of differing durations at various times in the working day. As predicted, their work output began to increase. However, when the rest periods were eliminated, the work output continued to increase dramatically and kept rising almost without interruption with every change in working conditions—whether the changes were favorable or unfavorable.

The Work of Elton Mayo

Dr. Elton Mayo of Harvard interpreted the Hawthorne Experiments in a series of papers and books that made him famous. According to Mayo, in experiments like the one involving the telephone component, assembly workers demonstrated the importance of informal social groupings that were often more meaningful to them than the formal organization of a company, changes in physical surroundings, or money incentives. The young women assemblers, he explained, increased production because of the friendship and trust they developed among themselves and because of the special recognition given them as a group when they were singled out for the experiment. They felt special and acted that way. Mayo also pointed out that some of the other informal groups observed in the experiments operated to limit production and to fight controls even when better effort would have brought about higher pay. The reasons, Mayo suggested, lay in the suspicion and distrust these groups felt toward management and the need they felt to build barriers and intra-group rules for their own protection.

Mayo's broadest conclusions were highly controversial. He disturbed many readers with his sweeping view of the informal group as the workers' last refuge in a cold, inhumane society. His prescriptions for management, involving tactics with which managers could identify and control informal workers' groups, angered many liberal observers who interpreted these prescriptions as anti-union. Whatever the arguments against Mayo, he had publicized a remarkable series of experiments that included more than 20,000 individual interviews with workers and their supervisors. These interviews underscored the existence of a psychology and a sociology of work previously unexplored, and thus laid the major foundation for the complex, interdisciplinary behavioral sciences which gradually emerged.

With the advent of the Hawthorne experiments, management theory had been extended beyond physical movement and efficiency questions to a study of noneconomic questions concerning how workers behaved and why. The study of management had thus grown in one leap to embrace a large segment of behavioral science inquiry into motivation, communications, the nature of leadership, the social characteristics of organizations, and the best conditions for employee development and career growth.

Scientific management and industrial engineering had by no means been displaced by this human relations school of management. Extensive follow-up on the findings of the Hawthorne Experiments was delayed many years by the higher urgencies brought about by the Great Depression and then World War II. (During this time the term "human relations approach" gradually appeared and declined in use and the term "behavioral science approach" grew in popularity.)

The behavioral sciences are so important to modern management theory that various findings of researchers will be discussed when they supply the foundation for one of the Linking Elements.

The Management Cycle

So far this chapter has discussed only management science and behavioral science, two of the legs on which management theory rests. Management science, as was pointed out, focuses on the work of employees. As society needed more and more managers to manage increasingly complex tasks and the larger number of people in industrial and government work forces, more thought had to be given to the work of the managers themselves.

Henri Fayol's Work—The Basis of the Management Cycle

Of all the people who studied how a manager's work should be organized, few showed greater understanding or wrote about it more clearly and intelligently than a French mining director named Henri Fayol. Fayol spent his entire business career (over 50 years) as the industrial manager of a coal mine. He used the same scientific, rationally derived methods of attacking management problems as Taylor and Gantt (see Appendix B), but in an entirely new area.

In his book titled *General and Industrial Management* (written in French in 1916 and translated into English in 1949), he outlined what managers should do, how they should do it, and how they should relate to each other. Fayol saw the role of management as a cycle that keeps repeating itself. Managers perform a specific set of functions that gradually lead every project or task to a satisfactory completion.

Management Skills

Fayol divided a manager's duties into five primary functions: (1) planning, (2) organizing, (3) commanding, (4) coordinating, and (5) controlling. These functions, as Fayol saw them, form a cycle of management because they blend in with one another to form a total concept of management (see Figure 2.1).

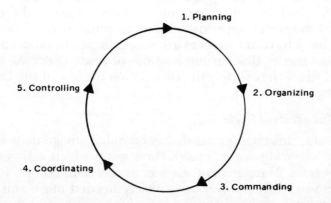

Figure 2.1. Pictorial Representation of Henri Fayol's Management Cycle (From Henri Fayol, GENERAL AND INDUSTRIAL MANAGEMENT, by Pitman Publishing Corporation, New York, Copyright © 1949. Reprinted by permission of the publisher; artwork courtesy NFPA.)

Other theorists who have studied and written about a manager's duties have used various terms to overcome the misunderstandings and problems that Fayol's original definitions sometimes created. For example, although planning and organizing are commonly used for the first steps, some theorists follow these with steps such as "executing," "implementing," "staffing," "leading," "follow-up," and "evaluating"—all words that describe one or the other of the remaining functions in the cycle.

Even though the management cycle applies to specific projects or activities, as well as to a manager's overall responsibilities, it is not as practical as it may at first seem to be. While it recognizes the importance of the manager's team, it provides little guidance for the manager's relationships with team members and concentrates on the disciplines which managers should impose upon themselves to increase their personal effectiveness. Despite this shortcoming, the management cycle has been a major foundation for management education and training for over 50 years. It continues to be taught as a fundamental concept in many management training programs today.

Management by Objectives

Management by Objectives is the fourth major foundation of management theory. It will be discussed in great detail in Chapters 4 and 5. The brief discussion here serves only to complete the historical picture.

Management theorists have always spoken about objectives and goals. So, for that matter, have people from areas other than management. There is, therefore, some question as to where the formal concept of MBO originated. Most people credit Peter Drucker, the famous author and consultant, while others point to Chester Barnard.

Chester Barnard,* for many years Vice-President of the Jersey Bell Telephone Company, spoke of the need for managers to develop a cooperative system which would be capable of satisfying the personal objectives of employees as well as meeting the objectives of the organization. Barnard thus recognized the existence of two separate sets of objectives and that the success of an organization depended on satisfying both.

Peter Drucker** spoke more specifically about an organization's objectives, particularly those of a business, since Drucker's main work was, at that time, at General Motors. He identified eight key areas in which objectives of performance and results have to be set: market standings, innovation, productivity, physical and financial resources, profitability, workers' per-

---

*Chester I. Barnard, FUNCTIONS OF THE EXECUTIVE (Cambridge: Harvard University Press, 1938).

**Peter F. Drucker, THE PRACTICE OF MANAGEMENT, (New York: Harper Brothers, 1954).

formance and development, work performance and attitude, and public responsibility. He was aware that some of the goals or objectives in these functions could be quantified quite readily while others were much more difficult to state precisely and without ambiguity.

While Drucker and Barnard were speaking primarily of the objectives of the entire organization rather than specific work and development objectives for each unit, possibly even for each individual employee, their thinking is fundamental to much of modern management theory. And, as noted previously, that portion of it dealing with MBO is relevant to the Linking Elements concept, which is described in the next chapter. The Linking Elements concept can furnish practical, sound approaches to management problems and management tasks to those managers who have mastered it. It can do this because it satisfies all the criteria for a comprehensive theory of management:

1. It accommodates all four foundations of management theory—management science, the management cycle, MBO, and the behavioral sciences.
2. It gives appropriate consideration to the organizational unit's need for performance (productivity, quality, response flexibility) *and* to the individual's right to gain maximum satisfaction at work.
3. It provides for consideration of three influences (situation, manager, and subordinate) on all decisions.
4. It applies with equal validity at all organizational levels, even though at lower levels freedom of action is limited to a greater degree.
5. It provides a guide for accurate diagnosis of performance problems.

Chapter 3

How the Linking Elements Concept Works

CHANGING VIEWS OF THE MANAGEMENT FUNCTION

It is interesting to note that in the case of each of the management theories discussed in the last chapter—management science, the management cycle, behavioral science, and management by objectives—it was hoped that a relatively simple system could be devised to help managers manage more effectively. It seemed as though, with intelligent and reasonable people, not too much would be required to help them overcome what appeared to be relatively minor obstacles to better management.

The management scientists thought that a lack of understanding of how to set standards prevented people from achieving more. After Fayol, it was inadequate awareness of the manager's role which had to be overcome. The management cycle, it was hoped, would bring better performance. Then, with the advent of the human relations approach to management, it was showing managers how to be more democratic that would unlock the door to higher achievement and greater job satisfaction at the same time. And so it went. One of the last major attempts to create an easy route to management effectiveness was based on the Managerial Grid (see page 150), a device highly popular when it was introduced and still widely used throughout the world today, though it is now seen in somewhat clearer perspective. Gone are the days when people seriously believed that significant changes in behavior, particularly in managerial competence, could be achieved with a program of five days or 10 days or even 30 days.

It has become abundantly evident, for instance, that there is more to motivation than just good leadership style and that management by objectives is not the simple concept it once seemed to be. There is no longer any hope that easy answers can be found. It is clear that good management requires either thorough understanding or a high level of innate ability to balance a far larger number of considerations than had heretofore been thought necessary.

The old definitions still hold, though—management means getting things done with and through people—but the meaning of this has changed. Not too long ago, this definition was believed to mean that a good manager who delegates properly is doing the best job possible without having to work hard. Gradually it has become clear that this is not really true because a manager's function is to provide support and help to immediate subordinates. Even with excellent delegation, there is a lot that is left to do, from searching out opportunities for improvement to helping subordinates overcome those stubborn problems that are beyond their capabilities or resources.

Nor is it simply a matter of being democratic or autocratic—task-oriented or people-oriented. One form of management or one specific leadership style will not do for all situations. It is now obvious that the three influences referred to earlier (see page 8)—the situation, the characteristics of subordinates, the characteristics and styles of managers—create a highly complex environment so that no single idea can serve as an adequate guide. All three of these influences have to be considered in decision making, and managers must feel comfortable with a wide range of leadership styles, from the highly participative to the highly autocratic, from the highly supportive to the rigidly demanding. Managers also must either have high competence in one of the technical fields that is important to their organizational units, or they need to have exceptionally good diagnostic and analytical skills so that they can determine where their unit's performance is weakest and so that they can quickly get to the source of problems as they develop. Even more important is the need to perceive the frontiers of the field so that they can help their teams identify significant opportunities and take advantage of them.

In addition to being good leaders, modern managers must also be good planners, good organizers, and competent decision makers. That is a difficult task and appears to be an almost impossible one. But it is really not more difficult today than it was in the past—just more complex. For instance, in the past there has been no doubt that different styles of leadership were called for in a factory or office with unskilled or semi-skilled people and in a lab with highly educated scientists or in an organization with widely dispersed salespeople. But today there are more technical variations, higher employee expectations, more demanding competitive requirements, etc. The manager who is bent on rapidly improving competence must dig through the wealth of existing theories and gradually shape a philosophy and a framework that can serve as a guide.

How many capable managers, however, have the time and the inclination to do so? It would seem that there is a need for a blueprint with which managerial decisions as well as self-development decisions can be made. The Linking Elements concept presented in this book can furnish such a guide. It stands squarely on research and research findings and it covers most, if not all, the skills managers need to be effective. It does not sidestep the contradictions that exist between theory and practice, but faces them and resolves them as best as can be done within the limits of existing knowledge. This does not mean, though, that the Linking Elements concept provides an easy road to greater effectiveness. It is mainly the roadmap for very difficult self-development and self-discipline that can bring results to the manager who persists in developing the awareness and the habits that are needed.

THE LINKING ELEMENTS CONCEPT

The Linking Elements concept is based on the fundamental truth that an organizational unit will achieve the highest level of performance which its environment permits if the manager can bring a high level of alignment between the needs of the unit and the characteristics and needs of the people in it.

The Organization

As illustrated in Figure 3.1, the Linking Elements concept begins by stating the obvious—that an organizational unit, whether it is an entire company, a governmental agency, a small office, or a voluntary organization, wants to achieve a high level of performance, whatever meaning the word "performance" has for it. For business organizations, for instance, performance might be measured in many terms, among them: quality of products or services; return to stockholders; growth and stability; quality as an employer, as a customer to suppliers, and as a member of the community and of society at large.

In order to achieve performance:

1. An organizational unit must have control.
   a. This means, first of all, that the unit must have direc-

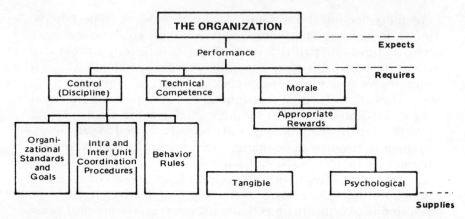

Figure 3.1. The Organizational Basis for the Linking Elements Concept (Artwork courtesy NFPA)

tion. It must know where it wants to go and how fast it wants to get there. That is, it must have *goals* that it wants to achieve and must have *standards of performance* so that everyone knows what to contribute towards the achievement of these goals. Control also means *discipline*. Not discipline in the sense of punishment, but discipline in the sense of a disciplined team, where every individual recognizes the needs of the team and is willing to forego personal interests for the sake of achieving the goals of the team.

b. Besides direction, an organizational unit needs *coordination* if it is to have control. Coordination means that everybody knows what to do relative to other people. For instance, everybody in a fire company can agree with the goal that hose lines should be laid as quickly as possible when apparatus arrives at the scene; but if coordination is lacking, a lot of wasted motion will delay the company in achieving this goal. A well drilled, tightly disciplined team can lay hoses and connect them to the water supply much faster than a team that has not attempted to coordinate its actions.

c. For good control, there must also be behavior rules for the individual which establish what the unit can expect from an employee and which tell employees what is expected of them.

2. An organizational unit must have high technical competence if it expects to achieve a high level of performance. Each individual on the team must have the necessary capabilities, knowledge, and skills to perform well on the assigned tasks.

3. An effective unit team must have a high level of morale. Morale depends on the satisfaction that people get from their work. There are two kinds of satisfaction, tangible and psychological. An organizational unit must provide adequately for both kinds of satisfaction.

An organization unit can achieve control, technical competence, and morale only if the people in the unit have the characteristics and abilities that are needed and are willing to devote them to the goals of the organization. The relationship of the individual to the organization is a critical factor in the achievement of performance goals; and the manager, the person in the middle, can do much to shape it.

The Individual

Figure 3.2 illustrates the characteristics and needs of the individual which the manager must balance with the characteristics and needs of the organization.

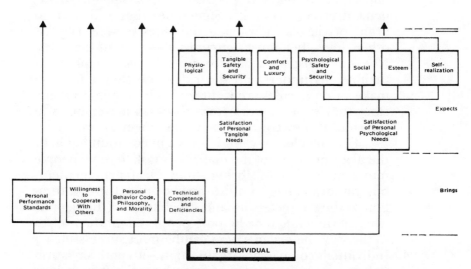

Figure 3.2. The Employee Basis for the Linking Elements Concept (Artwork courtesy NFPA)

1. Individuals come to an organization with personal performance standards and a willingness to work—which
   may or may not meet the requirements necessary to
   achieve organizational goals. If willingness to work on
   required tasks and assignments is sufficient to meet unit
   needs, then the manager has very little to do. If, on the
   other hand, it is not, as frequently is the case, then there
   is a whole series of skills which a manager must apply to
   gradually bring an employee to more willingly accept
   organizational goals.
2. The coordination which an organization needs so that
   all sub-units can move towards goals in an organized
   fashion requires cooperation. People must work
   smoothly with each other and with other teams. Good
   coordination depends on willing cooperation. There
   are many obstacles to cooperation between individuals
   and between teams. A manager must be able to recognize serious problems and must have the skills to remove all obstacles to cooperation and coordination.
3. An individual brings attitudes and a philosophy of life,
   or a morality, that may be compatible with organization
   rules. Often, though, individuals feel that some rules
   are wrong or that they should not be applied in a certain situation. When this is the case, managers have difficult decisions to make. Sometimes they will have to
   grant privileges by waiving the rules temporarily. At
   other times they must demand adherence to the rules.
   Not only must managers be sure that all members of
   their teams understand the rules, but they must also
   make sure the rules are right for their people. In many
   cases they have to work towards obtaining changes in
   the rules if they consider them no longer appropriate.
      This, incidentally, highlights a major foundation of
   the diagram. It is not the manager's task to force people
   into a mold that will bring some 'ideal' arrangement;
   but, rather, managers must work to adapt the organization to the competencies and capabilities of the people,
   while at the same time helping people adapt themselves
   to the way the organization can be most successful.
4. Individuals come to an organization with both skills and
   deficiencies. As a matter of fact, throughout their lives
   most people have some deficiencies relative to the tasks

on which they work. And they usually lack the knowledge and skills needed for higher level jobs which they would like to obtain and which they hope will bring greater work satisfaction to their lives.

It is a manager's task to help people eliminate these deficiencies so they can develop their abilities in ways that increase their effectiveness in the organization. The manager should also help them as they prepare themselves for jobs or assignments from which they will gain greater work satisfaction as they progress in their careers.

5. Finally, every individual expects from the organization the satisfaction of a complex set of both tangible and

Figure 3.3. The Linking Elements Concept. Note the relationship between the individual and the organizational unit. (Artwork courtesy NFPA)

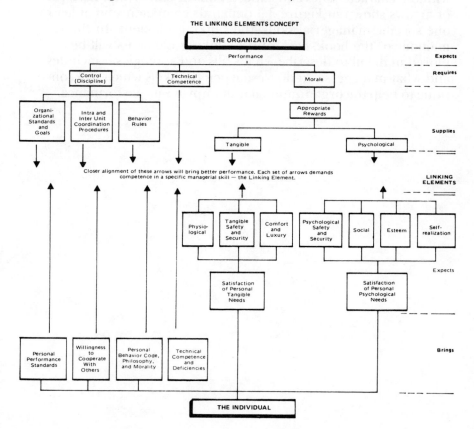

psychological needs. On the tangible side, there is the
need for adequate income to satisfy the physiological
needs of food, clothing, and shelter as well as some of
the safety and security needs and a certain level of comfort and luxury. On the psychological side, there is the
need to feel secure, the need to belong and to be respected, and the need to find a measure of satisfaction
in one's work. There is a great deal that managers can
do to raise the satisfaction which their employees and
subordinate managers obtain from their work.

The Linking Elements

Linking Elements are the skills and strategies which a manager must apply so that the organization's needs and the rewards which it can supply achieve the greatest possible balance
with the characteristics and expectations of employees. Each set
of arrows shown in Figure 3.3 demands competence in at least
one specific managerial skill—the Linking Element. In the remainder of the book, each of the Linking Elements will be explored in detail to describe what skills and strategies it includes
and what managers can do to sharpen the skills which will continue to help the organizational unit improve its performance.

Chapter 4

Managing With Goals

THE GOALS OF AN ORGANIZATIONAL UNIT

Most managers will agree that a day started without a plan, without some goals to achieve, will result in less accomplishment than a day for which objectives have been set. The concept of goals and objectives is such a simple one. It seems so logical that setting appropriate goals with and for employees and subordinate managers should, at the very least, clarify what demands concentration and what is to be handled in a more routine manner. Goal setting can and should provide the discipline to help managers think through the things that need to be done and thus help to establish a regular habit of planning. Appropriate participation by subordinates in goal setting can assure that their knowledge, and not only the manager's, is brought to bear on the problems and on the opportunities that face the team.

The advantages that a regular goals program can bring—in communications, in putting first things first, in establishing a clear view of respective responsibilities, in developing employees—are so significant that it would seem the concept of managing with objectives, or towards results, should have swept like wildfire through the industrialized nations and have become a standard process everywhere. This, however, has not happened.

In an article in *MBA* magazine, Stephen Singular* explained that organizational goals programs often appear under different names. According to Singular, these programs are most frequently called "Management by Objectives" ("MbO" or "MBO") or "Managing by Objectives/Results," or they are hidden behind labels such as "Performance Appraisal" or "Performance Objective" programs. The different names are used because the words "goal" and "objective" have different meanings in different organizations.** Whatever the label, Singular

---

*Singular, Stephen, "Has MBO Failed?", MBA, Oct. 1975, pp. 47–50. Reprinted by permission from the October 1975 MBA. Copyright ©1975 by MBA Communications, Inc.

**For purposes of this text, the words "goal" and "objective" are used synonymously; distinctions are covered later in this chapter in the section titled "The Hierarchy of Objectives."

cites a research study by professors Fred Schuster of Florida
Atlantic University and Alva Kindall of the Harvard Business
School that estimates that fewer than half of *Fortune Magazine's*
list of the largest 500 industrial companies manage their businesses with systems that can be termed MBO based. According
to Singular, this is so in spite of the fact that MBO "is a technique based on real planning and thought and is, most agree,
the best theoretical management program ever conceived."
Moreover, on the basis of research results, "less than 10 percent of those 500 corporations—somewhere between 36 and 50
companies—have MBO-based programs that are considered a
success. And only 10 companies, or 2 percent, have programs
that are considered "highly successful."

This chapter will explore the concept of managing with
goals, whether it is called Management by Objectives, management by results, or some other name, as a central strategy in
achieving the desired balance between needs of organizations
and of their people. It will review several reasons why MBO has
failed to approach its potential for creating more effective organizations and will briefly discuss possible solutions to the
problems of MBO. The next chapter will cover these solutions
more thoroughly and will attempt, in the process, to come to
grips with some widely held beliefs that are in conflict with reality, beliefs that stand in the way of more rational administration
of goals programs.

The Management Cycle and MBO

Though it is frequently not recognized, MBO is a fairly
practical approach to applying the management cycle to a manager's everyday work. When you, as manager of your organizational unit, go through the process of selecting goals for the
coming period, you are really doing little else but good planning. The action plans which lead to the achievement of the
goals make up the balance of the planning process.

In the language of planners, you conduct a situation analysis to determine the strengths and weaknesses of the current
situation, as well as the opportunities inherent in it, so that you
can select appropriate goals. Then you prepare strategic and
tactical plans to achieve these goals. Whether you approach this
operation in an informal or formal manner, it still is planning.
A thorough set of goals and an appropriate (though not necessarily detailed) set of action steps constitute a complete plan—
and probably a better plan than one not specifically expressed

in terms of goals. Arriving at agreement on goals, deciding who will assume responsibility for the achievement of each goal, and providing the necessary resources are the steps that are generally included under the term "Organizing" in the management cycle. Implementing action plans falls under "Implementing" or "Executing" in the cycle, and progress reviews of a goals program fall under the "Follow-up" or "Controlling" phase of the cycle. In this last phase, the steps needed to improve low achievement are determined, and plans and goals are revised.

Goals for Individuals

Everybody has goals, even people who do not realize that they set them. Some take their goals seriously; others do not. But almost everybody, even most people who lead very simple lives, have some vague, general idea about where they would like to be sometime in the future.

For people who think seriously about the future, though, and who expect to accomplish something in life, goals are not merely guesses about the future; they are real and meaningful targets to strive for. Some of these goals are complex and distant in the future. Others are simple and short term. For instance, if you have decided to go on a vacation in three months, you have set a goal. It is a very clear and direct goal, and you probably see clearly what steps you must take to accomplish it. Obviously, you have to decide on destination or itinerary. You must arrange for tickets and for money, possibly for traveler's cheques, and for the clothing and sports gear you may need. If no emergency arises, you will then be able to leave on your vacation as intended.

Not all goals are as easily accomplished. Many goals are not as specific. They may not have a date when they should be accomplished, and even the goal itself may be somewhat vague. For instance, consider the example of a college graduate with a degree in management whose career goal is to become a top-level manager, possibly the president of some organization. This goal, of course, is clear but nowhere near as specific as the one in the preceding example. It does not state the exact position or the size of the company or the industry, or a date by which it will be accomplished.

There are some fundamental differences between the two types of goals just described, differences which significantly affect planning. Taking a vacation is a short-term goal, which can

be achieved easily unless an emergency or really unusual circumstances interfere. Becoming a high-level manager is a long-
range objective. It usually would not be very productive to tie it
down with specifics such as the company and executive level or
the date by which it is to be achieved. It is clearly important to
distinguish between long-term and short-term goals and to
work with them differently.

HIERARCHIES OF GOALS

Most organizations working with goals have therefore tried
to identify different kinds of goals. Some talk about objectives
as being long range, general targets, while they view goals as
specific, relatively short-range targets. Other organizations reverse these definitions of goals and objectives. For the purpose
of this book, as has already been pointed out, the words "objective" and "goal" will be used interchangeably. The distinction
between long and short-term goals is fundamental; but beyond
this there is a need to further identify the various types of goals.
Thus, goals may be arranged in two hierarchies, one in time,
and one in scope, as shown in Figure 4.1.

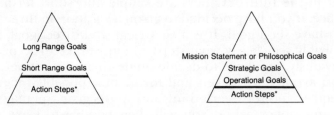

*Action steps are not goals. Their significance is explained in this and later chapters.

Figure 4.1. Hierarchies of Goals

Each hierarchy rests on *action steps*, the specific tasks that
have to be accomplished so that the goals will be reached. Action steps are not goals. While the distinctions between the various levels of goals are not of great significance, the distinction
between goals and action steps has broad implications. From
the point of view of making a goals program successful, the
distinction between action steps and goals is of crucial importance. Whereas goals are ends to be reached, action steps are
the means to these ends.

Philosophical Goals/Mission Statements

Philosophical goals are not meant to be achieved. They include such qualifying words as "best," "fastest," and "most." They aim towards the future. For instance, one philosophical goal for an organization could be to provide the best service for its public or to provide the best product of a certain kind to its customers. An organization can have philosophical goals in many areas. Some could refer to the public or to customers, others to the interests of employees, shareholders, the community, and so on.

Philosophical goals exist for organizational units as well as for the entire organization. For example, an engineering department could have as its philosophical goal the objective of designing better quality, less costly products than those of any competitor. Philosophical goals describe in the broadest possible terms the overall aims of an organization or a subunit. Thus, the term "mission statement" is often considered an accurate definition of philosophical goals. The individual members of an organization seldom are directly concerned with achieving the organization's philosophical goals because these merely define the environment within which more specific goals should be set. People work primarily on operational levels; and, as the goals at these levels are being achieved, the entire organization also achieves strategic goals, and thus moves in the direction of its mission statements.

Although philosophical goals are rarely guides for action, they do offer a sense of direction and purpose. Frequently they are not in writing and exist only as a consensus within the organization. Individuals, of course, often have mission statements for which they strive. "To be an excellent manager" is such a statement. Individuals also work toward achieving their own personal philosophical goals, in their careers and in their lives, by setting their own strategic and operational goals. For instance, in order to achieve the philosophical goal of becoming an excellent manager, a high school graduate would have to set strategic goals such as obtaining appropriate degrees, serving an internship in an appropriate discipline, being successful in a series of positions with increasing responsibilities, and so forth. Operational goals within these strategic goals would concern taking specific courses, obtaining good grades, establishing good performance records in respective positions, and so forth.

Strategic Goals

Strategic goals are the big goals, usually fairly long range, which help to move the organization in the direction of one of its mission statements (see Figure 4.2).

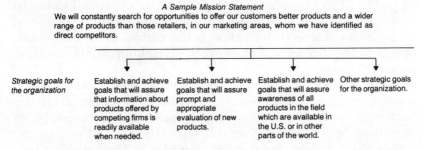

Figure 4.2. Organizational Strategic Goals in Support of One Mission Statement

As Figure 4.3 shows, the organization's strategic goals are specific enough so that departments, divisions, bureaus, or offices can set strategic goals for their respective units to support organizational strategic goals. For instance, in the example, Unit A could be the Merchandising Department, Unit B could be the Personnel Department, and Unit C could be the Quality Assurance Department. Each of these departments has strate-

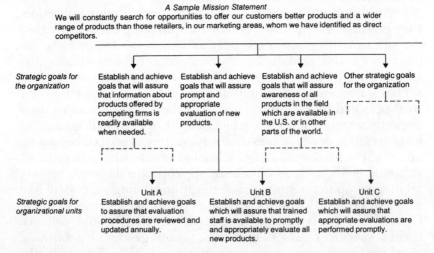

Figure 4.3. Unit Strategic Goals in Support of One Organizational Strategic Goal

gic goals supporting all the strategic goals of the organization that are relevant to its function.

Note that in this example all strategic goals merely specify requirements for operational goals. Such goals are very common because they, in effect, define the areas in which operational goals could, and often should, be set regularly. Strategic goals can be of a different nature, though, pertaining to results that are to be achieved only once. Here are some examples:

- Develop and market a new product line or a new line of services.
- Penetrate a new geographic market.
- Achieve industry agreement on a new set of standards.
- Solve a major scientific problem.
- Mount an expedition to explore. . . .

A unit's strategic goals can then be allocated to the various subunits (or managers) in such a way (see Figure 4.4) that they will be accomplished if every subunit achieves its own. How this allocation of goals takes place and how the decisions are made concerning who gets what will be discussed in Chapter 5. If all subunits achieve their strategic goals, then larger organizational units will achieve theirs all the way up the entire organizational structure.

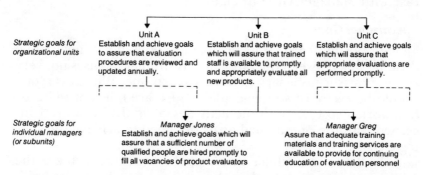

Figure 4.4. Subunit Strategic Goals in Support of One Unit Strategic Goal

It is important to keep in mind, as this picture becomes more complicated, that the organization referred to here can be a corporation, an institution, one government agency, or an entire government; but it can also be a division, a department, or even a single office. Wherever a goals program originates, mission statements, expressed or implied, exist; and strategic goals should be prepared in a more or less formal way if people are to communicate effectively with higher and lower levels, as well as the same level, of an organization hierarchy. Each strategic goal, then, should be supported by strategic goals of the various lower organizational units, or managers; and these managers must accept their share of the particular goal. Please note that this discussion is intended only to assure a common viewpoint on the structure of the goals hierarchy. In no way does it suggest how many goals should be set, or how formally they should be expressed. These questions will be explored in Chapter 5. The point here is that for a goals system to work properly everyone should understand how the various goals in different levels relate to each other.

Very often an organizational unit's strategic goal is simply parceled out among the subunits of the organizational unit. This is especially true of those functional units where each subunit assumes a proportionate share of the organizational unit's strategic goal. Goals which specify at what rate sales should grow, for instance, would be divided among the various regional or functional sections of the sales department.

Some strategic goals are not parceled out though, but apply only to one individual or one organizational unit. This is the case with Manager Greg in Figure 4.4.

Operational Goals

Supporting each strategic goal are operational goals. The dividing line between operational and strategic goals is not very sharp, nor is it necessary to have a sharp one. While everyone should be aware of strategic goals which are relevant to his or her work, most of the time activities of individuals are concerned with the operational goals designed to achieve the strategic goals.

If all the individuals in an operational unit achieve the unit's operational goals, then they will either achieve the unit's strategic goals or else they will be as close to achieving them as they can possibly come. This is true, of course, only if the goals were set properly in the first place.

Operational goals are more specific than strategic ones. As a matter of fact, much that is being taught about the importance of goals being stated properly and measurably, with specific completion dates, applies primarily to operational goals. It does apply, to some extent, to strategic goals; but if those are not as specific, it is not likely that problems will arise as long as the operational goals supporting a strategic goal are clarified quantitatively, qualitatively, and in time.

Operational goals are different for different functions but can be quite similar for people in the same function. For example, sales representatives could all have sales goals for the same products or services, but with respective dollar amounts of sales determined by each of the territories. Similarly, production goals could be almost identical for different units and people performing the same kind of work. There would still be some operational goals that would be different, however; and these would pertain to the development of individuals or to correcting specific problems unique to certain individuals or organizational subunits. Examples of operational goals are given in Figure 4.5, which shows at least one goal at each level of the entire hierarchy.

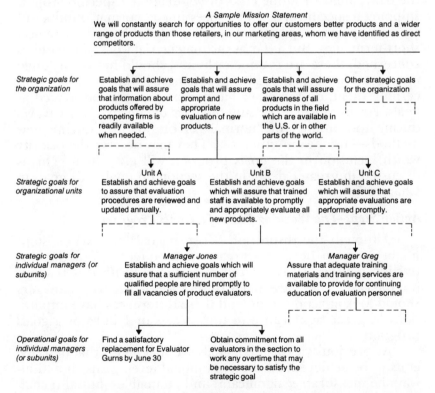

Figure 4.5. Diagram Illustrating the Relationships Between Strategic Goals at Different Organizational Levels, and Operational Goals at the Lowest Level. (At each level only a few goals are shown in support of only one of the goals at the next higher level. Many others, of course, could exist at each level.)

Operational goals as well as strategic goals can be long range and short range. For instance, the operational goal of achieving a certain production level by a certain date can be a short range goal, but there could be the longer operational goal of achieving an even higher production level—a record level—by a later date. There is, of course, nothing wrong with considering the record goal as a strategic one or with calling all goals which are supported by operational goals strategic goals.

Usually it is not necessary to have a clear picture of the line that separates strategic goals from operational goals. Sometimes that line is quite fuzzy and at other times it is unimportant. What is important, though, is that all operational goals be clearly measurable.

One other point deserves mention here. Many managers consider all short targets as goals, and, of course, they are. Even the daily, almost routine tasks of completing a specific project; shipping a specific order; or processing a "normal" number of forms, reports, inquiries, etc., are goals, although extremely short-term ones. But as far as the managerial work of the unit is concerned, these are routine tasks and should not be included in a goals program. Major problems or opportunities concerning them, on the other hand, may properly be treated as goals. For instance, increasing the level of "normal" activity, reducing the number of "normal" errors, or introducing new methods—are meaningful goals. They may deserve the priority which inclusion in the goals program will give them. This is discussed in greater detail in the section on quality of goals in Chapter 5.

Action Steps–The Working Ends of a Goals Program

Although the distinction between goals and action steps might seem to be of no greater consequence than the distinction between strategic and operational goals, this really is not the case. There are major differences in the way managers should look at action steps, and these differences have implications of great significance to the success or failure of a goals program.

As previously explained, goals are statements that describe ends to be achieved. At the operational level, goals should always be measurable, significant, and attainable—but also challenging. *Action steps*, the specific steps that are necessary and desirable in order to come closer to accomplishing a goal, are not ends to be reached; but, rather, they are the steps necessary to achieve the end results.

Action steps must also be measurable, of course, but it does not matter whether they are challenging. Action steps by definition are achievable. Examples of action steps for the goal of assuring that a qualified person will be found by the end of June to replace Evaluator Gurns who is retiring include placing of advertisements and other specific recruiting and selecting activities.* Action steps for the goal of providing adequate training on a specified topic to current employees include such items as searching for and purchasing training materials, scheduling specific seminars, conducting the seminars, etc.

The most important characteristic of action steps is that they are generally *under the control* of the person or group which has been assigned and/or has accepted the responsibility for carrying them out. Thus, the individual or group can properly be held responsible for the completion of action steps.

Goals, because they are also subject to external and uncontrollable events and circumstances, may never be achieved even if all appropriate action steps have been taken. The goal of having adequate personnel available at a specific salary scale can be achieved only if enough qualified people are available and willing to accept positions at the specified salary scale.

Action steps can be large or small, short term or long term. The length of time or the size of task is not the key factor. The only thing that is of importance is that an action step is essentially under full control of the person or people responsible for it.

Sometimes what appears to be an action step prior to its completion may turn out in retrospect to be a goal. The action step of driving to a certain place and arriving there at a certain time can turn out to be a goal if exceptionally inclement weather or a major, sudden obstruction prevents the trip from being completed on time. As a rule, it is fairly easy to tell whether someone can be held accountable for completing an action step because only unusual and unexpected events will prevent its achievement.

---

*Note that many such steps could possibly be taken—without finding a qualified replacement for Evaluator Gurns by June 30, at the salary which can be offered. That is why the distinction between a goal and an action step is so important.

Chapter 5

Making Goals Programs Successful: Part One

Conceptually, there is nothing unusually complicated about goals programs. It would therefore seem as though it should be quite easy to make such programs work well. The fact that few are successful is proof that there are subtleties that can become very important.

Since this chapter concerns the first Linking Element, it might be useful if you gave some thought to the skills that a manager must apply to achieve the best balance of the goals and performance standards of an organizational unit with the performance standards of the various individuals in the unit. These skills are the linking element as shown in the segment of the Linking Elements diagram, Figure 5.1.

Figuré 5.1. Segment of Linking Elements Diagram

If you can spare the time before you read on, you should write out, either in the book itself or on a separate paper, what skills you believe belong in the Linking Element box in the diagram. At the end of the chapter you will then be able to refer back to your notes. You will see that you were aware of many facets of the necessary skills but that you have gained, from your reading, clearer organization of your thoughts and some deeper insights.

You will be given a similar opportunity to collect your thoughts before the discussion of the other Linking Elements.

THE EIGHT POTENTIAL PROBLEM AREAS IN GOALS PROGRAMS

Analysis reveals eight areas in which goals programs can fail to achieve their potential and thus lose the opportunity to become a way of life. In any organization, all eight areas are rarely involved at the same time, though they can be. The eight problem areas can be summarized by the acronym EQIFAPPO as shown below.

POTENTIAL PROBLEM AREAS IN MANAGEMENT BY OBJECTIVE/GOALS PROGRAMS

Extent of Goal Setting

Quality of Goals and Goals Statements

Involvement by Managers in the Way Employees and Lower Level Managers Work Towards Achievement of Their Goals

Frequency of Goals Reviews

Accountability of Subordinates—The Bases on Which Performance Will Be Evaluated

Participation by Subordinates—The Voice Which Subordinates Have in Setting Goals that Affect Them

Performance Appraisal/Evaluation—the Relationship Between the Goals Program and the Performance Evaluation Process

Operational/Developmental Goals Considerations—Where Developmental Goals for Individuals Fit into the Goals Program

Improving the ability to cope with all eight of these problem areas can help a manager achieve higher morale and better performance, the results of a successful goals program.

All eight problem areas are briefly summarized below. The first five areas will be discussed in detail in this chapter. The sixth one, participation by the subordinate, has so many ramifications that it requires a chapter by itself. The last two areas will be covered in Chapter VII. In all three chapters emphasis will be on the way the Linking Elements concept can provide practical suggestions to a manager on how to make better decisions in all these areas.

As you read on, please keep in mind that the way the potential problems are approached depends on the three considerations emphasized throughout this book as crucial to all decisions: (1) the manager's own capabilities, (2) the capabilities and competence of subordinates, and (3) the particular situation. These considerations are especially important with respect to all the aspects of goal setting.

Extent of Goal Setting—Potential Problem Area One

On how many goals should one person concentrate during one review period? *

The number of goals on which one person should be working during any period is an important aspect of a goals program. On one hand, if a goals program exists in an organizational unit, it is desirable that each one of the managers in the unit and possibly also the employees think about and try to achieve goals in all areas of their respective responsibilities. At the same time, they cannot possibly pay equal attention, and devote above-normal effort, to every one of their duties and responsibilities. The most important matters deserve and should be given special attention in planning and preparation. And it may be of equal importance that managers and their subordinates both have the same view on what is important.

The Quality of Goals—Potential Problem Area Two

What aspects of goals and goal statements help to assure that people will understand goals clearly and that goals can become the foundation for serious effort?

---

*Review period is the time between a semiformal or a formal review of progress against goals. How long this period should be is discussed in greater detail under Frequency of Goals Reviews in this chapter and in Chapter 4.

Quality has many dimensions; with respect to goals, these dimensions fall into two major categories: (1) the quality of the goals statements (the way they are expressed) and (2) various quality aspects of the goals themselves.

Quality of Goal Statements

Goals must communicate the same meaning to all those who are concerned with them. To communicate appropriately, goals, especially operational goals, must be measurable so that it is easy to determine to what extent they have been accomplished.

Quality Aspects of Goals

There are two major aspects of goals which impart quality. First, *goals must be relevant and must be perceived as being relevant and important.* Goals that are not so perceived will hurt an entire goals program because people do not respect a goals program that they do not consider to be of genuine value to the organizational unit. If anyone is to devote the extra effort that goals may require, that person must be basically in agreement that the goals are indeed worthwhile ones in relation to higher level goals of the organization. Goals must therefore be relevant to the organization's overall mission and to the strategic goals of an organizational unit.

Secondly, *goals must be both challenging and realistic* (capable of being achieved). This is one of the most difficult requirements to achieve and is a major reason why attempts to manage with goals become paper programs instead of a way of life.

Involvement—Potential Problem Area Three

How extensively should a manager be involved in supervising subordinates while they work to achieve the goals?

Another area where goals programs can lose their chance to become a way of life concerns the amount of involvement by the manager in the action steps which lower level managers or employees set and in the way they implement them. What should the manager's role be? (The subordinate's role in the setting of goals is examined under "Participation" later on in this chapter).

Frequency of Reviews—Potential Problem Area Four

How frequently should progress toward goals be reviewed and goals priorities be rearranged?

Progress reviews are reviews during which managers and the people reporting to them sit down, in a fairly formal way, to review all the goals that have been set at some previous time. Such reviews can have several purposes, among them:

- To inform the manager of progress on goals that have been achieved or will soon be reached
- To review progress on goals that are targeted for the future
- To change goals that are no longer realistic or appropriate
- To set new goals for which a need has arisen
- To review and realign priorities
- To assure that goals and priorities are clearly seen the same way by both managers and subordinates
- To provide additional support and possibly even resources for goals that retain their priorities, but may not be achieved without some additional steps.
- To review whether other people who are affected by the goals are being kept informed.

In light of these reasons, it seems desirable that managers conduct progress reviews regularly.

Accountability—Potential Problem Area Five

What really is it that people should be held accountable for? Goal achievement? Action-step achievement? Both?

The questions involved here ask what it is that a manager can reasonably expect from employees. To what extent can anyone be held accountable for accomplishment of goals if outside interferences prevent their achievement despite intelligently directed and extensive effort?

When goals are not achieved, whose fault is it? And what will be the consequences of establishing responsibility? These questions are closely related to performance evaluation, which will be discussed in Chapter 6.

Participation in the Decision-Making Process—Potential Problem Area Six

How much influence should people have in the selection of goals that affect them directly?

This potential problem area is possibly the most fundamental one. If goals are to be a way of life, then the most important question, it would seem, concerns whose goals they are to be. To whose music should the band be marching?

Performance Evaluation—Potential Problem Area Seven

What should be the role of performance evaluation in a goals program?

Many managers consider performance evaluation a task that they have to perform once or twice a year to provide the personnel department with justification for the increases that their subordinates should receive. In some organizations, performance evaluation is held in even lower esteem; managers go through it in a perfunctory way to satisfy what they perceive to be an ornery organizational requirement. Some organizations, of course, see performance evaluations in proper perspective—as an essential step to fair salary and career administration.

The problem is that performance appraisals determine who gets the promotions as well as who gets the money, and that is close to everybody's heart. Unless they are conducted properly, the rewards may go to those who are lucky rather than those who are competent over the long run, and that ultimately works to everybody's detriment.

Operational and Developmental Goals—Potential Problem Area Eight

How do the goals of employees and subordinate managers fit into a goals program?

That human resources are the most important resources of an organization is generally accepted, although there are many managers who cannot translate this conviction into specific actions. Yet, if an organization neither shows concern for the development of its individuals nor helps them define what work environment changes would provide greater job satisfaction for them, then it is not likely that a high level of enthusiasm for organizational goals will develop. One of the difficulties lies in the fact that only some of an individual's goals are directly in line with those of the organization. Certainly the desire to complete projects successfully is directly related to work achievement. But most personal goals concern career direction and these, while related to organizational goals, are not connected to work achievement. There are many skills involved in helping subordinates select realistic developmental goals—from determining appropriate participation level to career counseling.

The organizational unit in which everyone prepares to be a chief will be an unhappy place if few vacancies occur when people have acquired the qualifications. However, an organizational unit in which all members are competent and strive for higher levels of performance can be a little like a ball team that wants to win every game. It presents a spirited atmosphere in which it can be a pleasure to work. Development of all employees to the limit of their respective capabilities can be an important ingredient, therefore, in the success of the goals program.

A DEFINITION OF GOALS

Before discussing potential problem areas, it might be worthwhile to take a closer look at what a goal really is, or should be, in a work environment. In conventional practice all production targets are called goals or objectives, and that's where the trouble often starts—because a goals program that tries to cover all the bases is stretched too thin to do much good. Goals should be set on only the important matters that determine whether production figures or quality results or sales or costs will maintain a satisfactory trend. The line between expected accomplishments that deserve to be on the exclusive list of goals and those that don't is not a very sharp one. For instance, to get a certain number of batches out this week, to hold costs during the coming month to a certain amount, or to reach a monthly sales target are not really goals in a good goals program. If they were, the goals program would become a treadmill and a bore, not a stimulating, challenging aspect of work that can make work akin to a sport. Just as in a sport, developing the foundations for better performance on a broader scale—and seeing the performance actually improve—can be an exciting experience.

The distinction between accomplishments that deserve to be included in a list of goals and those that do not will become clearer when you actually try to follow the suggestions listed below under "Extent of Goal Setting" and make the difficult choices that are involved.

AN ANALYSIS OF THE EIGHT POTENTIAL PROBLEM AREAS IN A GOALS PROGRAM

The Extent of Goal Setting

Recordkeeping and Goal Setting

There are many managers who believe that goals should be set on all activities. Other managers will set goals on all those

activities which they consider important enough so that the expected results should be specified in advance. Often they expect these to be in writing, together with summaries of plans
for achieving them. The attempt to make a goals program so
comprehensive can easily bring a heavy load of paperwork and
may therefore be self-defeating. People see such goals programs primarily as just another task that must be done according to some schedule. They resent the unnecessary effort, the
thick books of goals and action steps, and the excessive re-
straints these place on their freedom to react to changing situations in a creative way. Management can thus lose its chance to
make goal setting an integral part of the working habits of employees—to stress goal achievement as the essence of competent performance.

The more successful programs, therefore, carefully identify from the goals that could be set those that deserve priority,
and the programs assure that these priorities are clearly understood by the people involved. During any period, each person
can then give priority for extra effort and time to those action
steps which will help to achieve priority goals. Such attention to
a limited number of goals during any review period requires
good communications and enough contact between manager
and subordinate manager or employee to assure that priorities
are seen the same way by both. This is especially important because the matters for which goals should be set are usually not
those which are of the highest urgency and importance.
Rather, they are those which, while very important, may be far
less urgent at the moment. (See below, page 66.)

If fewer goals are to be set than there are responsibilities
and important activities, however, it is necessary to select priorities. This is not easy, but considering two major influences can
help in the decision-making process. The influences are the capabilities of subordinates and the characteristics of the goal itself.

One question that many managers ask when it is suggested
that goals be set only on some selected areas concerns the other
functional responsibilities: What will prevent them from being
ignored? If it weren't for that question, however, managers
would not attempt to cover too many or too few responsibilities
with goals; and this potential problem area would not exist.

Here is where the science of management ends, and where
the art begins. If you work at it, you will undoubtedly not find it

too difficult to establish for each of the people reporting directly to you what an acceptable and normal level of performance is
with respect to those duties not currently covered by goals.
Since the frequency with which you hold reviews varies, as will
be discussed soon, this is not really as much of a problem as it
appears at first sight. As soon as it turns out that a problem
develops or opportunities become apparent and no goals exist
to deal with them, a goals review can be called and the priorities
can be changed, or some goals can be dropped and new ones
can be set.

No matter how many goals are set, every subordinate,
highly competent or not so competent, still has to work on all
the duties which are part of the job. However, during any period, there should also be one or several tasks or responsibilities
which deserve greatest attention because they are the ones
where maximum improvement is especially important during
the coming months or weeks. These are the tasks on which the
extra effort is required, and this is where goals should be set.

In deciding how many goals to set, it therefore is important
to look at the capabilities of a subordinate. Then, to decide
what functions or projects should be emphasized with goals, it
is necessary to look at the functions which are being performed
and to select those that deserve highest priority.

How Many Goals to Set—The Capabilities of Subordinates

With some subordinates a manager can agree on several
goals because they are competent enough to work on several
goals at the same time. There are other subordinates for whom
only one single goal can be set. Determining how many goals to
set requires an assessment of the subordinate's capabilities in
terms of technical competence as well as maturity.

As far as this book is concerned, maturity of a subordinate
does not refer to age, nor does it refer to personal psychological
maturity, though it is related to it to some extent. It refers instead to the maturity of the person with respect to the management process discussed here. A mature subordinate makes decisions on a rational basis, understands and accepts the need to
forecast, sets goals, plans the work, and works the plan. Such a
person does not resent planning and goal setting as an imposi-
tion. He or she is keenly aware of the benefits of thorough analysis and will assure that emotional reactions are kept out of the
goal setting and decision making processes. Lack of emotional-

ism in goal setting does not, however, mean denial of self-interest. On the contrary, a mature person gives high and proper weight to the personal benefits which an alternative will bring. If the system is such that low, easy-to-achieve goals are in his or her best interest, then the mature person will strive to set such goals. Conversely, if the (psychological and/or tangible) reward system favors challenging goals, such an individual will set goals that way.

A mature individual usually will not be concerned about exposing lack of knowledge or inadequate training on any topic, or about asking the manager for help and advice sincerely when he/she believes this to be useful for greater achievement.

Technical competence is usually quite easy to assess. Maturity, on the other hand, is not simple to recognize; but the findings of researchers can help to provide some guidelines. There are two schools of thought on the subject of maturity, both of which have much in common. One looks at the life cycle, traces the maturity of a person from birth to full adulthood, and draws a parallel to the job situation. The other one looks at the levels of psychological existence and draws conclusions about appropriate leadership styles from these.

Life Cycle Theory of Leadership

In helping to decide how many goals can be set, an interesting diagram provides some guidelines. It was developed by two professors at Ohio State University, Dr. Paul Hersey and Dr. Kenneth Blanchard. They entitle it the Life Cycle Theory of Leadership. The diagram shows the development of an individual from infancy to self-sufficiency, or the development of a new employee from the first day on the job to full job competence.

In considering Figure 5.2 it is first necessary to understand the two coordinates, the vertical and horizontal axes. The horizontal axis depicts the extent to which a parent, or a manager, assigns tasks. If near the left end of the line, the manager or parent assigns very few tasks and the subordinate or offspring makes all or most of the decisions about what task to work on. Towards the right end of the line, the manager or parent assigns most, if not all, tasks. In other words, the farther to the right one moves, the more the manager or parent decides what has to be done.

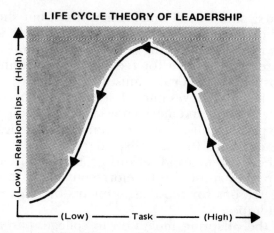

Figure 5.2. A Representation of the Life Cycle Theory of Leadership (Based on the work of Paul Hersey and Kenneth Blanchard. Reproduced by special permission from the February 1974 Training and Development Journal, by the American Society for Training and Development, Inc., Copyright © 1974; artwork courtesy NFPA.)

On the vertical axis, the parent's or the manager's concern for establishing a good *work* relationship is depicted. At the bottom of the diagram, the parent or manager has little concern about how well the subordinate likes the decisions which are made. At the top of the diagram, the parent shows maximum concern about the way the decisions or work arrangements are accepted by the offspring or subordinate.

It is important to notice that love or warm feelings do not enter this diagram. A parent can have, and show, great love for an offspring and still show little concern about whether a child likes to be told what to do and what not to do.

To understand the meaning of the diagram follow the line, from right to left, first for an offspring:

1. On the lower righthand side of the diagram, the parent must assign a great many tasks to the infant, and there is little need for the parent to be concerned about whether or not the child likes the decisions which are made.

2. As the child begins to mature and becomes aware of the world, the parent must explain the reasons for decisions. This is shown by the way the curve rises to the left toward greater concern for relationship. In the early

years, parents still must assign tasks, but should allow the offspring increasing freedom to decide what he or she may do. But as the child grows, parents must show increasing concern for feelings by explaining the reasons why certain rules must be followed.

3. As the child moves into adolescence and becomes more independent and more knowledgeable about the world, the parents must relinquish some of their right to make the decisions for the offspring; but at the same time, if they wish to avoid serious problems in their relationship, they must also be more convincing in explaining the reasons for those assignments or rules which they still impose.

4. As the offspring moves on to college, parents can no longer be deeply involved in making decisions for the offspring because they are no longer in close or continuous contact. The offspring must accept more of the responsibility for decisions. At the same time, the responsibility for initiative in the relationship begins to pass to the offspring and the parents have less opportunity to shape the relationship the way they would like to see it.

5. Finally, when the offspring is married and is established in his/her own career, the parents can no longer assign tasks at all; and the initiative for the relationship has moved almost exclusively to the offspring.

What is true for the child as it matures is true for an employee who enters and becomes established in a new job. The diagram therefore applies to new employees and managers. It also applies to experienced people in new assignments. There is one difference between the life cycle for the relationship between parent and offspring and the life cycle for the relationship between manager and employee. While the development of the child toward the mature adult is a fairly steady path, the employee does not necessarily progress steadily from right to left. Job changes, changes in the organization or in reporting relationships, or the more nebulous personal matters affecting employee behavior can bring shifts on the curve in either direction.

New employees or managers must be introduced to their jobs. They must receive orientation and on-the-job training.

They must be told the rules of the organization, the procedures in effect, and all the requirements of the job. If they are people with little experience and education, they must accept what they are told, and usually do so willingly. As they become acquainted with the job, there is greater need to explain reasons for procedures or instructions, if the person is to perform well. Even people with extensive experience and/or education first have to be oriented to the job and have to be told what is expected of them.

Depending on previous experience and personal capabilities, new employees move up the curve more or less rapidly. As they progress in their careers and competence, their superiors must relinquish the specific assignment of tasks more and more. They must increase their concern for the relationship as the subordinates reach higher capabilities or possibly higher positions. There comes a time when superiors can no longer be very specific in telling them how or what they have to do.

How fast and far along the curve a person can move, from right to left on the curve, depends on ability and potential. For instance, retarded persons whose capabilities allow them to master only the most routine tasks live permanently on the right side of the curve, able to assume only a low level of responsibility. They always have to be given assignments and told what to do. While there must be some concern about how they like their tasks and assignments, such concern can only be quite limited. The majority of employees in a technologically advanced society such as the United States, however, once established in their jobs, work either near the peak of the curve or somewhat to the left of it. Their superiors must still assign much of the work, but assignments must be made with a high degree of concern about how employees like them and with appropriate explanations of the reasons for them.

Most managers and highly educated knowledge industry professionals work on the left side of the curve. They are capable of accepting assignments in more general terms. They make many of the decisions about what they should do, when it should be done, and how it should be done. At the same time, their superiors cannot have as much concern about the relationships that exist between them, and the subordinates themselves have to accept a considerable amount of responsibility for these relationships. This places a fairly heavy responsibility on them to establish their own goals in consultation with their superiors, to work independently toward the achievement of the goals, and to keep their superiors informed of progress.

There are people who live at the lower left corner of the diagram. In the extreme, in another environment, if a manager were to have Albert Einstein or any of the great inventive geniuses in the history of mankind working for him or her, the supervisory role of that manager vis-á-vis the subordinate would probably be extremely limited, perhaps non-existent. "Good morning Albert, glad you were able to come in today. Is there anything I can do for you?" That would possibly be the extent of the supervision that would bring the greatest and best performance from Albert Einstein.

Highly competent, highly motivated people, as they climb the career ladder also come closer and closer to that ultimate point on the curve. As was pointed out before, the curve does not depict warmth in the relationship, nor does it show such matters as trust and mutual confidence. These are outside the scope of the diagram in many ways. The diagram really applies only if there is a good interpersonal relationship, characterized by friendliness, mutual respect, and, in case of family, the love and warmth that family life should provide.

Conclusions From the Life Cycle Theory

With respect to the extent of goal setting, the conclusions from the curve shown in the diagram are fairly clear:

1. With a new employee, or one who is limited in potential for personal development, only very few goals can be set.
2. With more experienced, competent, and mature individuals, several goals can be set at one time. It is clear that toward the left bottom of the curve goals can exist for most of the important activities and responsibilities.
3. A major goal for every manager is to help every unit employee continue to move along the curve to the left, i.e., the path to maturity.

The diagram, of course, does not supply clear-cut guidelines, but a manager who understands the diagram fully can find in it a guide to the number of goals which can be set with a subordinate.

Levels of Psychological Existence

M. Scott Myers and Susan S. Myers described seven levels of psychological existence which were based on the extensive research work of Dr. Clare Graves. The seven levels, as phrased by the Myers, are outlined in Figure 5.3.

7. *EXISTENTIAL*—High tolerance for ambiguity and people with differing values. Likes to do jobs in his own way without constraints of authority or bureaucracy. Goal-oriented but toward a broader arena and longer time perspective.

6. *SOCIOCENTRIC*—High affiliation needs. Dislikes violence, conformity, materialism, and manipulative management. Concerned with social issues and the dignity of man.

5. *MANIPULATIVE*—Ambitious to achieve higher status and recognition. Strives to manipulate people and things. May achieve goals through gamesmanship, persuasion, bribery, or official authority.

4. *CONFORMIST*—Low tolerance for ambiguity and for people whose values differ from his own. Attracted to rigidly defined roles in accounting, engineering, military, and tends to perpetuate the status quo. Motivated by a cause, philosophy, or religion.

3. *EGOCENTRIC*—Rugged individualism. Selfish, thoughtless, unscrupulous, dishonest. Has not learned to function within the constraints imposed by society. Responds primarily to power.

2. *TRIBALISTIC*—Found mostly in primitive societies and ghettos. Lives in a world of magic, witchcraft, and superstition. Strongly influenced by tradition and the power exerted by the boss, tribal chieftain, policeman, school teacher, politician, and other authority figures.

1. *REACTIVE*—Not aware of self or others as individuals or human beings. Reacts to basic physiological needs. Mostly restricted to infants.

Figure 5.3. Levels of Psychological Existence, by M. Scott Myers and Susan S. Myers (Reproduced with permission from the Winter 1973 issue of THE BUSINESS QUARTERLY, Copyright © 1973 by THE BUSINESS QUARTERLY, School of Business Administration, The University of Western Ontario, London, Canada.)

It appears as though in many ways these seven levels roughly parallel the Life Cycle diagram. For each level, certain leadership approaches are better than others. In general, the lower the level, the fewer the number of goals with which the individual can work at any one time. People at the two or possibly three lowest levels probably cannot cope with a goals concept at all and have to be assigned tasks. People at the fourth level are likely to perform well with a very small number of specifically delineated goals. At higher levels, people can undoubtedly cope with larger numbers of goals and work with them in a more competent fashion.

The seven levels of psychological existence are similar to the Life Cycle diagram in another way. The levels are not sharply defined, particularly since every individual, at any moment, may be living at more than one level, and people switch back and forth between levels just as they may move up and down on the life cycle line as their situation changes. Despite this lack of precision, the separation into seven distinct levels is quite helpful. It highlights the difficulties that a manager can face if he or she misjudges the psychological existence level of an individual or a group. For instance, an egocentric manager who attempts to work with a group that lives at the existential level is bound to be highly ineffective and create considerable friction. The same is true of an exceptionally mature manager who lives at that highest level and has to work with a group that is at a much lower level.

An autocratic manager in a sophisticated, mature group will be unable to gain the group's respect. If his or her instructions are incomplete or inadequate, as they frequently are likely to be, the group may either ignore them or may follow them to the letter, in either case to the organization's detriment. Such a manager cannot last very long in that environment.

Conversely, a highly sociocentric manager is likely to fail in a conformist environment because he or she will be perceived as weak, unable to make decisions, and ill prepared for the task. Conformists might even expect the manager to make decisions that require high acceptance. They would, of course, expect him or her to make decisions in their best interest and convince them of their correctness rather than to make them jointly with the group.

Individuals in a group and especially the group as a whole must be ready for the managerial style used by the manager. This is of great importance in every environment. In one instance an instructor in an evening course in a college attempted to conduct the course in a highly participative way. The particular instructor recognized that the students were not ready to rise to the psychological level required but thought that it would be an interesting experiment to try anyway. He thought this would be especially true since it was an evening course in management and most of the students were adults who were at least two to three years older than their daytime counterparts.

On the first evening of the course, he told the class that they would be making many of the decisions normally reserved for the instructor. They would decide on what basis they would be graded, how fast the instruction would proceed, what emphasis should be given to the various topic segments, and what instructional techniques were to be used. They could decide, for instance, on the ratio of lectures to group discussion and problem solving activities and on the types of tests they were to receive.

As it happened, the class did not turn into a highly motivated group. It was, in fact, a disaster, except for a few students who rated it exceedingly high. Students complained that the instructor did not seem to know what he expected from them or seemed ill prepared to present the subject to the class. Members of the class, with few exceptions, were totally unprepared to cope with a psychological environment far above the one that existed in their other classes. They were asked, fairly abruptly and without adequate preparation, to assume responsibility for their own learning, to set learning goals, and to live at a psychological level of existence far above the one which they were capable of achieving at their respective stages of development.

It is quite likely that with adequate preparation and gradual development the students could have accepted the new environment. The few who were able to make the transition turned in outstanding work as the sessions progressed. Whether that was due to their own capabilities or at least partly attributable to the approach of the instructor has not been verified through further experiments.

What this example highlights is something that many managers have noticed or have experienced either to their satisfaction or dismay. A team or group must be prepared for a change in leadership style and must learn how to cope with it before it can respond favorably to it.

Just as the levels of psychological existence appear to apply to groups, the life cycle diagram also appears to apply to them. Newly formed committees or other groups whose members have not previously worked with each other sometimes need considerable structure and task assignment to organize themselves into effective teams. If they are composed of people who have considerable experience in working and contributing to group effort, they can free themselves quickly from external direction and move rapidly along the life cycle line from right to left. If, on the other hand, a group lacks enough individuals with experience and knowledge, it requires considerable patience and good understanding on the part of the manager to slowly wean the group away from highly structured leadership toward a more mature, participative style in which individuals contribute effectively to the group. Without careful direction, the group may experience the problems that arise from the attempts by some team members to assume leadership in the group, from the fear of the less-assertive members to expose thoughts that may be rejected, or from game playing by those who are not fully in agreement with team objectives or assignment.

Characteristics of the Goal Itself

The Life Cycle Theory primarily concerns the influence which the competence of subordinates has on the extent of goal setting. It determines how many goals should be set. The manager's capabilities and the situation are also involved in deciding the functions or projects for which goals should be established—and that involves setting priorities.

Setting Priorities

Deciding on priorities is necessary to assure that the limited number of goals which are set are for the most important functions or projects and not for those with lower significance. Priorities are useful, not only for a goals program, but also for good management of time. There is no question that managers who want to make best use of the time available to them must allocate their time to activities in proportion to their respective priorities. Competent managers attempt to spend as much of their time as possible on the high priority matters and delegate accordingly.

Adequate attention to priorities can assure that when more work has to be done than the available time permits, those goals which deserve maximum attention indeed receive it and that if anything has to remain undone, it will be the project with the lowest priority. This means that the manager has to decide, sometimes alone and sometimes in conjunction with the subordinate, what operational goals deserve highest priority for the upcoming period. Sometimes these priorities are easy to set, but sometimes many complications exist which make setting them difficult.

Several factors must be considered when setting priorities. The most significant are (1) the urgency of the goal and (2) the importance of the goal. Sometimes goals are both urgent and important. Sometimes they are urgent but not important—for example, filling low-level vacancies quickly whenever they arise. The latter type of goal obviously cannot qualify as a goal on which effort should be concentrated during the upcoming period. Sometimes goals are important but not urgent. An important project, for instance, might have a completion date in the distant future.

Other less significant considerations for determining priorities are:

1. How quickly the particular goal can be achieved. There often is a desire to work for those goals which can be achieved quickly because that simplifies scheduling and allows full concentration on goals that are more time consuming.

2. The extent to which completion of the goal might help with other goals. For instance, if, during the next period, one goal calls for obtaining agreement on new procedures, then such a goal would deserve a higher priority than goals which will be easier to achieve once the new procedures are in effect.

Most of the time considerations related to priority are not easy to sort out and consequently goals that appear to be urgent often receive higher priority than they deserve. Goals on important matters that are not urgent are thus postponed longer than they should be, resulting in crises at a later time. Figure 5.4 can help, to some extent, to dramatize the necessity to keep

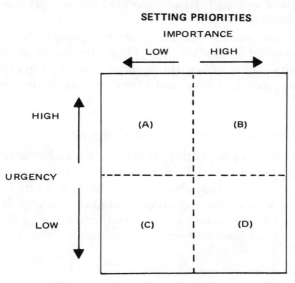

Figure 5.4. An Importance/Urgency Diagram That Helps Determine Priorities for Particular Goals

important matters in mind. First priority must go to those goals that are both important and urgent; they appear in area B of the figure. In defining goals that belong to this category, it is necessary to exercise restraint; otherwise specific production or quality goals for the upcoming months are the only goals which will be set. As one articulate rancher once phrased the problem: "These guys are forever chasing the cows, and no one ever builds the fences so they can stop the chasing." Area B matters rarely allow enough time for significant reviews and therefore do not deserve inclusion on the list of priority goals.

The next priority seems difficult to decide. How does one choose between low importance and high urgency (area A) and high importance and low urgency (area D)? Things that are urgent certainly deserve attention even if they are not very important. These matters, however, should be completed quickly and, from the point of view of an effective goals program, if they are not important, they belong with the regular routines of the job.

This leaves the matters in area D, which require planning so they will be completed on time. More so than any other projects, these deserve careful thought to decide on goals and action steps and on completion dates. Only careful planning will prevent matters in area D from becoming emergencies at some time in the future.

Finally, those matters that are neither important nor urgent are rarely involved in goal setting. They are shown in area C. When the workload is heavy, there should be some question as to whether any work at all should be done on matters in this area.

Conclusions From the Importance/Urgency Diagram

With respect to goal setting, there is a somewhat surprising conclusion. It is not the matters in area B—those most important *and* most urgent—that require the highest priority for goal setting. These will receive maximum attention anyway. It is the matters in area D that need to be covered with goals so that they assume greater urgency and receive the attention they deserve.

Conclusions on Extent of Goal Setting

It may sometimes appear difficult to limit the number of operational goals which are set with a person and to decide on those which deserve the highest priority. One practical way for you to do this might be to come to an agreement with each individual reporting to you at the beginning of the year on strategic goals for each area of responsibility. As soon as these goals have been set, you and your subordinate could together select one or several operational goals that deserve primary emphasis during the first one- to three-month period. All the other goals could be lumped under a single goal: "To maintain performance in all other areas of responsibility." The subordinate would have to have a clear view of the action steps and their completion dates only for the goals singled out. Any extra or special effort will be devoted to these goals rather than others. Usual responsibilities would be discharged as well as they had been in the past.

Since you can conduct reviews fairly frequently, a new goal can easily be added whenever the need for one becomes apparent. At the end of the review period, progress on the priority goals for the period is reviewed. New priorities for the coming period are then discussed. This is when other goals may be considered.

In deciding on the number of goals that should be selected with a specific subordinate, you can look at the capabilities of the subordinate as well as at the requirements of the situation. There is great temptation to set more goals, of course, in order to obtain improvement or above-normal effort in many areas. It should be obvious, though, that this is quickly self-defeating. If more goals are set with a person than that person is capable of working on simultaneously, the results will undoubtedly be disappointing. If more effort is required than the maximum which he or she is prepared to give, then the goals will not be taken seriously and resentment will arise. In the end, less will be accomplished than if the number of formal goals is limited to what is appropriate for the situation and the capabilities of the subordinate.

Summary–Extent of Goal Setting

1. The number of goals which can be set with any one subordinate depend on that person's capabilities.
2. The more mature and competent a subordinate, the more goals can be set with him or her.
3. Goal selection requires great personal restraint on your part. Setting too many priority goals with any one per-

son can cause serious damage to a goals program's via-
bility.
4. While strategic goals can be set in all areas of responsibility, operational goals should only be set on those matters that deserve highest priority for the upcoming period, until the next review.
5. Goals will bring the best results if they are set on those
matters that are important, but not urgent.

Quality of Goals and Goal Statements

There are several aspects of goals and goal statements that
determine their quality, among them:

1. The mechanical aspects of goal statements must be in
order. This refers to the clarity and precision of goal statements. Goal statements must communicate the same meaning
to all parties. To do this, several requirements must be met:

a. The goal statement must either state or clearly imply
who is to accomplish the goal.
b. The goal statement must have a specific date by which
the goal is to be accomplished.
c. The goal statement must specify or must clearly imply
the quantity that is to be achieved.
d. The goal statement must specify or clearly imply, based
on the organization's environment, what level of quality
is sought.

For example, a goal statement may say, "We will prepare a
monthly report." This clearly is not definite enough even
though it appears to be specific. Such a goal statement is inadequate because it does not name the date by which the report
will be provided, nor does it specify either quantity (the information that is to be contained in the report) or quality level of
the information in the report. It may very well be that quantity
and quality is known because the statement refers to reports
previously prepared, thereby specifying standards by implication. But, lacking previous standards and a completion date,
the goal statement is inadequate. A more appropriate goals
statement might say: "We will submit, by the fifth of every
month, a report on our activities similar to those previously
filed," or "covering at least the following topics," or "of (00)
pages, covering at least the following topics . . . ."

2. All goals must be in line with the mission. This was discussed under "Extent of Goal Setting," especially with respect

to the selection of priorities. If a manager insists on priorities that are not perceived by subordinates as very relevant to the mission of the organizational unit, then subordinates will obviously not take the goals program very seriously.

3. Goals must be challenging. This means that they must be set high, but not so high that they are beyond achievement. Goals that are not challenging usually need not be set. Chances are they will be achieved whether anyone makes a special effort to achieve them or not. On the other hand, goals that are so high that they are not likely to be achieved are usually "demotivating." People will rarely strive for something that they feel they cannot reach. A few famous studies by Dr. David McClelland* and his associates at Harvard University attempted to gain greater insight into achievement motivation, the need people feel for doing something particularly well. McClelland's studies used people from many fields who seemed to demonstrate a high need for achievement.

McClelland's research disclosed a pattern of behavior characteristics for high achievers that was unexpectedly different, in some ways, from traditional views of how successful people behaved. The research indicated that those people who strove for a high degree of achievement enjoyed moderate risks and challenges that were neither too easy nor too hard, risks and challenges that offered an approximately 50/50 probability of accomplishment with a high level of effort. These people also wanted steady feedback about how they were doing, and they readily accepted help when it was useful to them. Their fear of failure and their enjoyment of success were far more intense than were similar feelings in other people; and this, in part, explained their willingness to devote the extra effort that often is necessary for success. Money and other material benefits of accomplishment were important to the high achievers only to the extent that these rewards helped to prove that goals had been achieved. Many high achievers were happiest competing against their own previous best efforts.

The subjects of the studies obviously set challenging goals that were not unrealistic. McClelland's work has been confirmed by research in schools, which has shown that pupils with a history of success will usually set realistic goals, while those

---

*David C. McClelland, J. W. Atkinson, R. A. Clark, and E. L. Lowell, THE ACHIEVEMENT MOTIVE (New York: Appleton-Century-Crofts, 1953).

who fail regularly tend to set goals too high or too low (see Chapter 9, page 186).

The odd thing about managers or employees who are not experienced with goal setting is that, when asked to set goals, they will set unrealistic goals for themselves, seriously hoping or believing them to be achievable. When later they realize that they were overly optimistic, they will then justify failure to achieve the goals by pointing out that they had been unrealistic in the first place.

Learning how to set goals so that they are both realistic and challenging therefore appears to be an important foundation for achievement motivation. As McClelland's studies indicate, managers and individuals who are high achievers usually set challenging but fairly safe goals.

While helping subordinates set realistic goals will not necessarily turn them into high achievers, it is true that unrealistic goals will hinder the creation of an atmosphere where subordinates can find higher levels of motivation. It would seem, therefore, that goals are most beneficial to the organization *and* to the individual when they are set just below the point where they would be unrealistic but where most of them are still achievable. At this level, the joy of achievement will be high and failure is likely to be minimal. Goals may be missed by a small margin or by a short period of time, but that's all.

Helping employees and subordinate managers set realistic goals is a big challenge for a manager. This is why competent managers are careful and resourceful in coaching their subordinates in goal setting. Managers need to work not only with those who set their goals too low, but also with those who set them unrealistically high.

Determining how challenging a goal actually is is most difficult. It is relatively easy to write each goal statement so that it communicates properly, or to choose only goals that are thoroughly relevant to the mission of the organizational unit. It is an entirely different matter, though, to determine in advance what goal will turn out to be challenging. When managers and their subordinates try to determine what quantity or quality levels are to be accomplished and a completion date, they are relying on forecasts or estimates. Depending on the environment, the availability of data, and the goal setters' ability to forecast, the goals will be more or less accurate. They are targets that appear to be achievable. But are they challenging?

One way managers can tell whether goals are really set at a level which is realistic but challenging is to look at effort as well as the percentage of instances when goals are exceeded. If effort is high, about 50 percent of the goals will be exceeded and 50 percent will not be fully achieved when they are really set at a challenging and realistic level.

For the manager, it is partly a matter of judging the situation correctly, but even more a matter of being aware of the attitudes of the individual subordinate. What complicates matters is that certain people inevitably set goals much higher or lower than is realistic for them. Some set them higher because they wish to please the manager, while others are just unrealistic and feel they can achieve much more than can realistically be expected. Others either because the environment punishes the setting of challenging goals or because they like to play it safe, set goals that lack challenge. The climate of the organizational unit exerts great influence over goal setting. If people are aware that they will not suffer when they do not fully achieve goals which challenge, then there is a much greater likelihood that they will set challenging goals.

One-hundred percent batting averages are impossible in the goal-setting game. The trick is to strive for steady improvement in setting goals that stretch abilities. Managers must be alert to subordinates' needs for coaching and assistance and they must keep alert for problems. Reluctance of most subordinates to set challenging goals is a clear indication that something is not completely right in the motivational climate. The extent to which subordinates are willing to set challenging goals is an important diagnostic indicator of the confidence of subordinates in the manager and the system, and in the competence of the manager to cope with the system.

Summary–Quality of Goals

1. Goals statements must be clear, concise, and measurable in quantity and quality as well as in time. Goals statements should also specify or clearly imply who is responsible, particularly if the goal requires more than one person's work to achieve it.
2. Goals must be perceived to be important so that employees do not feel that they are asked to spend extra effort on that which they believe to be trivial.
3. Goals must be challenging, but at the same time they

must be realistic so that about 50 percent of them can be achieved or exceeded with intelligently directed effort consistently applied.

Involvement by Managers in the Way Subordinates Work Towards the Achievement of Their Goals

A goal for an office or plant may call for a 5-percent productivity increase, or a field sales force's goal may call for an overall 10-percent increase in sales. These goals would be divided up among the various sub-units of the staff in the office or plant or among the members of the sales force.

The subunits, in turn, would decide on implementation goals and action steps to carry out their respective share. The plant or office departments would decide what would be analyzed in detail to determine where opportunities for savings exist, where additional equipment should be purchased, or where new methods should be installed. For the sales force, they would decide what market areas should receive special emphasis, what specific accounts should receive more careful planning, and so forth.

The question which the office manager, the plant manager, or the sales manager should not take lightly is the extent to which he or she should be supervising work so that it is being done, and done correctly. How much checking is necessary?

Among the factors which must be considered with regard to extent of supervision are workload and competence of the lower level managers. Also involved is the question of how much confidence managers have in the ability and the competence of the subordinates to take assignments to a successful conclusion. Subordinates are quite aware of this factor. Many managers give their subordinates the feeling that they are constantly looking over their shoulder and that they do not permit creative thinking and freedom to do the job as they (the subordinates) feel it should be done. This is often derisively referred to as "snoopervision."

Then there are those managers who are rarely available for questions or help, even when needed. Such managers, though they sometimes believe themselves to be good delegators, can be most frustrating to the people who work for them. There is inevitably considerable information and authority to which subordinates do not have easy access. Managers control the limits of the resources available to the group and represent the only legitimate route to help from higher levels of management. Those who refuse to become involved with complex, difficult, or risky decisions or who are unavailable when such decisions have to be made are not the competent delegators that they sometimes believe themselves to be.

The question of supervision is not at all theoretical. Managers have to decide for each individual who reports to them how frequently and in how much detail they should be checking progress toward goals. This involves deciding not only how frequently they should set formal reviews for all goals (see page 78 below) but also how often they should check progress on the goal of greatest interest to them at the moment. It also concerns how specific they should be when making suggestions about steps that should be taken to achieve a goal if it appears as though subordinates are not taking appropriate steps.

Clear and simple guidelines on extent of supervision are not easy to come by. Some general principles can be followed, though, which will assure that the question has received careful thought.

In deciding how deeply to become involved in helping subordinates or in checking how they approach their assignments, managers should keep the two theories of maturation discussed previously in mind—i.e., the Myers' Levels of Psychological Existence and the Hersey-Blanchard Life Cycle Theory. Those subordinates who have either limited experience or limited capabilities and are less mature, in a business sense, than they might be (who, in theoretical terms, live below their sociocentric level or have not grown past the peak of the life-cycle curve) require fairly careful checking to see that they are approaching their assignments in a competent way. More competent or mature people require considerably less of this over-the-shoulder watching; and, in fact, to do it would lead to considerable dissatisfaction on their part.

Management involvement in supervision not only concerns the frequency of progress checks but also the detail with which managers expect action steps to be set and the level of formality of the action plan. With some subordinates, as part of their development and training process, it may indeed be necessary to lay out a very detailed action program in writing for each of the limited number of goals that have been selected as priorities. With more experienced and mature employees, less formality is required. Detailed discussion of action programs may be needed only on a very few goals. Highly competent and mature subordinates can best decide themselves how detailed or formal the action plans for almost all goals should be. The manager might rarely, if ever, check them, except when the subordinate asks for a review of the action plan to take advantage of any ideas the manager might contribute. However, when a project is critical, it may call for fairly detailed involvement on the part of the manager, even if the subordinates are quite competent, if for no other reason than to show that the manager accepts full responsibility for the results.

With respect to involvement, here as elsewhere three factors should influence the manager's behavior—the situation, subordinate capability, and the manager's own personality and needs. For instance, as one of several goals a subordinate may take a course at a local college on a topic relevant to work. With a highly motivated and mature person, the manager may do little more than occasionally ask the subordinate how the course is going and whether help is needed. With one who is less motivated or less capable of learning, much more would be appropriate. The manager should probably inquire regularly how the course is going and what help the subordinate may need to gain full advantage from the course. The manager might also attempt to provide assignments which would put to immediate use any new knowledge the learner had acquired. With the least competent employees, it might be necessary, after every class, to briefly review the lesson and to help them clarify the more difficult concepts.

Detailed follow-up of this type could be deeply resented by competent people as interference. On the other hand, for many who feel insecure or lacking in knowledge but would still like to do well, such "interference" might be considered very helpful and could be sincerely appreciated.

There is one question which managers frequently ask when it is suggested they allow their subordinates more freedom in working toward goals: "How do I know that action plans have really been considered and that they are being followed?" That question is, of course, not always easy to answer because they really know very little about the plans of subordinates in whom they have confidence. However, managers have access to some information about progress from day to day contacts or from the reports they receive. Furthermore, managers routinely receive considerable information about action plans and how they have been revised during each goals review and whenever subordinates encounter difficulties. A subordinate who does not provide such information voluntarily is not yet sufficiently mature, and more detailed monitoring or checking is required, as well as training or coaching to provide the subordinate with greater awareness of the manager's need for up-to-date information. The highly competent subordinate recognizes his/her responsibility to keep the manager informed so that the manager has a general idea on progress in all areas for which he or she is responsible. One of the major responsibilities of the manager, therefore, is to help subordinates develop a thorough understanding of their responsibility for communicating any obstacles or occurrences that may prevent the achievement of a goal. Two very common characteristics of less mature subordinates are the desire to be left alone to complete projects as they see fit long before they have achieved the experience and competence to consistently reach good results and an aversion to filing regular verbal or written reports. Competent subordinates, on the other hand, keep their managers informed about developments by providing brief synopses of events and progress on a regular basis. They recognize that managers too have to report to someone who expects them to be knowledgeable about the status of major projects and aware of significant problems.

Summary—Involvement of Managers in the Work of Subordinates

1. Involvement concerns (a) how much discussion there should be about action steps necessary to achieve a goal and (b) the frequency and detail with which you check on how well the subordinate implements action steps.
2. The extent of desirable involvement on your part depends on the capabilities and maturity of your subordinates.
3. The more competent a subordinate, the less welcome is your involvement, except when requested. The less competent a subordinate, the more necessary is your involvement.
4. Involvement is viewed as desirable by subordinates only if it is clearly intended to provide help rather than to evaluate performance.
5. Your expressed goal should be to help subordinates develop so that progressively less involvement will be needed.

Frequency of Goals Reviews

A goals review is simply this: At least once a year the manager and each subordinate set strategic and operational goals on all the major responsibilities in the subordinate's job. At the same time, they select those few operational goals (see"Extent of Goal Setting") appropriate for the subordinate and the situation for priority attention during the period until the next review, which may come between one and three months later. This assures that while goals have been set in all areas of responsibility, at the next review emphasis is on high-priority goals. During this review priorities may be shifted or new high-priority goals added. As an alternative to this approach, the manager and the subordinate could select only priority goals and lump all other duties and responsibilities under one priority goal stating that all other functions would receive their normal attention.

Goals review sessions have an important communications function since they allow both the manager and the subordinate to gain clearer perspective on many aspects of their joint responsibilities. Daily contact usually deals with specific problems of the moment or with small issues; it rarely provides a comprehensive review of goals. If it does, it qualifies as one of the goals reviews under discussion here. Even managers who are in continuous contact with their people can gain many benefits from regular, semiformal reviews of all the goals on which their people are working. Not only do such reviews assure that the planning process is a continuous one and that the horizon is searched regularly for new opportunities, but also they maintain a more open communications climate which presents opportunities for a relaxed exchange of views.

One of the questions that managers must resolve about reviews concerns how frequently they should be held with different people in different situations. Should reviews be on a rigid schedule? Should they be held more often with the competent or with the less competent people? What is the influence of organizational level and of physical proximity? How does the type of work affect a review?

There are several significant benefits which fairly formal, regular reviews can bring:

1. They are likely to prevent the common complaint that the manager does not really know what employees are doing or what they are contributing to the achievement of the organizational unit's goals.

2. They provide evidence that the manager is serious about the goals program, that he or she supports it, that it receives the necessary emphasis and is not just a flash in the pan or eyewash for higher level managers.
3. They also provide opportunities for managers to become more knowledgeable about the capabilities and potential of each of their people so they can help them individually develop greater competence and higher levels of success.

Some specific purposes of goals reviews are:

1. To pinpoint those areas in which the manager should provide additional help or support and to discuss the specific support the manager should provide
2. To keep the manager informed of progress about goals on which work is proceeding essentially as expected
3. To review what new goals, if any, should be added for the upcoming period
4. To review which goals have become unrealistic as a result of changing events and should therefore be modified
5. To drop any goals that are no longer important enough to keep on the list of goals
6. To review the adequacy of coordination and communication with the people who are affected by the goal
7. To assign priorities to the goals for the upcoming period.

Of these, the first purpose is the most important. The manager has to determine how he or she can help a subordinate achieve realistic goals, decide whether additional help should be provided, or allow the goals to slip.

Goals review sessions provide marvelous opportunities for managers to talk, face-to-face, with each of their people. Such regular sessions can open up communications in a totally different manner than the discussions that take place daily. When clearly understood by both manager and subordinate, goal reviews can do many things. To the employee they say:

- Here is another chance to tell your boss all the great things you have been doing lately,
- This is the time to ask for any help you need with goals you want to achieve, the personal, career-related goals as well as the job-related ones.
- This is also the time to get some advice and help with problems you are facing.

For the manager they represent opportunities to get to know the employee or subordinate manager better. The manager learns a great deal about aspirations as well as capabilities and knowledge/skill deficiencies and has a chance to take a general look at the past performance, to review plans for the immediate future, to provide recognition, and to help the subordinate take another step along the life cycle or just gain a slightly more realistic perspective on some aspect of the work environment.

To obtain the maximum benefit from these reviews, a manager must thoroughly understand how they contribute to the motivational climate, how they can provide the foundation for factual performance evaluations, and how they relate to the other aspects of managerial style. These issues are discussed further in later sections of this chapter and in sections entitled "Holding Subordinates Accountable" and "Relationship of Performance Appraisal to Goals Review" and in Chapters 7 and 10, respectively.

Extensive experiments on the motivational aspects of reviews were conducted by behavioral scientists at General Electric and the University of Virginia.* A system of regular reviews, called Work Planning and Review, was established. Review sessions were scheduled at different intervals depending on the nature of the job and on the manager's style of operating. Some were as frequent as once a month. The results of the study showed significant changes in attitude and actions on the part of the subordinate managers. Those whose managers conducted regular reviews displayed significantly better attitudes toward their superiors and the goals toward which they were working. It was also determined that managers who conducted regular reviews took actions to improve performance more frequently than those who did not conduct regular performance reviews.

There are few hard and fast rules as to how many times a year goals review should be held. However, many organizations which have reasonably effective goals programs require managers to hold goals reviews with each direct subordinate at least once every three months. It is possible to hold reviews as frequently as needed—every other week or perhaps even every week.

---

*H. H. Meyer, E. Kay, and J. R. P. French, *Split Roles in Performance Appraisal*, HARVARD BUSINESS REVIEW, Jan.-Feb. 1965, p. 123.

With highly competent subordinates who can work on several goals at the same time, it would be wise to hold a review once a month because with such subordinates there is relatively little need for detailed discussions about how goals are being approached. Since there is relatively little involvement by the manager in the way the competent subordinate works toward achieving the goal, then there may be a need for frequent goals reviews in which progress towards goals is explored and the subordinate has an opportunity to call on the skills and capabilities of the manager to help with the difficult problems. At the same time, the manager receives an up-date on the status of the various projects which are in progress.

Goal reviews can be less frequent for subordinates whose work the manager must closely follow. Some subordinates are constantly in need of help or guidance with regard to action steps. With such subordinates a manager can hold formal goals reviews once every three months because he or she has kept informed of progress, and the subordinate provides information continuously about the adequacy of work.

Some managers believe that they do not need regular, semiformal goals reviews for subordinates with whom they are in constant touch because they are aware of the status of all goals. These managers often fail to realize that the world looks different from the perspective of the subordinate. Not only does the subordinate lose some of the benefits of the goals review; but, especially because of the frequent contacts, the subordinate rarely ever sees the total picture and often is more confused about priorities than his or her manager believes could be possible. Information that comes in bits and pieces and which is rarely placed in perspective is just not as useful as information placed in perspective—i.e., information that may be received in review.

Furthermore, without regular, semiformal goals reviews some of the functions of the goals review can be slighted, especially its usefulness in coordinating activities, in analyzing the relative priorities of goals, and in establishing new goals. Also, without reviews, information for performance evaluation is less comprehensive and reliable.

Goals reviews can help managers think of their roles in a different light, such as that depicted by the revised organization chart in Figure 5.5. Organization charts are usually drawn as pyramids with the highest position on top. This implies a com-

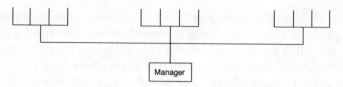

Figure 5.5. Organizational Chart Showing Need for Manager to Provide Support

mand order and a communications order in which, as Alvin
Toffler pointed out in his book *Future Shock*, communications
cannot proceed horizontally but rather must follow a complex
path. For instance, Toffler cites the example of a furnace operator who cannot call a maintenance person directly when there
is a breakdown of the furnace but must go to the supervisor
who must go to the general foreman who is the lowest level
person authorized to contact the maintenance department.
The general foreman must call the general maintenance foreman, who, in turn, can send instructions to the appropriate repair department so that the repair is scheduled.

Toffler concludes that such a system does not place adequate confidence in the individual who does the work and
therefore is detrimental to a healthy psychological climate.
While Toffler is, of course, right about this aspect, he overlooks
an equally and possibly more important principle—the one
which says the decision must be made at the lowest possible
level at which *all* information is available. A furnace operator
cannot possibly have the information about the schedules and
priorities in the maintenance department or in the furnace department and therefore should not directly affect either. Decisions must be made by people who have access to the information that allows them to determine alternate ways the furnace
operator may be used, the relative importance of the work
being done on the furnace in question, the work load of the
maintenance people who can repair the furnace, and so forth.

If the organizational ladder were visualized upside down,
with the manager at the bottom, as sometimes has been done,
then the situation becomes totally different. In goals reviews, as
well as in most problem-solving areas, the manager must support the people who report to him or her because if the manager does not do so, the portion of the pyramid above that
manager's position can collapse. From this point of view, it is
the manager's function to supply the repair services when they

are required by the furnace operator; and it is quite natural for the furnace operator to turn to the boss for help when furnace difficulties develop. There is no implication here about lack of confidence in the furnace operator.

This upside down pyramid has profound implications for managers who accept its philosophical implications, especially in goals review sessions. When a manager sees his or her function as supportive, it becomes obvious that one of the primary purposes of the goals review concerns the help the individual subordinate and his or her team should receive so that work can proceed most effectively.

A good goals review follows a pattern that assures that all subjects are covered thoroughly. One useful procedure might be as follows:

1. With respect to all completed goals, ask these questions:

   How well was the goal achieved?

   How difficult/easy was it to achieve the goal?

   What was the quality and quantity of effort needed to achieve the goal?

   Was there adequate communication on progress towards goal achievement?

   How adequate was your support in helping your subordinate achieve the goal?

2. With respect to all open goals, ask these questions:

   Will the goal be achieved? If not, what is the problem and what should be done about it?

   What is needed from you, as manager, to help your subordinate achieve the goal?

   How adequate are communications, so far, between all parties?

   How appropriate is the involvement of those people who are affected by this goal?

   Is the goal still appropriate in light of changes in environment?

3. Determine what new goals should be set.

4. Review priorities and realign them in the light of the current situation.

In deciding on the frequency of reviews, it is important to keep in mind that more frequent goals reviews often provide more factual data about the way subordinates work towards goals and thus help to make performance appraisals less subjective. It is also important to remember that monthly production goals are not valid candidates for the list of priority goals for any one period, although maybe the quarterly production goal is. Examples of more important goals that must be included are programs that lead to accomplishment of production goals—improvements in work methods and procedures, skills development, work force plans, communications improvements, etc.

An example may help to clarify this picture. A manager, Jean, may have set jointly with a subordinate manager, Helen, the following strategic goals for Helen and Helen's unit for the coming calendar year:

1. Develop and achieve production goals which will bring an overall productivity increase of 5 percent.
2. Develop the capability, by midyear, to absorb schedule changes which are announced on the day preceding the day on which they are to go into effect, without more than 5 percent nonproductive time.
3. Reduce rework time by 10 percent from the preceding year.
4. Decrease cost of supplies used by 3 percent.
5. Assure better coordination with the XYZ department and develop ways to measure such coordination jointly with the manager of the XYZ department.
6. Develop a standards manual by midyear.
7. Establish and achieve self-development goals which will reduce the number of times when it is recognized too late that a specific goal has not been achieved.
8. Establish and achieve self-development goals in the (*relevant*) technology.

If Helen were a fairly competent person, she would use these strategic goals to develop some very specific operational goals for the first quarter, which she would review with Jean. Her operational goals might be:

1. Reduce time per unit by 2 percent by March 30.
2. By Feb. 27 prepare specific plans, including a training program outline, to improve the unit's ability to cope with schedule changes.
3. Enroll in an evening technology course and achieve a good grade.
4. Obtain an analysis of causes of rework by February 10.

Just because Helen would pay primary attention to these four goals during the first month, or possibly even longer, does not mean that she would neglect her normal supervisory duties. She certainly would keep closer tabs on the use of supplies, talk to the manager of the XYZ department about coordination, collect data for the standards manual, and think about how she can recognize when a goal is in trouble earlier. But, while working on these things, she would make certain that none of them interfered with her efforts to achieve the four primary goals for the period.

If Jean usually meets with Helen on a monthly basis, the end of the January review might show that:

- Helen has enrolled in an appropriate course.
- She is well on her way to completing the analysis of causes of rework.
- The cost-reduction goal appears to be roughly on target.
- Helen has some ideas on how to deal with schedule changes, but she is not at all certain that these will come close to meeting the goals. She has prepared a preliminary outline of the training program which she wants to discuss with Jean, together with the entire approach to this goal.

During the discussion, in addition to pleasantries and some discussion of matters of mutual personal interest, Jean might:

- Commend Helen on enrolling in an excellent course and, if she is knowledgeable, offer any help that Helen might need.
- Ask Helen whether she would like to review what could be done to make faster progress on the March production target, but not pursue it further if Helen feels she can handle it.
- Discuss the schedule-change goal in detail with Helen and review the training program, make suggestions, contribute any ideas she can think of, and agree to review its status with Helen in two weeks to see how else she could help.
- Decide with Helen that the goals on rework analysis can be dropped and that Helen should submit a new goal for the strategic rework goal.
- Decide that the self-development goal of passing a course can be dropped since Helen will undoubtedly complete it satisfactorily.
- Decide that a specific goal should be set with respect to the standards manual.
- Decide that a new matter pertaining to a new service has

become sufficiently clear and important so that a goal can be set for it.

- Discuss the general situation in Helen's unit to see whether all priorities are still appropriate and whether any problems or opportunities exist that should receive more attention.

As a result of this review meeting, Helen would submit new goals and priorities within a few days, and at the end of February a new review would follow a similar pattern. During the month there is little need for Jean to follow up with Helen on these matters, except for the one on schedule changes on which she had promised further help.

Summary—Frequency of Goals Reviews

1. Goals reviews are important to an open communications climate.
2. There are many purposes which goals reviews satisfy. They provide, for instance, perspective on the total situation and foster an exchange of views that helps to satisfy everyone's needs—the manager's, the subordinate's, the unit's.
3. Goals reviews should be scheduled regularly; there should be at least one review each quarter.
4. The frequency of goals reviews depends on the situation (the closeness of contact between manager and subordinate and the importance or complexity of the goals), on the capabilities of the subordinate, and on the need to obtain adequate factual data for performance evaluations.

Holding Subordinates Accountable*

If managers want their subordinates to have confidence in them, it is important that they hold subordinates accountable only for those matters that are under the control of the subordinate and that they are factual and fair in this. They should not forget that goals are primarily forecasts, and even the best forecasts are only estimates of what will occur. This means that

---

*Some people make a distinction between the use of the phrases "holding someone responsible" and "holding someone accountable." For the purposes of this book, the two expressions, as well as the words accountable and responsible, will be used to mean the same thing.

even carefully planned and well-implemented steps still may not bring full achievement of a goal.

Can someone be held accountable, for instance, if unexpected emergencies pop up? For instance, if a supervisor is striving to improve quality and, just as he or she is making progress, three of the more competent employees, the ones with the best quality record, are in a car accident together that keeps them out of work for several months, how should this supervisor be rated if quality deteriorates temporarily and then again resumes its upward trend—without making the goal? How good is performance? Is the performance poor because the goal was not reached, or is it excellent because an improving trend existed before, as well as soon after, the accident?

The question of accountability concerns, first of all, the extent to which an individual can be expected to achieve a goal and how performance can be judged if the goal is not reached. Many goals programs fail, as do larger attempts at organizational planning, at least in part because they are not able to deal with accountability.

It does not seem particularly useful for managers to place *full* responsibility for the achievement of goals on the people who have accepted them. Higher level managers, it would seem, have to accept their share of the responsibility. It is often meaningless to observe that 80 or 90 percent of a goal has been achieved or to note that the goal has been achieved exactly on the day planned or a few days earlier or later. The original goal may have been totally unrealistic and impossible to achieve, or it may have been very easy. In either case, to measure percentage of achievement for each goal or for the number of goals which were achieved does not represent a useful way to judge a subordinate's performance. On the other hand, there are many activities or categories of action steps related to goal achievement that a subordinate can and should be held specifically accountable for. Use of these can make it easier for managers to place less reliance on actual achievement of goals when deciding what to expect from subordinates. There are eight major activities related to goal achievement that are fully under the control of the person working on a goal and for which he or she can accept complete responsibility:

1. Setting challenging but realistic goals
2. Setting thorough action steps
3. Maintaining continuity and consistency in planning

4. Assuring the quality of action steps
5. Keeping to schedule
6. Solving problems
7. Communicating problems in a timely manner
8. Maintaining good relationships with others.

Setting Challenging but Realistic Goals

Managers must keep in mind that subordinates will set both high and realistic goals only if they do not feel threatened when they do so. (This will be discussed in detail later on.) A manager can hold subordinates accountable for the skill and conscientiousness with which they set goals in the first place and the extent to which goals are set so that they are realistic and yet challenging. Even though this first criterion of accountability speaks of goals and possibly may appear to be a goal, it really is only an action step because anyone in a responsible job can learn how to forecast what can be accomplished in his or her position. It is therefore reasonable to expect competent people to set realistic and challenging goals.

If someone does not wish to set goals that are challenging yet realistic, this will soon be evident. The person will generally set goals too low even though it is apparent that he or she could do better. On the other hand, someone who consistently sets goals too low because he or she does not know how to set challenging goals, or sets them too high so that they are not realistic can usually be helped through training in forecasting and in realistic goal setting.

However, obstacles other than competence and desire to perform well are involved. If people are forced to play a game in which they try to obtain the lowest possible goal to gain the greatest assurance that it will indeed be achieved, then mutual goal setting cannot be effective. Since the people working on goals usually know more about what can be accomplished than their managers, especially if they have been trained to do such forecasting, their managers need their cooperation in helping to set really appropriate goals. How difficult this is has already been discussed on page 72.

If a goals program exists and the manager wants it to become a way of life rather than a paper program, then the manager cannot expect people to set challenging goals and discipline them when they do not achieve them. Most managers make allowance for effort and do look at events or conditions which are beyond the subordinate's control when reviewing the reasons why a goal was not achieved or why, for that matter, much more was accomplished than had been expected. But rarely do subordinates know what the manager will consider valid or how the manager actually looks at performance. Unless they know the manager's standards, it is not likely that they can develop the full confidence that is needed to go out on a limb with tough goals.

A manager must be prepared to look at goals only as *predictions* of achievement. The manager can expect that the employee will make a serious effort to attain them, but he or she must recognize that some goals may not be achieved, even with the best action program and the most untiring effort. If you accept this fact, you can hold subordinates accountable for setting realistic goals that are quite high, and you can use the record of how they set their goals as a measure of performance.

Setting Thorough Action Steps

Subordinates can also be held accountable for the thoroughness with which they develop action steps in support of their goals. A person working on goals should be aware at all times of the action steps that should be taken next and the dates by which they should be completed. Even though you would not frequently ask a competent subordinate what progress was being made towards the accomplishment of a goal or what actual steps were being taken, the subordinates should know what steps were necessary. There need not be many steps, nor need they be formalized on paper. However, should you ask a subordinate the planned action steps for a specific goal, the subordinate should have a plan or schedule and should readily be able to list and explain the steps.

Therefore, you can hold your subordinates responsible for being constantly aware of the next appropriate action steps for every goal on their priority list. In this as in other areas of accountability, factual data can be obtained on performance. Not only do regular contacts with subordinates provide much valid data, but the records from the regular goals reviews yield additional information on which to base a valid judgment. If the subordinate, at every contact and at the goals reviews, provides evidence that appropriate action steps are being taken and are planned for each goal, then that subordinate clearly is thorough in setting action steps for each goal.

Maintaining Continuity and Consistency in Planning

You can also hold your subordinates accountable for maintaining the continuity of their plans—for not allowing their plans to lapse. Competent people will think about their goals at all times. Less competent people will forget about goals during very busy periods. The least competent ones will remember goals only when they know their managers will ask about them.

Continuity of effort is desirable when carrying out action steps and may be used as a measure of performance. Subordinates who are striving to achieve their goals will think of them every day, which will be clear from the way they approach their tasks. Evidence of continuity will be found in the contacts which occur between manager and subordinate in the period between goals reviews. Subordinates who regularly and voluntarily update their managers on progress provide ample evidence of their continuing attention to their goals planning.

Assuring the Quality of Action Steps

Quality of effort is another aspect of work for which you can hold subordinates accountable. When looking at the action steps that the subordinate takes, you obviously must evaluate them to see whether they are the best that could be taken. A subordinate who regularly takes action steps which you consider as good as any that you would take certainly deserves to be commended. Those who take inadequate action steps can be held accountable. When an employee or subordinate manager's action steps are frequently less than adequate, then it is necessary to provide training. While training proceeds, the evaluation of the subordinate's work can reflect the fact that full competence has not yet been reached.

This criterion requires somewhat more personal judgment by the manager since there are no absolute criteria upon which to base the measurement of quality. The manager has to judge whether the action steps are the best that could be taken and whether they are being executed competently. In making such judgments the higher level manager must rely in part on his or her experience and in part on the results of the action steps.

Keeping to Schedule

Completing action steps on time is also entirely under the control of subordinates, and they therefore can be held accountable. If a subordinate agrees to complete some project by a certain time and then accomplishes it by that time, then he or she clearly has performed satisfactorily. Conversely, if an action step is not completed on time, something is wrong. The quality of the action step or the amount of effort which had to be devoted to its completion may have been misjudged, for example. Once someone has made a commitment to a plan of action, that plan should be implemented as decided; and since, by definition, matters beyond his or her control are not involved, the manager can reasonably expect that steps will be completed as agreed.

Keeping to the schedule—timeliness—is probably the easiest criterion of accountability to measure and evaluate. Clear statements of action steps require the specification of completion time as well as quantity and quality. It will be clear at goals reviews whether deadlines have been met. The reviews create a permanent record that may be used for evaluating later performance.

Solving Problems

It sometimes becomes apparent that action steps will not, in fact, lead to the achievement of the desired goal. When that happens, the person working towards the goal should be expected to reconsider the action steps and take any additional steps that may be necessary to reach the goal.

There are many benefits in making a clear policy that everyone is expected to be creative in solving the problem whenever achievement of a goal is threatened. Such a policy is evidence of management confidence in the competence of employees, and it sets the stage for the feeling of accomplishment which comes whenever new approaches prove to be better than previous ones. It is necessary, of course, to make it clear that help is available when difficulties cannot be overcome. The quality of the revised action plan may be used to judge performance fairly and factually.

This criterion is also fairly difficult to evaluate and must be based on the evaluator's judgment, even though, as in other instances, goals reviews can provide a basis for judgment.

Communicating Problems in a Timely Manner

Once an organization understands how to work with a goals system, everyone knows that it is essential to notify the manager as soon as it becomes clear that a goal will not be achieved. This gives the manager an opportunity to decide whether to (a) provide additional resources or help in order to assure that the goal can be achieved and (b) change the goal if it appears that all has been done to achieve it and it still cannot be achieved, or that it does not warrant the additional resources needed for on-time achievement.

For instance, suppose someone must find out what equipment would be best for a particular operation. The person may have committed himself or herself to completion of the investigation and trials by a certain date but may find, as time progresses, that more urgent matters have come up and the tests will not be finished in time. At this point the person has several choices. He or she can let the goal slide or inform his or her manager that the goal will not be achieved unless more time is allocated to investigation and trial or unless additional personnel are brought in to help. If this notification is given early enough so that the goal can still be achieved, the manager has the opportunity to rescue the goal or to move its completion date back.

If everyone in an organization accepts the responsibility of providing timely notification when a goal is in trouble, then there is greater likelihood that the most important organization goals will be achieved on time. Factually evaluating how promptly employees notify managers of trouble is fairly easy. Notification must be early enough so the manager can still rescue the goal if that is possible or desirable. Since about 50 percent of all goals will not be fully achieved, as discussed on page 73, much data regarding a subordinate's actions when missing a goal is available, and a fair evaluation will rarely be difficult.

Maintaining Good Relationships With Others

There is one more aspect of goal programs for which subordinates can be held accountable, and this concerns their relationships with others. Subordinates can be judged on the extent to which they coordinate with others who are affected by their goals, how thoroughly they communicate with these people, and probably even on how well they obtain cooperation from others in order to achieve their own goals. Of course, subordinates should be judged on the basis of the cooperation they elicit from others and especially the cooperation they give to others.

A number of questions relating to goals reviews appear on page 83. Those which concern communications can aid in evaluating how well subordinates maintain their working relationships.

Accountability is a complex responsibility which cannot be satisfied by simply checking how well employees have achieved their goals. Holding people accountable for the way in which they work to achieve their goals will bring a much better chance that they will accept goal setting as a useful process.

Summary—Holding Subordinates Accountable

A manager can gain higher levels of confidence and greater assurance that subordinates will be willing to set challenging goals if the manager says something like this:

"So that we do not misunderstand each other on what I expect from you, it might be well if I explain my standards. I expect you to achieve all the goals on which we have agreed and you have accepted. However, when we review progress, and especially when we find it likely that a goal will not be achieved, I will look at the following:

- First, I will check whether that goal was set carefully in the first place—i.e., whether you had taken the responsibility for setting realistic but challenging goals requiring more than routine thought and effort to achieve.
- Secondly, I will look at the thoroughness with which you have laid out the action steps leading to the achievement of the goal.
- Then, I will look at the extent to which you have kept these action steps in mind.
- I will also look at how good these action steps were and compare them with those I might have chosen. Obviously, I do not expect you to take the same steps because many roads can be taken to reach the same result, but I will try to determine the extent to which the steps that you have taken were of high quality and reasonable.
- I will also take a look at whether your action steps were completed as you had planned, or whether many were delayed for various reasons even though they were fully under your control.
- Since we will be looking especially closely at those

goals that have not yet been achieved or are not likely to be achieved, I will be checking whether you have given some thought to changing the action steps that you originally contemplated to see if better ones can be substituted for them.

- If the new action steps still do not appear as though they will reach the goal, I will look at whether you have given me timely notification that a problem exists with respect to that goal so that I have the chance to do something about it.

- Finally, I will look at the way you have worked with others and the extent to which you have helped them and kept them informed so that they are able to help you as much as possible.

If you have done all these things and the goal is still not attainable, then it is clear that I have to provide additional help or relieve you from the responsibility of achieving the goal on time.

Summary—First Five Problems Areas

There are eight ways in which a goals program can fail to achieve its promise of improving performance and bringing greater satisfaction to people. These eight ways can be summarized in the acronym EQIFAPPO: Extent, Quality, Involvement, Frequency, Accountability, Participation, Performance Evaluation, and Operational/Developmental Goals.

This chapter has discussed the first five of the potential problem areas of goals programs. It has attempted to emphasize that working towards goals can become a way of life, not just a program, only if the manager understands the process of goal setting and achievement thoroughly, especially the many aspects of its impact on subordinates. Many of these are subtle but they have great influence in shaping attitudes. If people see goals programs as a management device to obtain more effort from employees, without consideration of the way employee need can be met at the same time, very little cooperation can be expected. To create an atmosphere which assures that the needs of the employees will be met and that they will gain many personal benefits from a successful program requires great care on the manager's part. The manager must see that action steps are well chosen and that responsibility is properly assigned.

The sixth potential problem area—an area in which managers can do a great deal to enhance the general climate in their organizational unit—concerns the extent of participation in goal setting which managers allow their subordinates and the timing of this participation. It is of such great importance and has so many ramifications that the entire next chapter is devoted to it.

Chapter 6

Making Goals Programs Successful: Part Two

This chapter discusses the sixth potential problem area in working with goals—participation. At one time management decided what was to be done; lower level managers and employees did it. If they reached the goals, then everything was fine. If they did not, sometimes they were blamed, whether it was their fault or not. A goals program in which lower levels have only token participation is not much different from this type of approach.

PARTICIPATION DEFINED

Participation is widely misunderstood. Many managers are not clear in their own minds as to whether participation means that many people must participate in every decision or whether participation applies only to decisions involving one or very few subordinates. Other managers believe that if they allow a great deal of participation, they have in effect given up their right and obligation to manage. Still other managers are concerned that they will be perceived as soft and indecisive if they allow a high degree of participation. Many believe that participation requires a lot of time; and, for most decisions, this time may not be available or may be too costly.

None of these views need necessarily apply, but all can in certain situations. Managers can and should allow a high degree of participation with some decisions or goals and with some of the people who report to them in some situations; but they cannot afford to make a high level of participation the rule in all situations with all, or even with most, goals or with all of their people. Goals or decisions that are made at higher levels, for instance, must be passed on. Rarely can a manager allow participation with these except in the ancillary decisions or goals pertaining to implementation.

A thorough understanding of how a manager can be highly participative without relinquishing the need to maintain control on important matters is a major issue in this book since it is so crucial to the climate which makes achievement and the satisfaction of people at work two major criteria of success. The key element is the general guideline: a manager should allow the maximum amount of participation which the particular situation and the capability of the subordinates permit *to those people who believe that a specific decision affects them and who want to be involved*. It is important to note that this guideline does *not* exclude fully autocratic decisions in some situations and/or with some subordinates.

Every manager has a wide range of participation options. In some decisions,* all those who will be affected can and probably should take part at the earliest moment. In other decisions, only those who have the expertise in the particular topic should be consulted. In some, the manager alone should quickly make the choice, while in others the manager's role should probably be minimal.

LEVELS OF PARTICIPATION AND TIMING

Sometimes several people should participate right from the beginning, while at other times the involvement of subordinates should start only at a later time. The questions below point up some of the many possible levels and time points at which subordinates could be brought into a decision/goal setting process.

1. Does the quality level need improvement?
2. By how much does the quality level need improvement? (Here the decision that improvement is needed has already been made.)
3. If the quality level is to be improved by 5 percent, how should the organization proceed? (Here the fact that improvement is required and the amount of improvement that is necessary has already been determined, and employees or lower level managers participate only in subsidiary decisions.)

Even more limited and later decision-making participation is possible. If quality level is to be improved by 5 percent through a training program, the influence of subordinates could be restricted to the choice of topics that should be cov-

---

*Goal setting and decision making are closely related topics. To set a goal requires at least one decision to be made.

ered in such a program and to when and how the program should be conducted.

An infinite array of timing and levels is possible. No one can choose the best ones all the time; but with a thorough understanding of the principles that are involved, more managers can make better selections more often. Every research project that has addressed itself to this topic has found that an overwhelming majority of employees and managers at every level feel that their respective superiors could do a much better job in the decisions pertaining to the extent and timing of participation that they allow.

Many of the actions that a manager should take to achieve a good climate for goal setting so that goal setting can become a way of life also create a climate which helps subordinates gain greater satisfaction from their job and thus increase their motivation to achieve better performance. The most important step in bringing satisfaction to subordinates concerns the amount of influence over goals which subordinates have, their level of participation in the goal setting process. People want opportunities to influence the decisions that affect their lives in the present as well as in the future. This includes the things with impact on their working conditions as well as on the work itself.

Today's goals have great effect on the environment of tomorrow. What the world will be like tomorrow, what equipment there will be, what policies will be followed, what work will be done—all these things are affected by the goals that are set today. It is, therefore, of considerable importance to people, once they understand the goal-setting process, that they have an adequate voice in the way goals are set.

Obviously, an organization cannot permit everyone to have equal influence on goals. Somehow an organization must perform many functions which are required because they are part of the mission. Volume of service, quality of service, sales volume, profit levels, new market penetrations, production goals, budgets are examples of goals in which it is impossible for all people who work in an organization to have an equal, or even a significant, voice. They are too basic to the very existence and performance of the department. These goals very often have to be set by the group of people who are most knowledgeable on what can reasonably be expected, who know what resources are available to devote to them, and how those resources can best be allocated. For instance, sales-volume goals or service-re-

quirement goals have to be determined by people who have
knowledge of market or service demand and who can make
decisions on prices and promotional activities; profit-level goals
have to be set by those who see the entire picture; new-market-
penetration goals must be set by managers who understand
what is required to penetrate a market and who have both the
information and the expertise with which to predict what can
be expected when various levels of resources are committed;
and so on. Some of these goals can conflict with one another, of
course; and all have to be balanced against the total resources
available to an organization. This is why top-level management
is often involved.

Many of these decisions have to be made by the most
knowledgeable specialists working in task forces or teams; and
it is obvious that once determined, they have to be accepted by
the organization. At lower levels especially, they become requirements which managers are expected to meet. This means
that the freedom to affect them becomes more limited the further down the organizational level a specific manager's position
is. It does not mean, though, that such a manager does not have
a wide range of opportunities for practical, self-motivated goal
setting on implementation goals relevant to the major strategic
goals that have been set for him/her. If the question of accountability is resolved as suggested in the preceding section, then
accepting such goals as reasonable, realistic, and challenging
even though one has not participated in their formation is not
necessarily a detriment to a healthy, positive climate.

Fortunately, in most organizations, people agree with most
of the numerical goals. These are the production goals which
are most commonly understood as being goals. Most of them
are not, however, the goals emphasized in this book because
few help an organization improve its performance overall.
They are not the primary influence on shaping people's beliefs
about their ability to influence their environment today and in
the future.

One of the reasons the objectives referred to above are not
goals in the most meaningful sense of the term is because they
must be set higher in the organization; and, therefore, as far as
lower levels are concerned, they are no longer goals. Rather,
they are commands or requirements. They may be very easy to
achieve, or they may be totally unrealistic. Therefore, the skills
of goal setting that lower level managers are expected to apply

do not apply to these goals. These goals or targets or quotas, as they are often called, do provide a useful framework, even when they are far from realistic, for setting the implementation goals and for the entire goal-setting process.

In deciding the level of participation that a manager should allow in the goal setting process, there is much in the literature that can provide guidance. The literature very often calls it decision making rather than goal setting, however. It should be clarified here, therefore, that goal setting and decision making have a great many things in common. The setting of any goal requires at least one, and possibly many, decisions. Therefore, almost anything that applies to decision making automatically applies to goal setting.

Styles of Leadership

Because of the importance of participation in goals and in other decisions affecting work, behavioral scientists have devoted considerable effort to investigating the way participation should be used. The more important of these theories will be discussed here and related to the goal-setting process so that they can become practical guides to action for the manager who wishes to create the best possible climate.

This discussion of participation in goal setting starts with a famous, widely used diagram. It was published in 1958 by Professors Robert Tannenbaum and Warren H. Schmidt of the University of California in Los Angeles and is called the Continuum of Leadership Behavior (see Figure 6.1).* The problem Tannenbaum and Schmidt addressed was the difficulty managers find in trying to be "democratic" while simultaneously maintaining authority and control. The solution they proposed involved the ability to operate effectively along the whole continuum from boss-centered to subordinate-centered leadership. This, of course, represents a difficult challenge but one which can be met if the leader pays attention to key questions about self, subordinates, and the situation. Some of the questions proposed by Tannenbaum and Schmidt are summarized as follows:

> *Leader:* What are my own values and convictions? Do I have confidence in my subordinates and a desire to see

---

*Robert Tannenbaum and Warren H. Schmidt, *How to Choose a Leadership Pattern*, HARVARD BUSINESS REVIEW, Vol. 36, No. 2, Mar.-Apr. 1958, pp. 95–101.

them grow and advance? Do I feel secure in certain situations?

Subordinates: What sort of behavior do they expect from the leader? Do they need independence and want responsibility? Do they feel the problem is important, and do they have the technical knowledge needed to discuss the problem? Do they trust the leader in various styles?

The Situation: What are the demands of organizational policy? What are the time pressures? Is there a need to keep some information confidential?

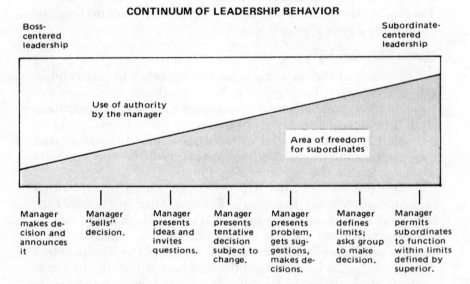

CONTINUUM OF LEADERSHIP BEHAVIOR

Boss-centered leadership

Subordinate-centered leadership

Use of authority by the manager

Area of freedom for subordinates

| Manager makes decision and announces it | Manager "sells" decision. | Manager presents ideas and invites questions. | Manager presents tentative decision subject to change. | Manager presents problem, gets suggestions, makes decisions. | Manager defines limits; asks group to make decision. | Manager permits subordinates to function within limits defined by superior. |

Figure 6.1. Continuum of Leadership Behavior (From Robert Tannenbaum and Warren H. Schmidt, *How to Choose a Leadership Pattern?* HARVARD BUSINESS REVIEW, March-April 1958, Copyright © 1958 by the President and Fellows of Harvard College; all rights reserved. Artwork courtesy NFPA.)

Such questions may help to clarify the leader's decisions about how to lead at any given time and may, in fact, confine leadership style to a particular segment of the Continuum of Leadership Behavior diagram (as may happen, for example, when both leaders and subordinates do not wish decision-making to be shared).

At least two points are considered essential by Tannenbaum and Schmidt: (1) The leader should never shirk responsibility for the decision, however it is made. (2) The leader should always make clear what style of leadership is being used. There should be no attempt, for example, to trick subordinates into thinking that the leader's decision was their decision. This requires that the manager make it clear, at the outset of every discussion about a decision, what level of participation he or she considers appropriate.

The important point is that a manager can rarely afford to give the impression that he or she plans to use one style and then, if the opinion runs counter to plans, change the rules of the game in midstream and insist on a particular course of action which he or she prefers.

The points along the Tannenbaum and Schmidt diagram can be renamed to make them sound more practical and realistic. Furthermore, for completeness, the continuum should really be extended further to show its full extent. Some of the points along the continuum could be described as follows:

1. The manager makes a decision and does not announce it until it has been implemented. While this is not a frequent situation, it does occur. For instance, a manager may have decided to leave the organization, or he or she may have decided that a specific employee has become so troublesome that steps will have to be taken to remove that employee. It is likely that such a decision will not be announced (to those concerned) for a long time, even though implementation steps are being taken. Little discussion occurs even at a later time.

2. The manager asks one employee or subordinate manager or a group to discuss a decision which the manager has already made. The manager in effect is announcing the decision only but does accept comments and thereby shows some willingness to do something about any problems or unhappiness which the decision may bring.

3. The manager announces an intended decision but asks for comments so that the decision can be changed if anything of major importance has been overlooked.

4. The manager calls a person or a group together and points out that a decision needs to be made, that it probably should be made in a certain way but that if the others feel very strongly about it, some modification of the decision would be possible.

5. The manager asks one person or several people to participate in the making of a decision, but points out that

the decision is of such a nature that if the group does not express clear direction or preference, the decision will be made according to the way the manager comes to see it during the discussion. (This level of leadership style falls at about the center of the diagram.)

6. The manager announces that a decision will be made jointly and that the manager's voice will be no greater than that of others in the group.

7. The manager suggests that a decision needs to be made and, unless the other persons or group objects, the decision should be made by them. The manager will provide whatever support is necessary, no matter what the decision is. While this type of decision appears to be rare, it is far more common than appears at first, particularly in the case of highly competent and motivated subordinates. In such situations this approach can be fully appropriate.

The last example is not the very highest level of participation in decisions. Theoretically, there is one more in which subordinates are so competent, mature, and informed and are so confident in their own abilities that they may make and implement decisions which are the boss' responsibility and inform the boss of them afterwards. Obviously, this is an extreme that could be desirable under some circumstances. It is not an option that a manager would choose for the more important decisions, and it may indicate that a manager has lost control over the unit.

Common Misconceptions

There are two common misconceptions about participation that probably deserve clarification at this point. Some managers believe that participation applies primarily to groups of subordinates. When Tannenbaum and Schmidt or, for that matter, any of the theorists speak about participation, they refer to participation by one individual, a few individuals, or a group as often as participation by all subordinates. The important thing is that the person or persons involved in or affected by the decision should have a say in it.

The second misconception, which is even more widespread since some of the theories do not clarify it and since the writers could possibly be in disagreement, concerns the extent of participation. There is a widespread belief that participation must be all-encompassing and that a manager who wants to be participative must allow a high degree of participation with all decisions. The view that Tannenbaum and Schmidt emphasize, and that is reinforced by other researchers, states that the competent manager should be able to use that particular style which is appropriate to the subordinate(s) and the situation. Since no one can be certain what style is most appropriate at any one moment, it is not important to be absolutely correct at all times but to develop a high batting average on the use of the right level of participation for decisions.

Equally important is intellectual honesty. Choosing a level of participation or timing that is not the very best at any one time may cause some temporary unhappiness. But if a manager gives the impression that subordinates will have considerable voice in a specific decision and then reverses himself (or herself) and insists on a course other than the one which the subordinate(s) prefers, then mutual trust has been damaged and that is a far more serious matter. It obviously is not easy to establish relationships where other people know at all times what level of participation is being used and why. Nevertheless this is a skill which every manager should continuously strive to improve.

As the diagram explains, the manager must choose the level of participation for every decision or for the setting of a goal which is correct for that particular situation and for the capability and competence of the subordinate. The manager who can make good decisions about how much participation to allow will establish a much better relationship with subordinates and will help to provide the climate that motivates them to greater achievement.

Selecting the Best Level of Participation

The difficult question is where along the range of possible participation choices is the best point for a specific situation. No specific guidelines exist. Managers who ask themselves that question automatically come closer to choosing an appropriate style for a specific decision or for a specific goal than those who do not pause to give it some thought.

Also, a manager can look to the following guideline: The more competent and capable a subordinate is, the more participation in goal setting can be allowed and the more likely it is that participation will lead to favorable results. In addition, Raymond Miles' Human Resources model provides another guideline. (See Figure 6.2.)

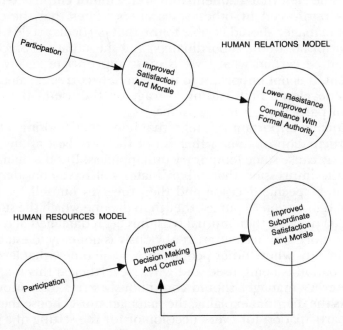

Figure 6.2. Raymond Miles' Human Relations and Human Resources Model (From Raymond E. Miles, *Human Relations or Human Resources?* HARVARD BUSINESS REVIEW, May-June 1966, Copyright © 1966 by the President and Fellows of Harvard College; all rights reserved. Reprinted by permission.)

Raymond E. Miles of the University of California at Berkeley interviewed hundreds of middle-level and upper-level managers in business and governmental organizations about participative decision making. He discovered what he claimed was "a great deal of confusion." Miles concluded that managers applied two models, which he described as follows:

> *"Human Relations Model:* The key element in the human relations approach is its basic objective of making organizational members feel they are useful and important parts of the overall effort. This process is viewed as the means of accomplishing the ultimate goal of building a cooperative and compliant work force. Participation, in this model, is a lubricant which oils away resistance to formal authority. . . . The manager lets his or her subordinates in on some departmental information and allows them to

discuss and state their opinions on various departmental problems. In return the manager hopes to obtain their cooperation in carrying out decisions for the accomplishment of department objectives where he or she does not allow participation. Implicit in this model is the idea that it might actually be easier and more efficient if the manager could merely make departmental decisions without bothering to involve subordinates. [It is, however, like a bank account. The manager "deposits" good will when subordinates are allowed to participate, and withdraws it when they are not.]. . . .

"Human Resources Model: This approach . . . focuses attention on all organization members as reservoirs of untapped resources. These resources include not only physical skills and energy, but also creative ability and the capacity for responsible, self-directed, self-controlled behavior. . . . In this model the manager does not share information, discuss departmental decisions, or encourage self-direction and self-control merely to improve subordinate satisfaction and morale. Rather, the purpose of these practices is to improve the decision-making and total performance efficiency of the organization. The human resources model suggests that many decisions may actually be made more efficiently by those directly involved in and affected by the decisions. . . . In fact, it suggests that the area over which subordinates exercise self-direction and control should be continually broadened in keeping with their growing experience and ability."

Miles reported some of his findings as follows:

"Which approach to participative management do managers actually follow? . . . Managers' views appear to reflect both models. When they talk about the kind and amount of participation appropriate for their subordinates, they express concepts that appear to be similar to those in the human relations model. On the other hand, when they consider their own relationships with their superiors, their views seem to flow from the human resources model. . . . They see themselves as reservoirs of creative resources. Moreover, the fact that they frequently view themselves as more flexible and willing to change than their superiors suggests that they feel their resources are frequently wasted. Correspondingly, they expect improvement in organizational performance to result from greater freedom for self-direction and self-control on their part."

Miles expressed his personal preference for the human resources model on grounds that "managers up and down the organizational hierarchy believe their superiors should follow this model."

Miles' work has not been widely recognized and accepted probably because its implication is that greater participation will always, or most of the time, lead to improved decision making and control. This, of course, does not mesh with the experi-

ence of most managers. Most managers find that it is only under certain circumstances that higher levels of participation will
indeed lead to improved decision making and control.

If the Human Resources Model is revised, though, as
shown in Figure 6.3, Miles' model takes on considerably more
meaning.

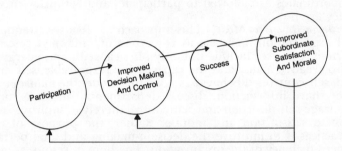

Figure 6.3. Raymond Miles' Human Resources Model, Modified

If managers see that the model does not suggest that they
should always allow maximum participation but rather that
they should decide what level of participation will bring the
highest level of success, then the model is a most useful one. It
says that, before setting a goal or making a decision, managers
should ask themselves what level of participation will bring success and then use that level on the Tannenbaum and Schmidt
continuum. It is important to notice here that the manager decides on the level of participation that should be allowed on any
one goal. The manager thus retains practically full control over
the operation of the organizational unit and the way decisions
are made. At the same time the manager allows the maximum
level of participation with respect to each decision and each
goal that subordinates can be given without any significant effect on the control process.

When stated this way, it sounds somewhat manipulative.
Yet it really is not if the manager's philosophy is truly that of
the Human Resources model and if the manager continues to
keep in mind that the level of participation should be influenced, as much as possible, by what subordinates perceive to be
the appropriate level. If better decisions are indeed made and
better goals are set, then more success is achieved; and success
in turn leads to much greater satisfaction. The subordinates

gain the satisfaction of having participated but also the satisfaction of seeing a successful outcome.

Thus, before setting a goal or before making a decision, the manager should decide what level of participation is most likely to lead to success. For instance, a manager may have been asked by superior officers to see that a certain task is completed by the end of the week. If it is important that the task indeed be completed by the end of the week, then this is not a decision that should be resolved participatively. On the other hand, the question of how the job should be accomplished could very well be a decision in which subordinates of the manager could be deeply involved.

One way to decide what level of participation would be best is to follow Miles and ask the question, "What level, timing and intensity of participation will bring the *highest level of success*?" That question alone can bring more appropriate participation levels and lead to more instances of successful joint decisions. They in turn lead to greater satisfaction, and a snowballing process has been started in which the manager, in the interest of the organizational unit and of its people, helps employees develop toward increasing ability to participate so that ever higher levels of participation lead to success. Success fuels the process, reinforcing good decisions and spreading satisfaction and the desire as well as the confidence for more participation.

The Miles model helps to come a little closer to the selection of the best point on the Tannenbaum and Schmidt continuum by asking what level of participation will bring the greatest success. It does not answer that question, however, and more specific guidelines are needed. There are no simple rules that can be used to help a manager; the issues which are involved are far too complex to permit the use of a simplistic formula. There are further considerations that lead to a more detailed analysis, which allows a more accurate selection of the participation level and timing. These considerations involve issues related to the characteristics of the subordinate and to the situation.

Issues Related to Characteristics of the Subordinate

First, there is a question of attitudes and maturity. This concerns the extent to which an individual is willing—and able—to accept responsibility and devote extra effort when required; the level of judgment which that person can apply; the willingness to accept the direction in which the goal takes the group, etc. If a person generally makes decisions based on emotional rather than factual considerations and does not analyze the facts carefully but instead jumps quickly to conclusions, then that person cannot participate at the same level, and in the same number of decisions or goals, as someone who has a more objective, rational approach.

Secondly, in addition to emotional maturity, the level of participation should take into account the extent to which the subordinate wants to be involved. There are many reasons why a subordinate may not wish to participate in a particular instance. They include the attitudes which the subordinate may have toward the decision or goal. If a subordinate thinks that the manager merely wants participation in order to have others share responsibility, then there might be a negative attitude towards participation. Similarly, if subordinates believe that a manager asks for participation only on a token basis and does not really want opinions or help with a decision or a goal—is likely to make the decision the way he or she wishes anyhow—then they often do not really want to spend time discussing the decision.

Thirdly, besides maturity and a willingness to participate, a thorough knowledge of the subject matter is required. If the subordinate has little technical knowledge of a subject, then certainly it would not be wise to give that subordinate a large voice with a decision related to that subject. An employee who knows little about pumps cannot contribute significantly to the selection of new pumping equipment. Furthermore it is likely that employees who know little about pumps would not want to be involved in a decision about pumps. Such employees may feel awkward in participating in a decision where they can contribute very little and might be concerned about exposing a lack of knowledge.

Often lack of knowledge is not based on education or experience of subordinates but rather on the amount of information about the decision which is available and can be made available to them. Without such background data and adequate perspective on the situation surrounding a decision or goal, the contribution of subordinates often cannot be a large one.

In a way these three guidelines on the extent to which a subordinate should be involved in goal setting or decision making are related to the Life Cycle concept that was discussed on pages 58–62. The further to the left the person has reached on the Life Cycle curve, the more extensively and the earlier that person can be involved in the goal-setting and decision-making process.

To summarize what has been covered so far, the extent and timing of participation by subordinates in the goal-setting process should be an important consideration which managers should not take lightly. Managers must give some thought to it with respect to every decision affecting subordinates.

The first question a manager can ask to find the best level of participation and timing is, "What is likely to lead to greatest success?" Success here should be thought of in terms of long- and short-term impact on task-related results as well as on people. The timing and the level of participation that will lead to the greatest success depends, in turn, on the capabilities of the subordinates who are being asked to participate.

Issues Related to the Situation

In addition to issues related to the characteristics of subordinates, considerations related to the requirements of the decision or the goal itself must be included. In order to make a decision or to set a goal in the best possible way, two things have to be considered: (1) the technical quality requirement—the knowledge that is required to make the decision successful or to set a high-quality goal—and (2) the acceptance quality requirement—the extent to which successful implementation of the decision or achievement of the goal requires acceptance on the part of the people who are affected. These two considerations were illustrated by Norman R. Maier of the University of Michigan in a grid (see Figure 6.4) which, while simple in appearance, is rich in complex questions.

Dr. Maier defines the quality requirements as follows:

"Technical Quality Requirements are the kinds of specialized knowledge and the amount of such knowledge needed to reach an effective decision.

"Acceptance Quality Requirements are the considerations of the amount of acceptance for the decision to be effectively implemented by those who are affected."

According to Maier's grid, a decision with high acceptance quality requirements and low technical quality requirements (quadrant A in Figure 6.4) might involve reassignment and rescheduling of working shifts. Little technical knowledge is necessary to make the decision, but a good decision must be acceptable to all the people involved. A decision with high technical quality requirements and low acceptance quality requirements (quadrant D) might involve a choice between two brands of a similar chemical on the basis of elaborate scientific specifications. Only one specialist may have the knowledge to make the choice, and no one in the organization would be affected or wish to be involved. Most difficult, perhaps, is a decision with high technical quality requirements and high acceptance quality requirements (quadrant B).

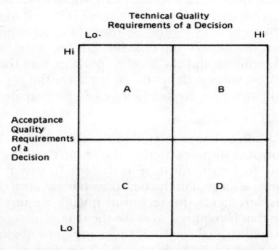

Figure 6.4. Simplified Leadership and Decision-Making Grid (From N. R. F. Maier, *Assets and Liabilities in Group Problem Solving: The Need for an Integrative Function,* PSYCHOLOGICAL REVIEW, Vol. 74, No. 4, April 1967, pp. 240–241, Copyright© 1967 by the American Psychological Association. Reprinted by permission; artwork courtesy NFPA.)

Maier concludes that participative decisions are usually more effective, especially in quadrants A and B but frequently also in quadrants C and D, because

> "there is more information in a group than in any of its members. Thus, problems that require the utilization of knowledge should give groups an advantage over individuals. Even if one member of the group (e.g.; the leader) knows much more than anyone else, the limited unique knowledge of lesser-informed individuals could serve to fill in some gaps in knowledge. For example, a skilled machinist might supply information on how a new machine might be received by workers."

Maier points out, however, that a strong leader may be needed to function as the group's "central nervous system" even when participation levels are highest. The leadership skill in this case involves the ability to keep discussion open, balanced, and fair.

In a way what Maier may be saying is that a "strong" leader knows what participation level to use in the many situations that arise with the various individuals and groups with whom he or she interacts. What participation level to use is easiest to decide in quadrant D, especially towards the lower right hand corner where technical quality requirements are highest and acceptance need is lowest. A knowledgeable manager can set such a goal or make such a decision. A technically competent person to whom the decision has been delegated can do it for the manager, and then the manager merely needs to explain or announce it. The development of a new data-processing program or the preparation of an article for a technical magazine could fall in this category.

For goals and decisions in quadrant C, neither high technical knowledge nor widespread acceptance is required. This quadrant generally involves matters about which nobody really cares what will be done. Everybody wishes that somebody else would make the decision and go on with the business at hand. There are, however, not too many decisions of this type in the work environment. Since goals should be set only on those activities that deserve high priority during a given period, it is unlikely that any goals would fall into this category.

Matters belonging to quadrant A are of a different nature. These require high acceptance for success. A goal in this quadrant could be to reduce absenteeism or increase the attention to certain specific quality details or the emphasis on certain types of customers. Most matters involving a significant amount of effort would be in this area, except for those decisions or goals for which, in addition to acceptance, high technical knowledge is required. For instance, the goal of reducing absenteeism by 20 percent does not require technical knowledge. Everybody knows what is involved. That does not mean that everybody can decide that 20 percent is the right amount of reduction to set as a goal, but everybody knows what the implications of the decision are and to what extent it will affect the people who have to implement it. Trivial decisions, such as whether to allocate parking spaces or change the coffee break time also lie in this box.

It is obvious that any goal or decision in which people believe that they can make a useful contribution and which affects them seriously will turn out better if high levels of participation can be used. If there are differences of opinion among group members, the manager must lead the group to a joint decision which will bring the minimum resentment from individuals so that all will exert the greatest effort toward making the decision successful.

Finally, those goals and decisions which involve many technical problems and which need high acceptance at the same time require the greatest skill on the part of the manager. Reducing the time required to improve the reliability of a technical product may call for considerable technical knowledge to set a realistic and challenging numerical goal. For successful implementation, though, a high level of acceptance may be necessary. For instance, the engineering department may believe that, based on tests, a product defect can be eliminated through a combination of component redesign and special attention to a number of critical operations during assembly. Or a research organization would be able to offer a highly desirable service if it could perfect a computer program and obtain the necessary data regularly within a tight deadline. Goals related to these situations must be decided by the people who have the technical knowledge to determine what is feasible. Success of the decisions and achievement of related goals, however, require implementation by several people. If the decisions and goals have high acceptance among these people, then the probability that challenging goals will be achieved is much higher than if such acceptance is lukewarm or lacking.

Decisions and goals of this type are most difficult, and therefore they require the greatest skill on the part of the manager. A good example, which concerns an emergency situation, comes out of a fairly popular training exercise in wide use by the armed services in management training. Trainees are told that during a flight across the desert their plane has to make an emergency landing. When it does so, it crashes. While all survive, they are now many miles away from the nearest habitation and the temperature during the day is excruciatingly high.

Rescued from the plane are a number of items such as raincoats for everyone, a mirror, a pistol, a parachute, and so forth. The trainees, working in small teams, are asked to decide which of these are of greatest importance to them and in what order they would want to keep them. Whether a team has an appointed leader or not, it usually tries to make these decisions by some democratic process. If a team does so, it is very likely that its members will perish within 2 or 3 days because the items that are of greatest importance are not the obvious ones. The team, first of all, has to understand that it cannot try to escape and must rely, rather, on the hope that someone will find it. Things like the mirror and the plastic raincoats are of primary importance, though they are generally not selected by people who would like to strike out to reach inhabited areas. (The raincoats should be worn so that less moisture evaporates from the body because it is loss of moisture that leads to death in the high heat).

Here is a typical decision that requires high technical knowledge and a high level of acceptance. While it is not immediately obvious what the leader should do in this kind of situation, many managers believe that the leader should obtain a consensus. But a consensus frequently results in a pooling of ignorance and brings disastrous results in the training exercise. In such a situation the leader should help the group identify the people who have the technical knowledge required to do the best possible job, then take advantage of the available knowledge to reach the decision jointly with the experts. Finally, if the manager wishes a decision to be successful or a goal to be a motivating one, the other people involved must be convinced that the decision is indeed the best.

This approach would undoubtedly be the best for goals such as those to improve product reliability or to offer a new research service. These goals require consultation with experts first and possibly joint decisions with them and then good communications to convince others who are affected—or, when possible, the development of action plans and subsidiary goals by those who have to contribute their efforts. Often such additional decisions concern the best ways to achieve implementation and to identify as well as overcome those obstacles which can be predicted.

A PARTICIPATIVE CLIMATE

In evaluating the actual level of participation in an organizational unit one has to look closely at the individual situation. For instance, if a manager says to a subordinate, "John I would like you to achieve sales of $300,000 in the next quarter," this may sound like a command; and, in some environments, that is exactly what it is. It is a quota that has been imposed on the

subordinate. But there could conceivably be high level participation.

An environment in which the subordinate is responsible
only for those things for which he or she can be accountable is
not an autocratic command but, rather, is much like joint goal
setting. The manager, based on the goal which has been passed
down from above or based on information received either from
specialists or from other data, in effect says to the subordinate:
"Tom, I think for you a $300,000 goal is appropriate. Please
take a look at it and let me know if this presents any special
difficulties for you."

The subordinate in this situation obviously has the right to
object and to say, "I have analyzed this and I don't think
$300,000 is a reasonable amount; I don't think we can achieve
$300,000 because . . . .." If the subordinate responds in such a
manner, then further review is in line to check on the reason-
ableness of the goal. If the subordinate does not respond, the
subordinate in effect is saying, "Okay, I understand that
$300,000 could be reasonable in view of the fact that you are
suggesting that it be the goal. I will do all I can to guide my
people to achieve that or to do everything that I have to do so
that it can be achieved. As soon as I see that I may have difficulty achieving it, I will let you know and then we will talk about
it to see whether you have any ideas I did not consider. If you
cannot suggest any, you can decide then whether you want to
give me additional resources to achieve the goal or whether we
are going to let it slide."

In an environment in which subordinate and manager
both clearly understand the accountabilities, what could sound
like a command is one in outward appearance only. It is obvious that in this kind of an environment there is a much higher
level of understanding and mutual trust than in an autocratic
environment or one in which elaborate discussions have to be
held to convince a subordinate to accept a higher goal than he
or she is prepared to accept at the moment.

Impact of Goals on Lower Organizational Levels

One important consideration that must influence the setting of goals concerns the impact they have at lower levels.
Goals that may appear as challenging but achievable at one level can sometimes appear impossible at several levels below

where less information is available about future developments. For instance, in a manufacturing organization the market research department and the sales department may be aware that unique developments in the market may bring a very substantial increase in orders.

Field sales managers might consider programs geared to achieving increased sales as unrealistic, and factory people may feel that an expansion program is not likely to be very urgent. As a result, goals related to sales increases or plant expansion might be perceived at lower levels as excessively demanding.

This leads to the question of who really should set production and sales goals. Such goals, as was discussed before, are really not so much goals as production targets. Nevertheless, they are perceived by the vast majority of people as goals and therefore must be considered in any goals program. Just like any decisions requiring considerable expertise, overall production targets should be set by those people who have access to the appropriate data and who possess the skills with which best to translate the data into realistic goals.

Obviously, production goals and the like require a high level of acceptance for successful implementation. Acceptance, in turn, will be forthcoming only if the goals are perceived as reasonable and valid. If they are not considered reasonable, at the very least, they will reflect negatively on those who have set them. At worst, they will have a detrimental impact on the willingness with which others devote effort to them.

Challenging goals of this nature, therefore, require good communications and some broad-brush explanation of why they were set at the levels at which they were set. Furthermore, and more importantly, such goals can be meaningful only in an environment in which people are willing to accept them as the best effort of other people and not as devices for manipulating others into higher effort than they are capable of or willing to give. In an environment in which individuals are held responsible only for competent and sufficient effort in working toward goals, the thought that goals may have been set for such purely manipulative reasons are not likely to arise. In organizations, where a high level of confidence exists in the competence and sincerity of those who determine production goals there is considerable effort to communicate the appropriateness of the goals.

Summary of Participation Guidelines

This discussion has not pinpointed the *exact* level of participation which would be best in any one situation with a subordinate or a group. But going through the thought process summarized below can help one better determine the proper level of participation:

1. Before making a decision or discussing a goal, always ask the question, "What level of participation will lead to greatest success?" This automatically assures that the choice of participation level will receive serious consideration. Just asking the question, therefore, will lead to a better choice of level.

2. As a useful next step, look at the technical quality requirement as well as the acceptance quality requirement of the decision or the goal. This helps to narrow the choice of participation level and provides a few other ideas about how to approach the goal or decision.

3. Once this question has been resolved, look at the capabilities and other factors related to the subordinate or subordinates to help zero in even closer on the best level of participation. These include (a) emotional maturity and attitudes, (b) willingness to participate, and (c) knowledge of subject matter.

When the steps in this thought process have been completed, you must make the final choice. Nevertheless, going quickly through these steps should bring a more rational choice of participation level than you would select if you gave less thought to this crucial question. While the process is complicated, it need not be time consuming. Learning to stop before making a decision—to ask the proper question—is the difficult part. The rest goes quickly after some practice. When you can decide on the appropriate level of participation in a fairly factual manner and can follow through on your conclusion, you are practicing a wide range of leadership styles. You will select from the many dimensions of leadership style those aspects which fit the needs of the situation and of the subordinate. At one moment with respect to one situation you may rely on others to supply answers and decisions and in a different situation you may merely announce the decisions you have made. In one area you may be highly supportive and provide help, while elsewhere you may insist on strict compliance with previous requests without offering any additional resources.

Such flexibility to adapt to the needs of the situation can easily be mistaken for erratic, unreliable behavior if it is not based on careful thinking and practice and on a sound framework that allows you to communicate, at all times, the reasons for your choice of style. Such explanations are of utmost importance. Consistency and reliability of leadership do not mean rigidity, however, nor do they mean restriction to a limited number of leadership approaches. Instead, they are based on the soundness of the underlying principles which guide your actions and on your ability to explain these principles adequately.

This chapter has discussed only one of the eight potential problem areas of goals programs—participation. It should be obvious at this point how important participation is. In succeeding chapters dealing with psychological satisfaction and technical competence (Chapters 8 and 9) there will be frequent references to this discussion.

Chapter 7

MBO, Planning, Performance Evaluation, and Employee Development

This chapter deals with the last two potential problem areas of MBO—the relationship of performance evaluation to the goals process and the place of developmental goals in a goals system. Most of the considerations which concern these two have already been discussed during the exploration of the previous six segments.

PERFORMANCE EVALUATION AND THE GOALS PROCESS—POTENTIAL PROBLEM AREA SEVEN

Most effective managers would agree with the statement that good planning and goal setting are the backbones of successful individual and organizational performance. Careful planning provides a framework for clarifying direction and identifying those opportunities that are most likely to achieve success. But planning in and of itself is, of course, a useless managerial tool unless the plans themselves are implemented effectively and efficiently and individual manager performance is reviewed in terms of how appropriately each manager worked towards the achievement of plan goals. Thus, the planning process, the approaches used to monitor individual progress towards achievement of planned goals, and the ultimate evaluation of performance itself are all essential management functions that appear to be intimately linked.

Similarly, the most meaningful appraisal/evaluation systems are tied closely to plans and their specific objectives, and they evaluate the performance of each person in terms of how that person works toward the achievement of his or her objectives. Just as planning itself cannot be carried out in isolation from the realities of the organizational unit, so, too, performance appraisals should not be separated from the planning process. The best system of planning and performance apprais-

121

al will be achieved if it is possible to fully integrate the planning process and the performance appraisal system.

The Evolution of Performance Evaluation

At one time, performance appraisals were based primarily on the personal opinion of the superior. They were judgments about the subordinate's ambition, initiative, general reliability, loyalty, etc. The supervisor would also evaluate quantity and quality of the work, punctuality, and other aspects of the subordinate's work that were measurable. Very often, though, these evaluations were not based on facts but mainly on feelings and therefore were heavily influenced by how much the boss liked the subordinate.

Gradually there came an awareness that appraisals of this type were grossly unfair to many people and favored those who were able to establish a friendly relationship with their bosses. As a result, such employees often were resented by their co-workers and contributed to poor morale and controversy.

Many voices were raised, therefore, asking that performance appraisal be based on achievement and on factual standards of performance. The work of the management scientists, starting with Frederick Taylor, provided much of the foundation for measuring performance of production workers, first in the factory and then in the office. But when attention was turned to evaluating the work of managers, there was little in the way of standards at first. Only when goal programs became popular did it appear as though a fair and factual standard was available. The work of managers, many people felt, could be measured on the basis of goal accomplishment. As has been discussed before, this method of evaluation also turns out to leave a lot of freedom to the manager to use personal opinion because it is the manager who decides whether the subordinate has acceptable reasons for missing a goal. Since many difficult goals are not achieved and easy goals are exceeded, there is still a great deal left to personal feelings and to the opinion which a manager has about any one subordinate.

Obviously, there will never be a system that can completely eliminate these defects. Not even the many combinations of evaluation based on goals as well as characteristics can come close. Only a performance appraisal that is based on matters which are under the control of the subordinates has a chance to be fair to the organization and to the individuals involved. A system based on accountabilities (see page 86) which concentrates on the quality of effort that people devote towards the achievement of goals is such an approach.

A significant advantage of evaluating performance of individuals based on effort and intelligently applied creativity, as well as on the setting of realistic goals on all the actions steps involved in the goal setting *process*, lies in the benefits this method has for achieving goals that require co-operation between different segments of the organization. If individual managers are not held responsible for the achievement of any multi-departmental goals that they accept but only for the eight accountabilities discussed here, then there is really no problem for an individual who assumes responsibility for a goal that requires the co-operation of a number of different departments. Task forces can spring up spontaneously in an open environment because managers are aware that if they accept a multi-departmental goal, they are responsible only for taking the proper steps and for early notification of their respective managers if the team is not heading toward the achievement of the goal. The high-level manager to whom all the other team members report can then take the appropriate steps to resolve the problem or allow the goal to slide.

If performance evaluations are to support the organizational unit's plans and its goals, they must be as factual as possible, must be based on controllable accountabilities, and must provide an opportunity for the subordinate to participate in the process. The best performance appraisals are joint activities in which both the manager and the subordinate complete the required forms and then discuss any differences in the way they perceive the subordinate's performance in each area for which he or she is accountable. Such comparisons, of course, require considerable skill on the part of the manager and, what is even more important, close personal acquaintance with the way the subordinate performs the work.

Two appraisals can be conducted each year, one for preliminary evaluation and a second one for salary decisions. At the first one, the subordinate sees more clearly how his or her performance is judged and at the same time has an opportunity to plan improvement. Even though the second evaluation influences the amount of increase which the subordinate will receive, its *primary* purpose should be to identify development goals for the subordinate, goals which should be evident from the findings of the appraisal.

Planning and Performance Evaluation

An effective planning and performance appraisal requires a framework within which data for a meaningful evaluation can be collected and an adequate dialogue between manager and subordinate can take place. The process, therefore, might consist of three stages (see Figure 7.1): a planning process, a review process, and an evaluation process.

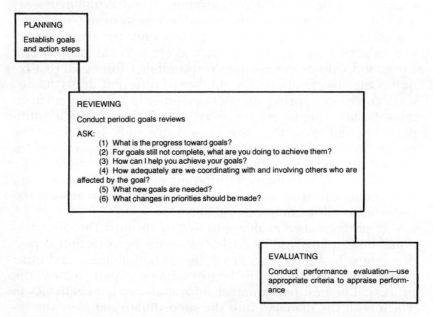

Figure 7.1. Planning and Performance Appraisal: A Three-Phase Process (Copyright © 1977 by Didactic Systems, Inc., Cranford, N.J. Reprinted by permission.)

- *Stage 1: Planning*—establishing goals and plans of action. This is the process in which manager and subordinate meet to see what has to be achieved and how it will be achieved. Specific goals are set and agreed to for the forthcoming period.
- *Stage 2: Reviewing*—reviewing goals regularly (see page 78). The goals review provides the data for evaluation and thus becomes the key link between planning and the ultimate performance appraisal.
- *Stage 3: Evaluating*—conducting the performance ap-

praisal itself. In this part of the process, manager meets with subordinate once or twice a year to evaluate his or her performance and to determine what specific personal development goals should be established for the future. Here, specific criteria are used to measure the *manner in which the individual has worked towards the goals which have been established during the previous goals reviews.* Evidence accumulated during these reviews can provide a firm foundation for the discussion of performance. The performance appraisal can also devote time to a discussion of specific knowledge, skills, and other items that the subordinate needs to develop in order to become better at his or her present job and to develop the background needed for positions towards which the individual might be aspiring.

Relationship of Performance Appraisal to Goals Reviews

Almost every employee and manager wants to know, and has a right to know, how superiors feel about his or her performance, and the manager who must evaluate performance has the obligation to obtain factual and adequate performance data. Most people want to do the best they can within the limits of their capabilities; they therefore need to know where they stand. If superiors meet with their subordinates in a thorough review session on some regular basis, they will become more factual in the way they evaluate performance and will rely less on personal preferences and expectations.

If deficiencies in knowledge and skills are to be corrected, they must first be identified, and goals review sessions provide excellent opportunities for finding them. All these benefits, however, will accrue only if the evaluation itself is fair and factual and based only on matters under the control of the subordinate.

The Inherent Contradictions

To make a goals program work, the reward system must match the goal-setting system. The two come together most sharply and formally during the annual or semi-annual performance review. If they are out of line, neither will work right. It is as simple as that. A goal setting system that involves you will work well only if you are willing to set the goals so that they are challenging yet still achievable.

If somebody wants you to set goals that way, how can you do it? Obviously, you don't know when a specific goal will be challenging and yet achievable. If you are experienced and knowledgeable, you can make some very good estimates of what will probably happen. You can set your goals higher than these estimates or you can set them lower. No matter what you do, you are only forecasting. You may make your goals or not, depending on your effort and the circumstances. You can't be sure.

What are the conditions, then, under which you would be willing to set a high goal even though you are not certain that you will make it?

Will you do it if it is likely that you will have to explain why you didn't make it and possibly find that your performance evaluation is affected negatively? Probably not. If performance is measured on the basis of goal achievement, chances are you will play it safe. You may still try hard to reach a tough goal, but the one you turn in will be a safe one—one that you are almost certain you can reach.

What has really happened here? You have begun to play a game. Communications on goals have broken down, for all practical purposes, between you and the person to whom you report. And the organizational unit which your boss heads has probably lost the chance to plan in an organized fashion that involves all levels if the boss is treating everyone alike. From here on in the boss is on his or her own. Any planning at this time has to be done with relatively little participation from you, your peers, and any level below you.

Let's take this scenario a step further. What if you were to treat your own subordinates somewhat differently? What if you were to say to them, in effect, that you would like them to list the areas in which goals should be set for the upcoming period and then assign priorities to them? Assume further that you then sit down with them to discuss their priorities so that both they and you see them the same way. There can be differences of opinion, of course, and these will have to be resolved. But assume for a moment that there are no differences of opinion, that you and one of your subordinates see the priorities in the same light and are in full agreement on them.

Assume further that so far there are no numbers or dates attached to these goals. They merely are listed to indicate where the priorities should be with respect to the effort that must be devoted to improving things. (Remember that the goals program should emphasize only those matters that are nonroutine). What would happen if you were next to ask your subordinates to set specific goals with dates and numbers on high-priority items. You would ask them to set the goals so that they were challenging but still possibly within reach, which means that they should have a 50/50 chance of making them with extra effort. Suppose you were to assure them that if they did not quite reach those goals, their performance evaluation would not suffer, that performance would be measured only on how competently they set their action steps and how seriously they took implementation of the steps and their own efforts to achieve the goals.

Not a very realistic scenario in many organizations in today's world, of course. But it is an intriguing one. What if it were indeed possible?

Resolving the Contradictions

There are several questions that need to be explored. In the first place, it would seem that your subordinates would now be free to set goals so that they are indeed challenging. Would they do it, though, you may ask, if there were nothing in it for them when they achieved the goals or, conversely, if there were no penalty for not achieving them? That, of course, is the key question, and the answer is very complex. It would seem that if there is indeed a climate that allows for maximum motivation, then there are significant rewards in goal achievement for the individual—the really important satisfaction from achievement, from accomplishing something that was difficult. There also would be the recognition which you provide directly and indirectly, the greater sense of security, the higher probability of faster career advancement. In short, there would be all the benefits which highly motivated, successful people enjoy—a potential cornucopia in setting and achieving tough goals.

But all this is loaded with a big IF. It will happen only IF the climate allows the highest possible level of motivation. A motivational climate requires the satisfaction of psychological and tangible rewards which are discussed in Chapter 8. If it is to exist day in and day out, it must take into account that most people may still not respond enthusiastically, exert substantial additional effort, give up some of their free moments, or even devote significantly more thought to their goals; but they are likely to do more than they would under a punitive system or under any other system.

A second question concerns another IF: If goal achievement itself is not a primary criterion for performance evaluation, then subordinates are not really responsible for goal achievement. If *they* are not, then who is? That's easy. You are!

You know this, of course, but you probably have always felt that while you are ultimately responsible to your superiors so your subordinates are responsible to you. In other words, you have felt that everybody, all the way up the line, is responsible or accountable for the achievement of goals.

In reality, the situation is different. As far as your subordinates are concerned, they are accountable for doing everything as though they were responsible for achieving the goal; but they are also aware that if they cannot achieve it, you consider yourself responsible. You are undoubtedly asking yourself now if it makes sense that you are responsible for the goal while your subordinate is working on it and he or she is not. "Why does the buck stop with me? Why am I treated differently?"

If you reflect on it for a moment, you can see there is logic to such an arrangement because you are the one who has accepted a goal from a subordinate that you know to be challenging. While it appears to be realistic at the moment when you accepted it, it may not turn out to be. If you accepted it, then you are the person who must help your subordinate achieve it. If he or she can't, even with significant and competent effort, and if you also can't do it when informed of problems in time, then obviously you have no choice but to take them off the hook. Does that leave you hanging? Maybe yes, maybe no. It depends on your relationship with your boss and on your boss' competence and understanding of what is involved. As far as your subordinates are concerned, however, the picture is clear. You have told them that you will evaluate their performance on *what they do* to achieve their goals and *not* on *whether* they achieve them.

If you have actually established a relationship with your subordinates that allows them to honestly submit challenging goals, do you build your own goals on these and turn them in to your boss? This, too, depends. Either your boss views goals programs as you do and has told you that you will be evaluated in terms of the criteria of accountability or your boss believes in expecting goal achievement from subordinates. If your boss holds the latter position, you may continue to play the same game that you probably are playing now. You chop as much off these goals as you think is wise and then turn them in as your goals.

If you are working for someone who thinks as you do, then you can set a challenging objective of your own, which would probably include fewer goals than submitted to you—what you consider to be within the realm of the feasible if everyone put in the necessary effort. In this case you are not playing a game. If your boss asks you how you arrived at these goals, you can safely show the challenging, ambitious, yet realistic goals of subordinates and explain how you arrived at your own goals based on these. Communications are free and open and planning can proceed, taking advantage of the best knowledge that is available at each level. There is nothing under the table; nothing is hidden.

Who Is Really Responsible for Goal Achievement?

You may be wondering who really is responsible for achievement of goals in such an environment as that described above. The answer is, essentially the same people responsible for them now. No one is really responsible for goal achievement! If this sounds like heresy it may be worthwhile to take a look at the actual situation as it exists in the world today. On the one hand, it often happens that some people are held accountable for goals that are not achieved, and sometimes a person's head may roll even when that person gives much time and effort to the achievement of the goal. On the other hand, certain people are commended for achieving goals that were not worth setting as goals because they were going to be achieved even if no one payed any attention to them.

The point which many people miss is that certain goals are simply not achievable, no matter how competent and complete the effort devoted to them. That is all there is to it. Responsibility goes all the way up to the executive director of an organization which has accepted a goal. At the end of the year, if the goal is not achieved, it is the executive director who has to explain why. If the board of trustees or the board of directors knows that the executive director has indeed done the very best that can be done by taking the most competent action steps possible and has put in all the effort that can reasonably be expected, then the board has to accept the fact that the goal was not achievable. The assumptions about the goal may have been wrong when the goal was set in the first place; the forecast might have been a good forecast, but it did not come true. One must be aware that about 50 percent of all goals that are set as they should be set will not be achieved.

Facing Reality

Although it may seem that holding people responsible for the quality and quantity of effort instead of the results is a new approach, it is really not that different from what happens now in well-managed organizations and organizational units. Today, if a goal is not achieved, the manager reviews what the subordinate has done in attempting to achieve it. If the manager is convinced that the effort was top notch and the reason for nonachievement was totally beyond the control of the subordinate, the competent manager may still give the subordinate an excellent evaluation.

Without clear understanding of what criteria the manager uses for evaluation, the subordinate may feel somewhat uneasy about being evaluated. There are, therefore, natural suspicions about the relationship between goal achievement and evaluation; or, at the very least, there are doubts, questions, and uncertainties that certainly do not make it easy for subordinates to trust the system implicitly. As a result, the planning process suffers because managers have to consider that some of their subordinates, at all levels, are building cushions into their plans. In an organization where subordinates are held responsible for goal achievement only when goals are indeed achievable, managers are really holding subordinates accountable only for action steps. In effect, managers are retaining responsibility and accountability for goal achievement themselves. Only the appearance that goal achievement is expected remains. But standards or criteria which subordinates can understand and which allow them to see for themselves how well they are performing may not have been communicated. Subordinates may have no guidelines except: "Do the best you can, and then hope that your boss will see your efforts the same way you do and will give proper weight to any obstacles that came in the way of goal achievement."

However, to suddenly release people from the requirement to achieve goals, even if a thorough system of new criteria were substituted, could be too sudden and be damaging to an organization which is accustomed to think of goals as targets which must be reached. The new concepts are more complex and people have to adjust to them gradually if they are to serve their purposes well.

Effectively Linking Planning and Factual Performance Evaluations

The following sections describe one possible approach to linking planning and performance evaluation. Several things are required for effective implementation of performance evaluations which support the planning effort of an organizational unit:

1. Managers must learn how they can fairly evaluate the performance of the individuals who report to them without basing that evaluation on goal achievement. This means that they have to clearly understand the eight accountability criteria which were discussed in Chapter 5 and also the way goal-review sessions can be used to provide the data which will allow a fair and factual performance evaluation. The form shown as Figure 7.2 is one way to approach data collection.

2. Goal-review sessions have to be used regularly to provide a forum for reviewing action steps and for establishing a data base for factual evaluation. Reviews have to be fairly disciplined and thorough to serve this function.

3. Performance evaluation must continue to be based, at least in part, on goal achievement, but it must also be based on action steps—on the quality and quantity of effort that went into attempting to achieve the goals. For instance, when performance evaluations are begun using this system, goal achievement can still count for 80 percent or even 90 percent of the evaluation base. But for those goals that were missed, or those where much more was achieved than the goal called for, the manager can look at the accountability criteria based on action steps. These criteria assure that the very best is being done to achieve goals. Even though they are based only on matters under control of the subordinate, they do not completely eliminate personal opinions of the evaluator; but they can go a long way towards establishing a fairly factual evaluation system, which can use data gathered in a systematic fashion throughout the year.

For Completed Goals, Use the Following Guidelines in Preparing Your Comments:

1. How well was the goal achieved?
2. How difficult/easy was it to achieve the goal?
3. What was the quality and quantity of effort to achieve the goal?
4. Was there adequate communication on status toward goal achievement?
5. How adequate was your support in helping your subordinate achieve the goal?

For Open Goals, Use the Following Guidelines in Preparing Your Comments:

1. Will the goal be achieved? If not, what is the problem and what should be done about it?
2. What is needed from you, as manager, to help your subordinate achieve the goal?
3. How adequate are communications so far in all directions?
4. How appropriate is the involvement of those people who are affected by this goal?
5. Is the goal still appropriate in light of changes in environment?

GOAL SUMMARIES	PRIORITIES	REVIEW COMMENTS

Figure 7.2. A Goals Review Form (Copyright © 1977 by Didactic Systems, Inc., Cranford, N.J. Reprinted by permission.)

The greatest benefit of such a system lies with its ability to communicate to people the fact that evaluations will not be arbitrary, that they are based on criteria that everyone knows and that the evaluations of managers can therefore be discussed— and even reviewed or challenged—in a systematic, organized way. This in turn can lead to improved confidence by managers when evaluating performance of their subordinates and in greater confidence by subordinates in the fairness of the evaluations.

The Benefits of Performance Evaluation and a Practical Evaluation Scale

There are four benefits to using the accountability criteria described previously:

1. The criteria are *based solely on matters under the direct control of the person working on the goals*.
2. They will, together, *bring the highest possible level of goal achievement*.
3. They can be used to help subordinates and managers communicate meaningfully on performance, and they serve as an excellent foundation for development of subordinate competency.
4. Feedback becomes much more factual and timely, and it is highly unlikely that a subordinate is not fully aware of the quality of his or her performance. In fact, subordinates have the same data available to them.

It might even be possible to use the evaluation scale on pages 134 and 135, or a similar one, to let subordinates rate themselves, based on the record of the goals reviews, and then to discuss only those ratings which the evaluator felt were not fully accurate. There are not likely to be many disagreements, however, especially if there are two performance evaluations each year.

A caution is necessary with respect to these scales. Though they carry numbers, these numbers cannot be added up to provide an evaluation total. Someone who scores a 4 on all eight criteria would score 32. That person is a very valuable staff member. Someone who scores 5's on six of the criteria but only 1's on Quality of Effort and Timeliness of Results also achieves a 32, but that person is hardly useful in any organization.

PERFORMANCE EVALUATION SCALE*

I. *Ambitiousness/Taking Initiative*

Sets goals at exceptionally high and reasonably attainable levels	5
Sets goals at high and clearly attainable levels	4
Sets goals at acceptable levels	3
Sets goals at levels somewhat below those appropriate for the individual and position	2
Sets goals at levels considerably below or unrealistically above those appropriate for the individual and position	1

II. *Thoroughness*

All goals have a thorough set of action steps appropriately prepared for them	5
Most goals have a thorough set of action steps, and other goals have action steps that are fairly complete	4
All goals have a fairly complete set of action steps	3
Some goals have a fairly complete set of action steps and other goals have action steps which are not adequate	2
Very few goals, or none at all, have an adequate set of action steps	1

III. *Planning*

Consistently thorough at planning goals and action steps	5
Some occasional difficulties at planning goals and action steps	4
About average, when compared to others in similar positions, at planning goals and action steps	3
Fairly regular difficulties at planning goals and action steps	2
Primarily a scattered and impulsive effort at setting goals and action steps	1

IV. *Quality of Effort*

All action steps set are those most likely to achieve goals most rapidly	5
Most action steps set will lead to achievement of goals rapidly, but some are of lower quality	4
All action steps are of good quality and are likely to achieve the goals, although they are not the best steps that could have been taken	3
Some action steps are of good quality and are likely to achieve goals, but others are not of good quality	2
Very few action steps, if any, are of good quality; they are not likely to lead to achievement of goals without significant changes	1

V. *Timeliness of Results*

All action steps are achieved on time	5

---

*Copyright ©1977 by Didactic Systems, Inc. Reprinted by permission.

Most action steps are achieved on time, with only short delays on others 4

Many action steps are achieved on time, with a few extensive delays on others 3

Some action steps are achieved on time, with quite a few significant delays on others 2

Very few action steps are achieved on time; there are many significant delays 1

VI. *Problem Solving*

Exceptionally imaginative action steps are added for all goals when it appears that a goal may not be achieved 5

Highly imaginative action steps are added for most goals, and good ones for others, where it appears that a goal may not be achieved 4

Good but not highly imaginative action steps are added for all goals where it appears that a goal may not be achieved 3

Good but not highly imaginative action steps are added for some goals and inadequate action steps are added for others when it appears that a goal may not be achieved 2

Very few imaginative action steps are added for any goal which may not be achieved 1

VII. *Communications*

Consistently notifies manager at earliest possible time when additional resources may be required to achieve all established goals 5

Consistently notifies manager in sufficient time when additional resources may be required to achieve most established goals 4

Generally notifies manager in sufficient time when additional resources may be required to achieve most established goals 3

Frequently fails to notify manager in sufficient time when application of additional resources may achieve established goals 2

Rarely or never notifies manager in time to apply additional resources to achieve established goals 1

VIII. *Inter-personal Relations*

Exceptionally thorough in keeping others informed of goals and action steps affecting them 5

Very thorough in keeping others informed of goals and action steps affecting them 4

Average in thoroughness with respect to keeping others informed on goals and action steps affecting them 3

Often fails in keeping others informed of goals and action steps affecting them 2

Rarely informs others of goals and action steps affecting them 1

Formal Performance Evaluations Versus Regular Goals Reviews

Formal performance reviews serve as foundations for deciding what knowledge or skills subordinates need for better performance and as preparation for possible promotion if they are to help improve the climate of an organization. The correction of knowledge and skill deficiencies discussed during the performance review can then become the basis for self-improvement goals which the subordinate needs to achieve.

One question that often arises about performance appraisal concerns comparisons with goals reviews. In what ways are performance appraisals and goals reviews similar, and how do they differ? They are similar because both are detailed contacts between a manager and a subordinate. Both provide an opportunity for the manager to learn more about the interests, views, and aspirations of each subordinate. Both can result in development goals for the subordinate.

The differences between the two are even more important, however. During a performance appraisal session, the manager is the evaluator and the subordinate is the person being evaluated. While in a well-conducted performance appraisal there are discussions of personal development goals and career goals and the subordinate's views receive a full hearing, the "evaluator/evaluatee" relationship directly affects income and career development.

During a well-conducted goals review, the discussion is between two people, both of whom have something to contribute to the achievement of the goal. The discussion does not stress successes and shortcomings. Instead, it concentrates on what needs to be done to achieve the goals which have been set, what new goals should be considered, what goals can be dropped, and, most importantly, how the manager can help with problems that the subordinate faces. Such discussions do not belong in the performance evaluations, except for exploration of personal development and career goals.

Performance Evaluation, Salary Reviews, and Promotions

The relationship between performance evaluations and salary reviews or salary actions needs to be clarified. There is a widespread belief that performance appraisals and salary adjustments should be separated in time to avoid defensiveness on the part of the subordinate during the evaluation. Organizations which attempt this separation are often underestimating the awareness of their people on a subject of such great interest to them. They thereby merely strengthen the conviction of their employees that the organization is not fully candid. It would be much simpler to say that there will be one or two performance reviews each year and that the amount of the salary increase will be affected to some extent by these reviews. It might even be useful to point out the several factors that will be weighed when decisions on salary are made, i.e.:

1. The actual evaluations relative to top-notch performance
2. The trend in improvement with respect to all eight accountability criteria
3. The money available for increases
4. Current salary level in relation to the top of the position's salary range.

At the same time, of course, it is useful to play the salary aspects down because within any one position the difference in the increase between good performance and excellent performance must, of necessity, be quite small. It is usually the job that has the greatest influence on salary level and not the quality of the performance. And that should probably be emphasized more extensively than is done in most organizations most of the time.

Subordinates sometimes question the relationship between performance evaluation and the tangible rewards. At such times, the managers should have a clear picture of these relationships so that they can be explained in a meaningful way. The tangible rewards most directly involved are incentive payments, bonuses, and salary.

Incentive payments usually are based on achievement of targets, and they therefore are likely to reflect the impact of external influences rather than the effort or competence of the individual. If business conditions become more difficult, sales in a profit-oriented organization will suffer, and sales people understand that their commissions will be lower. Similarly, in a factory where incentive payments are made for production, people understand that during product changes and at other times incentive payments may not be available and that their incomes may temporarily be affected in a negative way. Conversely, fortunate circumstances can bring fairly large payments even when there is little effort.

Bonuses are similar to incentives but they are easier to adjust to valid measurements of individual performance. While the total bonus pool may fluctuate, depending on the performance of the entire organizational unit as well as on the general political and economic conditions, the individual's share of the pool can have a direct relationship to performance. The manager who has established mutual trust with subordinates can distribute bonuses based on performance evaluation. Bonuses give managers a chance to tie performance evaluations directly to compensation.

The least direct relationship between performance and reward exists with salary increases. Here too most organizations make available to their managers a pool of salary increases that managers can distribute as they see fit. Sometimes the expectation exists in the minds of managers and staff members alike that everyone who turns in high performance should receive the highest possible salary increase. People often feel that high-level performance deserves high-level increases. For example, an organization may allow its managers to grant increases varying from 0 to 12 percent. At the same time, it may stipulate that each division or department may not grant more than an overall increase of 8 percent. In such a situation, all people who have earned an evaluation of excellent performance are likely to expect increases of 12 percent.

Obviously, this is impossible for the entire organization as a whole, and even for the staff members under the jurisdiction of a particular manager. The manager, therefore, has an obligation to explain to all staff members that salary increases are not tied directly and *immediately* to performance evaluation. High performance evaluations by large proportions of staff members can, of course, bring such high organizational performance that more money will be available, and everyone can enjoy large increases. In the short run, however, this is not possible; and, therefore, not only high performance but sustained high performance is important for the largest increases. A manager can and should rank all staff members in the organizational unit and then apportion the available salary pool of 8 percent of total salaries on the basis of that ranking.

The point is that staff members have to understand that salary increases cannot immediately reflect performance evaluation. In the long run, performance evaluations affect salary decisions in two different ways:

1. People with the best sustained performance receive higher salary increases than those with lower merit.
2. Organizational units with excellent performance receive larger salary pools, either because the organization earned more or because that particular organizational unit relative to others deserves a larger allotment.

People with the best sustained performance also deserve the greatest consideration for career preparation and career opportunities for which they are qualified.

Summary of the Relationship of Performance Evaluations and Compensation Programs

1. Contrary to popular impressions, it is not performance evaluation that should be separated from salary review but rather the performance improvement activities, especially goals reviews, as we have seen.
2. Hence performance evaluation and salary and bonus discussions *do* belong together, and career discussion should also be included.
3. These discussions represent excellent opportunities for making subordinates fully aware of the three influences on their salary increases, and on their bonuses: (a) their performance relative to the performance of others in the unit, (b) the available pool of money, and (c) the overall salary structure which places limits on jobs.
4. Bonuses should have a direct relationship to performance evaluation ratings.
5. Salary increases depend on performance evaluation ratings *and* continuity of high performance. (Otherwise game playing can occur.)
6. Continuity in high ratings will lead to higher competence and better positions—sooner or later.

A Few Implementation Problems

Managers who attempt to install a planning program with goals, and who would like to evaluate performance based on the seriousness and competence of effort, often find that some of the subordinate managers in their organizational unit do not really understand the distinction between goals and action steps. People who submit action steps in the belief that they are goals will usually insist that everyone should be evaluated on the basis of goal achievement because much of what they expect of their subordinates really constitutes action steps.

This is particularly true in those functional areas where goals are more difficult to define. For instance, a public relations manager may expect and set goals in terms of meetings with the community and legislative members, or a personnel manager may consider the publication of a newsletter and the prompt filing of insurance claims as goals. Defining work in these terms is not setting goals; instead, it outlines activities under the control of the individual responsible for them. If these are mistaken for goals, the respective manager may be very firm in insisting that people should be evaluated on the basis of goal achievement. Therefore, it is essential that the distinction between goals and action steps is clarified whenever a discussion arises about performance evaluation based on goals. This should be done with examples so that everyone clearly understands the distinctions and so that all see how the accountability criteria can help to focus on the critical action steps which a subordinate must take to assure that his or her best effort is devoted towards setting and achieving goals.

Performance evaluation based on effort to achieve goals is most difficult in situations in which the manager does not have direct contact with subordinates. In such an environment, which is particularly prevalent in sales organizations, the manager has little personal contact with subordinates, which makes it much more difficult to evaluate performance on the basis of the quality of effort devoted to action steps.

It is easy to evaluate the performance of some staff members. The results of their efforts clearly show that competence and significant efforts are being devoted to setting and achieving goals. It is more difficult to evaluate performance of other staff members, however. This is true where the manager either suspects or has evidence that a staff member does not devote the necessary effort or does not have the competence to achieve good results but where good results occur in any case. In such situations, more direct observation is necessary to make meaningful evaluation. Knowledge/skill diagrams and a knowledge/skill analysis can be of considerable help (see page 189).

Finally, there is the situation in which performance is poor but it appears as though the staff member devotes the necessary effort and is competent. Here, too, more personal contact is necessary to uncover the problems that exist in the situation—for example, whether the apparent competence and effort of the subordinate is real or is only an impression.

INCLUDING DEVELOPMENTAL GOALS IN A GOALS PROGRAM—POTENTIAL PROBLEM AREA EIGHT

The connection between on-the-job performance, career preparation, and goals programs is found in the last of the potential problem areas of MBO, which deals with the place of developmental goals in the total program. A goals program that covers only operational goals concerned with performance objectives is not complete. Employees need to see that the goals program includes some goals whose primary purpose is to help them, not just the organization unit. Only if this is the case can they take organizational goals seriously. Personal goals primarily involve personal development towards a career goal, and this starts with goals which help to improve competence on the current job. Personal development goals can also concern assignments which provide valuable experiences and satisfaction to the subordinate and thus lead to gradual but effective job enrichment. Job enrichment will be discussed in Chapter 8.

A manager who attempts to create a workable goals program has many opportunities to determine what the personal needs and aspirations of subordinates are and what specific knowledge or skills would most help them improve their performance. The manager can sometimes discuss these matters during the regular goals review after the work goals have been covered or, what is probably more meaningful, in a formal training and development needs analysis prior to, or in conjunction with, the performance evaluation. Such analysis will be discussed in detail in Chapter 9, which covers the Linking Element dealing with technical competence.

Developmental goals should become a regular part of the goals program since they provide opportunities for the manager to be totally supportive. Development goals usually can be set by the subordinate, with the manager providing guidance and counseling. In allowing the subordinate to set personal goals, the organization, through the manager, provides evidence that it does not consider the goals program a one way street aimed at better organizational performance alone; it also sees the program as a way to satisfy the needs of employees at all levels.

Motivational Impact of an Effective Goals Program

Many managers believe that it is their function to "motivate" their people. They are often told by researchers, lecturers, and other experts that if they are good "leaders," they can actually do so. There is some truth in this, of course; but this belief is also somewhat misleading. First of all, there are limits to motivation. Some people find work so distasteful that they can never really gain satisfaction from it. Fortunately, this is true only for a very small minority. Most people, however, cannot be "motivated" artificially, even by a very good leader. Much more is needed than just considerate leadership. A total management approach is required which creates a climate that allows employees to find motivation—the desire to accomplish more or better things. It may be said that all the activities in a well-managed goals program encourage people to find motivation.

Clearly, there is no single act, no simple way to provide an environment in which people will feel strong motivation to do all the things a manager would like them to do. A manager who helps employees attain greater satisfaction from their work usually finds that the motivation of employees increases. Unfortunately, however, it is very difficult to know how people will respond to help or what they would do if the manager behaved differently.

The studies that have been made consistently have shown that those managers who are technically competent and also skilled in providing job satisfaction to their people end up with best performance. The point here is that it is satisfaction with belonging to the work unit and achieving work-related goals, not just a happier outlook on life or personal liking for the manager, that is important in stimulating motivation. It is equally important to remember that not everyone can be motivated to the same extent and that even in the very best climate there are always some people who do not share the same level of enthusiasm as do others.

SUMMARY—MAKING A GOALS PROGRAM SUCCESSFUL

A smoothly operating goals program can help to bring a climate in which people can find motivation. Such a program can be developed and maintained if the necessary steps are taken to avoid the eight potential problem areas summarized in the acronym EQUIFAPPO:

1. If an appropriate number of goals are set, goals properly challenging the subordinate, and if priorities are selected so that they satisfy the desire to accomplish something worthwhile, then there is positive motivational impact.
2. The quality of goals and goal statements contributes to the motivational climate because accuracy and explicitness remove uncertainties and questions about what is

really expected and because good quality eliminates much confusion. Good goals give a feeling of direction that anyone can share. Winning the next game is a highly motivating goal for every ball team. In the work environment goals are rarely as challenging or as motivating as they are in sports, but if they are meaningful and clear, then they have the potential to challenge employees.

3. The level of involvement by the manager is important. The climate of motivation is enhanced if a manager exercises good judgment in providing help when members of the team need help and refrains from becoming involved when they would rather perform the jobs in their own way.

4. A manager who reviews progress on a fairly regular basis and who, during these reviews, explores what help the individual team members need to achieve their goals provides the kind of support and the kind of secure feeling that can add substantially to job satisfaction.

5. The manager who holds people accountable for the things that they can achieve and does not muddy the water by blaming them or giving them credit for things over which they have no control adds a feeling of confidence that also contributes to job satisfaction and thereby to a motivational climate.

6. The right amount of participation in goal setting brings many job satisfactions. If a manager allows the proper amount of participation in those matters that affect the members of the team, then team members gain the feeling that they have influence over their work and their future. They know that they have a voice in deciding the way the work is to be done. This knowledge contributes greatly to the feeling of satisfaction that they obtain from their work and to the confidence that they have in their organization and in their managers.

7. Performance evaluations can have a very significant impact on motivational climate if they are appropriately tied to the goals program and are based on accountabilities which consider only matters under the control of the person. Performance evaluations provide the feedback which tells people where they stand and what

they have to do to improve. These evaluations do much to enhance the confidence of people in their organization if they are factual and fair; if they are based on criteria which are known, understood, and accepted; and if they are reflected properly in compensation and career decisions.

8. Finally, a goals program can achieve a significant improvement in motivational climate if it is not restricted to operational goals but also covers developmental goals that help individuals improve performance on their current jobs and prepare them for the next higher jobs or for better jobs to which they may aspire.

This may be a good time to compare the notes you made at the beginning of Chapter 5 with this summary. To what extent has the discussion helped you to clarify your own thoughts on the way a goals program can be made more successful? Does the acronym EQIFAPPO represent a useful way to summarize the Linking Element which aligns organizational goals and performance standards with the performance standards of individuals? If it does, then the box between the arrows on page 49 can be completed by writing EQIFAPPO. If it requires other skills in addition in your view, then you can complete it accordingly.

Chapter 8

The Needs of People at Work

This chapter discusses the Linking Element encompassing the managerial skills which concern psychological rewards and the satisfaction of psychological needs.* At this point take the time to write out, either in the blank space in Figure 8.1 below

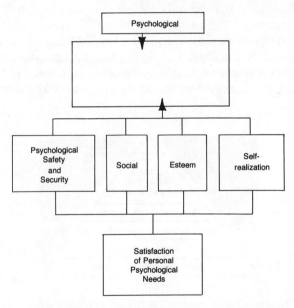

Figure 8.1. Segment of Linking Elements Diagram

or on a separate sheet of paper, what skills you believe to be important in aligning the psychological rewards an organization (or your organization) can provide with the yearning of the people in the organization for greater satisfaction of their psychological needs. This short exercise will again confirm for you

---

*See far right side of Figure 3.3, p. 35.

145

that you are indeed aware of most of the issues. Nevertheless this chapter will probably provide you with better organization for your thoughts and a more comprehensive view of the managerial skills which are necessary to satisfy this Linking Element.

RESEARCH OF OUTSTANDING BEHAVIORAL SCIENTISTS ON MOTIVATION

Much of the discussion in this chapter is based on Abraham Maslow's Hierarchy of Needs and on the work of Douglas McGregor, Frederick Herzberg, Rensis Likert, Robert Blake, Jane Mouton, and Chris Argyris.

The Work of Abraham Maslow

Psychologist Abraham H. Maslow concerned himself with the total range of the human mind and human relationships. His "Hierarchy of Needs," from the book *Motivation and Personality,* first widely published in 1954, has had a major influence on the development of current management theory. In simple form, Maslow's hierarchy can be diagrammed as shown in Figure 8.2.

Figure 8.2. Simplified Diagram of Maslow's Conceptualization of the Five Levels of Basic Human Needs (Adapted from A. H. Maslow, *Hierarchy of Needs,* MOTIVATION AND PERSONALITY, New York, Harper and Row, 1954; artwork courtesy NFPA.)

Maslow's basic premise is that people are motivated by the desire to satisfy needs that are not fully satisfied. He identifies five levels of needs and assigns them levels of relative importance, as follows:

- *Basic Physiological Needs:* Needs that are primarily related to bodily survival—the need for food and water to maintain life and the need for clothing and shelter to protect the body from harsh environments.

- *Safety and Security:* Needs that are concerned with safety and security—the need for self-preservation and the need to ensure future security. These needs essentially concern the protection of the basic physiological needs for the future.
- *Belonging and Social Activity:* The need to belong to a group, to have some means of group identification, to receive and give affection, and to participate in some form of social activity. These needs should be met at work as well as away from it.
- *Esteem and Status:* The need to have, to receive, and to give esteem and status (both of which are essential to human dignity). Self-respect and respect for others are important in a modern industrial society because the previous three needs are, to a large degree, satisfied.
- *Self-realization and Fulfillment:* The need to become all that one is capable of becoming. When this need dominates, work becomes a challenge and provides greater satisfaction.

While Maslow has drawn a picture that in many respects has stood up under the test of many challenges, in some ways it has been shown to be deficient. For instance, it does not adequately describe and highlight the impact of money on human needs. It also does little to explain what self-realization and fulfillment, or self-actualization, really is for people other than the few rare individuals to whom self-actualization is evident from childhood or becomes clearly evident at some later time (for example, the devoted artists and scientists who recognize their calling at some stage of their lives). These shortcomings will be discussed in greater detail later on.

The Work of Douglas M. McGregor

Professor Douglas M. McGregor, a social psychologist with the Massachusetts Institute of Technology, suggested that most organizations operated under certain traditional beliefs. McGregor called these beliefs Theory X and described them as follows:

"Management is a function which demands tight control over every aspect of the productive process. This is necessary because workers are naturally inclined to work as little as possible, to shirk responsibility, to be indifferent to organizational needs and to resist change. Workers must be regulated by 'hard' methods of strict discipline, or seduced by 'soft' methods which offer extensive benefits and constant efforts to achieve harmony."

Theory X did not really work, McGregor maintained, because it ignored some genuine basics of human nature. He proposed that managers would be able to see their subordinates more clearly in terms of beliefs that he called Theory Y: "People do not have an inherent dislike of work. They have motivation to work, a willingness to assume responsibility, and a readiness to help the organization reach its goals." McGregor proposed that ". . . the essential task of management is to arrange organizational conditions and methods of operation so that people can achieve their own goals best by directing their own efforts toward organizational objectives."*

McGregor pointed out that with Theory X, management takes both a hard and a soft line. He explained that the hard line—tight disciplinary measures when needed—is met by employee antagonism and leads to many forms of resistance. He described the soft line as including such benefits as vacations, pensions, and recreational programs. However, he went on to explain, these benefits are only enjoyable *off the job,* and each of them tends to encourage passivity on the job.

Theory Y, McGregor argued, would give workers a greater personal stake in their own work. They would be encouraged to use all their knowledge, skills, and ingenuity in accomplishing the organization's objectives. This would present a difficult challenge, McGregor allowed, but could be started in one way by the process of job enlargement (making workers responsible for larger and more complex parts of the production process).

The Work of Frederick Herzberg

In the 1950's a group of researchers led by Frederick Herzberg of Case Western Reserve University began an extensive survey process in which engineers and accountants were questioned concerning those aspects of their work that made them feel especially good and those that made them feel especially bad. Using the answers to these questions as a starting point, Herzberg developed the "motivation-hygiene theory of

---

*From THE HUMAN SIDE OF ENTERPRISE, by Douglas M. McGregor. Copyright ©1960, McGraw-Hill Book Company. Used with permission of McGraw-Hill Book Company.

job attitudes," which has since been tested at all levels of work throughout the world.*

Herzberg and his associates discovered a number of factors that were frequently listed as dissatisfactions but rarely as satisfactions. These factors included a surprising number of conditions that generally had been regarded as work incentives (or motivators)—for instance, salary, fringe benefits, and vacation and recreation policies. When these factors were deficient, they caused dissatisfaction. But when they were present, they did not represent important job satisfactions. Herzberg called these factors the "hygiene elements of work" or "dissatisfaction-avoiders." He considered their use in employment as a type of preventive medicine that helped keep people from being unhappy. However, they did not do much to make workers happy or to motivate them.

Virtually all the factors listed by workers as satisfactions turned out to be directly connected with the jobs they did. These "satisfiers" included the nature of the work itself, achievement in a work project, recognition for the work, responsibility for a job, and advancement to greater responsibility. Only satisfiers can help to bring higher levels of motivation.

After repeated studies, Herzberg concluded that most companywide efforts to improve workers' attitudes and motivation had little effect. These efforts included reductions in working hours, increased wages, improved fringe benefits, friendlier supervision, and company efforts to improve communications about policies. Much of the cost of these expensive programs, Herzberg proposed, should be shifted to job enrichment programs designed to make jobs more challenging and to give employees greater on-the-job opportunities for initiative, responsibility, recognition, and personal growth.

The Work of Rensis Likert

In the 1950's and the 1960's, University of Michigan researchers conducted an extensive series of experiments in which they observed the output of departments headed by supervisors who were "employee centered" and the output of departments headed by supervisors who were "production cen-

---

*M. Scott Myers, *Who are Your Motivated Workers?* HARVARD BUSINESS REVIEW, Jan.-Feb. 1964; Saul W. Gellerman, MOTIVATION AND PRODUCTIVITY, (New York: American Management Association, Inc., 1963), pp. 48–55.

tered." One typical experiment focused for a long period of time on the clerical departments of a major insurance company. The lowest production levels were consistently found in departments headed by supervisors who placed a major emphasis on production, who exercised strict controls over employees, and who frequently intervened in the work process. When the production-centered supervisors were transferred to departments that previously had employee-centered supervisors, production fell off.

Rensis Likert,* who summarized the experiments for publication, divided management practices into four categories: (1) exploitative-authoritative, (2) benevolent-authoritative, (3) consultative, and (4) participative. The participative type was probably best, he theorized, because employees actually worked in self-disciplined groups, which, to be productive, required little or no pressure. The most effective role for the supervisor, Likert concluded, was to provide information, materials, organizational support, and to "stay out of the way." Likert allowed, however, that authoritative control appeared to be necessary in certain exceptional crisis situations.

Likert also spoke of the manager as the Linking Pin between his or her organizational unit and the larger organization of which the unit was a part. Because the Linking Pin has some superficial resemblance, especially in name, to Linking Elements, the two are sometimes mistaken for each other.

The Work of Robert Blake and Jane S. Mouton

With the publication of their *Managerial Grid* in 1964, Robert R. Blake and Jane S. Mouton offered a model they felt appropriate to the realities of organizational life. The Grid® took into account a fact that many behavioral science researchers had noted earlier: high morale among workers did not necessarily equal high productivity. Ideally, they suggested, managers should move the organization to work equally toward maximum concern for people and maximum concern for production (Point 9,9 on the Managerial Grid shown in Fig. 8.3).

The Blake and Mouton *Managerial Grid* acknowledged that some organizations could survive under extreme leadership conditions. For example, at Point 1,1 on the Managerial Grid,

---

*Likert, Rensis, Human Organization: Its Management and Value (New York: McGraw-Hill, 1967).

work went on despite the fact that supervisors shunned responsibility or blame and might be almost totally out of contact with both higher management and subordinate workers. A Point 9,1 (Sweatshop Management) approach was considered possible if workers were uneducated and highly submissive to authority. A Point 5,5 position implied constant compromises between production needs and human needs, with little satisfaction of long duration in either direction. Though it accommodated these realities, the *Managerial Grid* also suggested a "road map" that could guide organized leadership towards circumstances considered better for the long-range effectiveness of the organization.

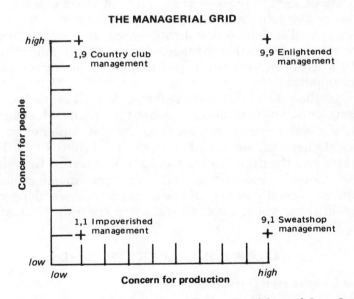

Figure 8.3. The Managerial Grid® (From Robert R. Blake and Jane Srygley Mouton, THE MANAGERIAL GRID, Houston, Texas, Gulf Publishing Company, Copyright © 1964, p. 10. Reproduced by permission; artwork courtesy NFPA.)

The Work of Chris Argyris

Professor Chris Argyris* of Yale used a parent-child analogy to describe problems between organizations and workers. On the one hand, he observed, while most employees come to

*Chris Argysis, PERSONALITY AND ORGANIZATION (New York: Harper and Row, 1957).

the job lacking experience, many begin to develop mature characteristics as people and workers. They are able to develop
more self-control, more patience, more ways of behaving, the
ability to give and take directions, and higher self-concepts. On
the other hand, he suggested, most organizations are like un-
bending parents who refuse to recognize growth and try to
keep their "children" childlike and immature; mature workers
become frustrated and angry under such management controls.

Argyris contended that these frustrations generally arise
because organizations believe they must be committed to one
unchanging management style. He felt that managers believe
they are obliged to press their authority at all times, even when
it may not be required, and that they must direct activity at all
times, even if such direction throttles ideas and suggestions. Argyris also suggested that managers believe that managerial controls, whether in the form of restrictions or incentives, cannot
be changed.

For the sake of their own survival, Argyris argued, organizations must learn to adopt a variety of management styles,
with workers contributing ideas to the development of such
styles. Otherwise, he stated, the mental health of both the
workers and the organization would be threatened by a vicious
cycle: controls designed to make workers "manageable and
spiritless" would cause workers to become more dependent.
This, in turn, would demand still more controls, thus continuing the cycle.

MASLOW'S HIERARCHY OF NEEDS

Some Unanswered Questions

Though it has survived for many years as one of the finest
explanations of human needs and perhaps still provides the
best available foundation for the discussion of motivation, there
are a number of questions which Maslow's hierarchy raises.
The three most important ones are: (1) What exactly is the role
of money in motivation? (2) How important are esteem and
social needs? (3) What is self-realization?

What Exactly Is the Role of Money?

As most managers know, people seem to think that money
motivates. There is certainly ample evidence to show that
people will come to work when they are paid, even though they

also work as volunteers on things they like when they are not paid. But people also talk a lot about money needs and it is not rare to hear someone say, "Well, if you want me to do that, then pay me for it."

Still, Maslow's diagram appears to be fairly mute on the question of money, and undoubtedly this is one of the reasons why managers do not see the hierarchy as a really practical concept which they can use in their work. Frederick Herzberg, too, relegates money to a secondary position. In a famous article, "One More Time: How Do You Motivate Employees," he has explained it this way:* "If I want a dog to come to where I am when the dog is on the other side of the room, I hold out a bone." Herzberg asks who is motivated, the dog or the person. His answer is that it is the person who is motivated, not the dog. The dog merely responds to the incentive, and as soon as the dog has received it and is satisfied, the dog may or may not remain where the person wants it to be. Herzberg concludes that motivation, rather than being an external incentive, is an internal sort of a generator which creates a desire to achieve a certain goal.

Herzberg's explanation is similar to that given by most behavioral scientists, who have all observed that the promise of a raise or the prospect of a raise seems to have a positive effect on people's efforts. It is a short-lived one, though, and wears off quickly. People generally revert to their pre-raise ways if their job and environment remain essentially unchanged.

There is little question in anybody's mind that, notwithstanding any theories to the contrary, people respond to money. To be of use to managers as a more practical model of motivation, Maslow's hierarchy must be modified to show where money is needed to satisfy needs. Thus, it can better serve as a guide to decision making. Incorporating money in the hierarchy will be done later on in this chapter, and the manager's role in supplying tangible need satisfaction will be taken up in the next chapter.

How Important Are Esteem and Social Needs?

Another problem with the Maslow diagram concerns the relative importance of esteem and social needs. The consid-

---

*Frederick Herzberg, *One More Time: How Do You Motivate Employees?* HARVARD BUSINESS REVIEW, Jan.-Feb. 1968. Copyright © 1967 by the President and Fellows of Harvard College; all rights reserved. Reprinted by permission.

erable research conducted to validate the hierarchy seems to indicate that the two lower levels—the physiological needs and the security needs—are indeed very important and can be considered foundation needs. There are, however, questions about the definition and the relationship of esteem and social needs.

There appear to be many people who place the satisfaction of esteem needs above that of social needs. To these people it is clearly more important to be recognized as individuals and to be valued for particular strengths and characteristics than to be submerged in a group. Most managers and innovators feel this way.

There are other people, however, who prefer being part of a group. They want to be liked, or loved, and this is more important to them than being esteemed. Some of these feelings may be the result of upbringing and culture. Some may be the result of a need for the security that a group provides. Whatever the cause, there are many people who prefer the warmth which a group can provide to the recognition of personal worth for outstanding characteristics.

Not only is there some question as to whether social needs or esteem should be higher on the pyramid but also whether these needs should be considered separately at all. In a way they support each other because they are both natural and require satisfaction regardless of which one is higher. They are in conflict too, though, because one's desire to be part of a group is, in a way, in conflict with one's desire to be recognized for outstanding characteristics.

Research has confirmed what analysis seems to show—that there are problems with the Maslow Hierarchy concerning social and esteem needs. It has been impossible to confirm through surveys and experiments that esteem needs are indeed at a higher level than social needs. It is important for managers to recognize the differences in attitudes toward esteem and social needs because awareness of these differences can help avoid a mistake which many managers make—to appeal to esteem needs which may be satisfied only at the expense of social need satisfaction.

What Is Self-Realization?

A third problem with Maslow's hierarchy involves the meaning of the highest need. For those lucky people who clearly understand what they want to do during any particular segment of their lives, or possibly with their entire lives, there is no doubt that self-realization or self-actualization is indeed the highest level of need. For most other people, however, self-realization is a somewhat nebulous concept. During certain periods of their lives, people seem to gain exceptional joy and satisfaction from doing certain things. However, these things have a tendency to change throughout life and in the course of a career.

Most people who think about "self-realization" often wonder what it really means for them. And those who are managers wonder even more how they can help employees find greater self-realization. How can they help someone else find more of something which that person probably seeks but cannot explain?

To make the Maslow Hierarchy a more practical guide to action, the three questions just posed must be resolved in a way which shows managers how they can better satisfy the various levels of needs. Fortunately, it appears that the Maslow Hierarchy can be revised without too much difficulty. Most of the basic framework can be retained because there is ample evidence that it holds true.

REEVALUATING THE MASLOW HIERARCHY

The Role of Money in the Maslow Hierarchy

Physiological Needs

If one questions the role of money in each of the levels of the Maslow Hierarchy, then it quickly becomes apparent that almost all physiological needs cost money. Some, such as air, appear to be free, but to the extent that an employer supplies air conditioning, substantial costs can be involved for air-moving and filtration equipment that prevents air from becoming stale or polluted.

In primitive worlds, the materials needed to sustain life were satisfied by each family directly from nature. In today's world, the salaries which employees receive are used to purchase most of the things which satisfy physiological needs. The point is that an employer's contribution to satisfaction of physiological needs requires expenditures of money.

Safety and Security Needs

Safety and security needs are more complicated. Many are satisfied with money, especially those which protect the physiological needs of food, shelter, and clothing for the future. An organization provides safety and security through pension programs, hospitalization insurance, other insurance programs, and so forth, all of which are expensive. Even the security clause in union contracts can cost an organization money when it forces the retention of employees who have seniority but lack appropriate experience to handle new equipment or to avoid a layoff. Salaries also contribute to satisfaction of safety and security needs when they are higher than necessary to meet expenditures and people are able to accumulate savings.

In addition to the tangible safety and security benefits money provides, there are psychological matters which also help make employees feel secure. These are primarily attitudes and beliefs about the stability of the organization and about the organization's managers. People who work for an effective organization with competent management and with supervisors who are highly trustworthy feel secure. On the other hand, people cannot feel secure when they work for an organization that is unstable and may not exist in the near future, or for a boss who is highly unreliable or in whom they cannot have confidence.

Figure 8.4 shows the separation of safety and security needs into their physical and psychological aspects. If this analysis is correct, then a manager's personal competence and ability to earn the confidence of subordinates can have a major influence on motivational climate.

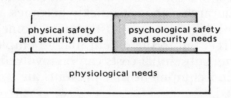

Figure 8.4. Modification of the Maslow Diagram, Which Shows the Separation of Safety and Security Needs into Tangible Areas (White) and Psychological Areas (Shaded) (Artwork courtesy NFPA)

Esteem and Social Needs

The traditional Maslow diagram shows esteem and social needs as two separate entities with the esteem need at the higher level, possibly because ambition was a more widespread characteristic during the early part of the century than it is today.

But, as was briefly discussed earlier, there is considerable evidence today that social and esteem needs cannot be separated in the same manner for most people. Since some people seem to value them differently than Maslow theorized, it would appear that they could best be shown together in one large step. This is how they are depicted in Figure 8.5

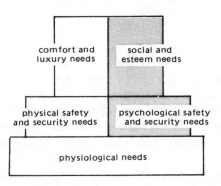

Figure 8.5. Modification of the Maslow Diagram, Which Shows Social and Esteem Needs as One Psychological Entity, and Comfort and Luxury as a Complementary Tangible Entity (Artwork courtesy NFPA)

Though esteem and social needs appear, at first glance, to be entirely psychological needs, this is not the case. Many people obtain gratification of social and esteem needs from their enjoyment and sharing of what they consider to be the "good things in life." Their esteem and social needs are highly satisfied when others admire and try to copy their lifestyle. "Keeping up with the Joneses" is a common phrase describing the desire which people feel for comfort and luxury equal to or better than that which their neighbors enjoy. Such a desire, which brings social and esteem need gratification, can only be satisfied with money.

It is important to note in Figure 8.5 that, though the vertical dividing line is shown in the center, its position is not meant to suggest that everyone needs an equal amount of tangible and psychological gratification. Every person is different in this respect. While some people satisfy most of their social and esteem needs through luxury items, other people look to the acclaim of peers and superiors.

There are segments of esteem and social needs that must be satisfied in other ways than through money. Policies and procedures that bring greater cooperation and give people a chance to help each other bring much more social and esteem needs satisfaction than those which lead to friction and conflict. Anything that managers can do to stimulate mutual support among the members of their unit, such as group assistance for personal emergencies or work sharing when someone is over-loaded, can help satisfy esteem and social needs. There are many ways to involve the group in work activities which strengthen the bonds between group members.

Opportunities to satisfy esteem needs are even more wide-spread. Few managers go out of their way to find things for which subordinates can be commended or seek out different ways to commend them. One of the greatest tools for creating a better motivational climate—the use of praise—is one of the least utilized ones. The result is that few employees and lower level managers receive much individual recognition from their superiors.

There are, of course, many perfectly legitimate reasons why few managers use praise as much as they could, for their own and their team's benefit. First of all, nobody wants praise to appear contrived or false, and it is usually difficult to find many things for which sincere praise can be given easily. Nonetheless, much more praise could be given honestly and would be well received. Most people hear in a word of praise the desire to be friendly; therefore, even if praise is recognized as being less than fully sincere, it still has favorable impact.

There are many other means besides using praise that can bring employees feelings of greater esteem. They include such things as asking for a subordinate's advice or giving a few words of commendation of an employee to a higher level manager. In addition, there are written commendations and many forms of formal recognition, among which may be found monetary awards for suggestions, for good safety records, for completion of training programs, and sometimes even for good atten-dance.

In industry one can find little evidence of commendations for serious effort, loyalty, attention to detail, or goal achieve-ment. The U.S. Armed Forces, by contrast, award medals not only for valor but also for meritorious service, and the Federal Government, as well as some state governments, has awards for outstanding achievement, with both tangible cash payments and less tangible awards. In view of the tendency of most people to see negative things first—the problems, mistakes, and failures—it is obvious that there are many things managers can do to better satisfy social and esteem needs. This chapter together with Appendix C describes a fairly comprehensive program to deliberately increase the satisfaction of the esteem needs of employees. Managers can work on creating an environment which provides many more work-related satisfactions, even if they recognize that there is little or nothing which can be done to add to the luxury and comfort needs of the employees. Many opportunities exist for managers to satisfy social and esteem needs—especially esteem needs—more fully. Undertaking this is important in itself, but it becomes even more important if one looks at the meaning of self-realization.

Self-Realization

Self-realization (Figure 8.6), as has been mentioned before, is difficult to define. Only a few fortunate people recognize early in life that they have a strong preference for a particular type of work.

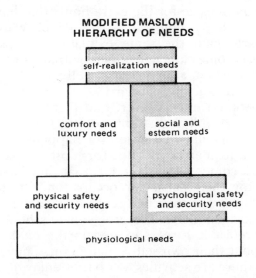

**MODIFIED MASLOW
HIERARCHY OF NEEDS**

self-realization needs

comfort and
luxury needs

social and
esteem needs

physical safety
and security needs

psychological safety
and security needs

physiological needs

Figure 8.6. Modification of the Maslow Diagram, Which Shows the Relationship of Self-Actualization Needs to Tangible and Psychological Needs (Artwork courtesy NFPA)

There is a true story about a pot washer in a New York City hospital who apparently was so devoted to his job that one could easily consider him to have found self-realization in his work. He reported to his kitchen happily every morning and was content on the job as long as his pots and pans were not mishandled by others. On the few occasions when he was out and others took care of them, he was clearly disturbed when he returned and found them neglected. While this individual certainly is somewhat unique, there are people in all walks of life and in all jobs who are happy with their work, mainly because they enjoy it. Their day passes quickly and they find the work interesting. They take pleasure in going to work in the morning; and they leave, most days, with the feeling of having accomplished something useful. Even when there were unpleasant events during a day, they can say to themselves that the next day will be better—and it usually is.

Not every executive, professional, or supervisor who works long hours is a workaholic. Some enjoy their work as well as, if not better than, the sports, socializing, or TV watching that they forego. The joy that comes from reaching for that which is difficult to attain, and to actually capture some of it, often does more than compensate for the extra hours that have to be devoted to what other people call "work". People who enjoy their work regularly gain the same exhilarating sensation from seeing projects come close to completion that painters or novelists experience when, after strenuous effort, their work finally meets their own exacting standards.

Some people rarely, if ever, find pleasure in their work. Their work is so dull and strenuous and their supervisors so lacking in competence that little ever happens to them which adds pleasure to their work. But for most people, the enjoyment of work comes despite the fact that they have no special preference for their particular occupation. Often they have drifted into it because their first real jobs gave them experience in it, or because an interesting professor in school led them to think that enjoyable careers existed in the field. They know very little about their own self-actualization. They do know, of course, that there are activities which they enjoy more than others, particularly some assignments and also certain hobbies, sports, and social activities. As far as their work is concerned, however, they would be hard pressed to indicate what kinds of activities could retain their interest continuously or get them to exert their best efforts most of the time.

Nevertheless, something akin to self-realization undoubtedly exists for most people. The same person who will work slowly and without enthusiasm on the job may work feverishly without pay during off-hours to help renovate a clubhouse or help the community organization with a difficult, time-consuming task. What then is it that makes people find greater satisfaction from work? What conditions must be met so that the work itself is more rewarding?

Even though self-realization is a need that everyone senses and even though it clearly is a higher level need, most people find it very difficult to identify work in which they would find such self-realization. Those who do ask themselves what kind of work would give them the greatest satisfaction find that it changes as they progress through life. For example, an individual, just beginning his career might consider a position as an engineer satisfying only to find, two or three years later, that a supervisory position is more appealing. A few years of supervisory activity might bring a yearning for creative self-expression; so the individual continues his search for fulfillment, perhaps with attempts to publish papers written in the evenings and on weekends.

Almost everyone will agree on the characteristics which work must have if it is to bring one closer to self-realization, even when they cannot define what self-realization may mean to them. Most people would consider their work to be close to fulfilling if they held a job they enjoyed going to every morning, a job in which the day flew by quickly and in which at the end of the day, they preferred to finish projects they were working on rather than leave on time. What kind of job would this be for you? Ask yourself the following question:

"If you think back to positions you have held or if you look at your current position, what actions could your superiors, especially your direct superior, take, or already have taken, without spending any money, that would bring, or have brought, additional job satisfaction to you?"

The author has tried to find the answer to this question by asking small teams of participants in hundreds of seminars, at the American Management Association, and in meetings of client organizations in order to prepare lists of the things that

supervisors can do to improve the jobs of individuals. Whether
people work in the public or private sector or in the professions
or the trades, the answers always are very similar. The statements that come up, almost invariably, are the following. Individuals want

- More information about what is going on
- More freedom to do the job
- More say on decisions at an earlier time
- More guidance
- More recognition
- Honest feedback about performance
- No promises that can't be kept
- More communication (The boss should know more about
  what it is I am doing.).
- More interesting assignments
- Less over-the-shoulder looking
- More support when needed
- More confidence from superior.

And the list goes on.

The startling thing about such lists is that they rarely refer
to any specific type of work. One would expect that if people
find self-realization in specific tasks, there would be requests
that say, "Let me do exactly this" or "Let me do exactly that."
This never seems to occur. People are not asking for more technical work, more supervisory duties, or more specialized assignments. Even the general statement "more interesting assignments" is exceedingly rare. To some extent, of course, this is so
because people are in jobs that appeal to them more than other
jobs. Nevertheless, one would expect many statements about
the specific work that the boss could give them or has given
them. In the rare instances in which someone says something
such as, "I wish my boss would give me more field work to do,
or more design projects," it usually comes from someone who is
in a job that he or she clearly does not like and who is therefore
yearning for other work.

The picture that emerges from these answers is that people
believe that they could obtain much greater satisfaction from
their existing jobs if only their managers treated them differently. They want to know more about what is happening in
the organization, and they want a bigger voice in decisions that
affect them. They want to be freer to do the job the way they
believe it can best be done, but they do want guidance and
training so they can be more confident and more successful at

it. Most importantly, it seems that they want to be recognized for their accomplishments. The fascinating part of these results is that for most people, apparently, self-realization lies not so much in a specific type of work as it does in the environment. People are in effect saying: "The work may not be the greatest, but it could come much closer to giving me some self-realization if the boss would provide more safety and security (by being honest, fair, and open) and more esteem satisfaction (by providing recognition and participation in decisions). Even though I don't know what job will give me full self-realization, I do know that I am fairly close to it when the job gives me

- Higher self-esteem and recognition,
- More meaningful social interactions with peers and with my boss, and
- A higher level of safety and security from greater confidence in the organization and in the boss."

Although self-realization is a nebulous concept, managers can indeed do a great deal to help subordinates find a higher level of it in their jobs by increasing the level of satisfaction of the "lower" needs identified in Maslow's hierarchy, especially security and esteem.

HELPING PEOPLE FIND MORE SELF-REALIZATION IN THEIR WORK

There are two approaches to helping employees find more self-realization. One of the approaches has already been touched upon and discussed in previous chapters. It concerns the impact of regular, though semiformal, goals reviews which may even be conducted by managers who regularly work closely with their subordinates. The other approach involves three strategies for improving the motivational climate through planned managerial action.

Three Strategies for Improving the Motivational Climate

There are many specific steps which managers can take in addition to holding regular goals review sessions and annual or semiannual performance reviews. These steps require considerable effort, but they can gradually create a climate in which there is substantially more motivation because they help to bring more satisfaction of psychological needs.

The steps are grouped into the three strategies to improve motivational climate—short-run, intermediate, and long-run— as shown in Figure 8.7. All three strategies start with the recog-

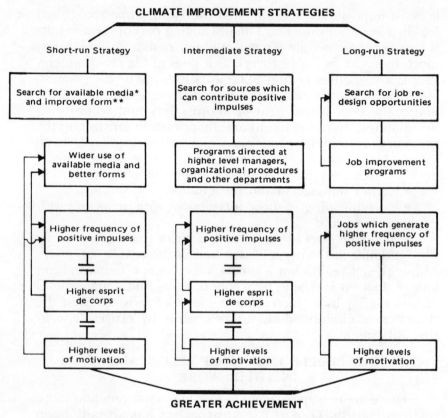

CLIMATE IMPROVEMENT STRATEGIES

Short-run Strategy	Intermediate Strategy	Long-run Strategy
Search for available media* and improved form**	Search for sources which can contribute positive impulses	Search for job re-design opportunities
Wider use of available media and better forms	Programs directed at higher level managers, organizational procedures and other departments	Job improvement programs
Higher frequency of positive impulses	Higher frequency of positive impulses	Jobs which generate higher frequency of positive impulses
Higher esprit de corps	Higher esprit de corps	
Higher levels of motivation	Higher levels of motivation	Higher levels of motivation

GREATER ACHIEVEMENT

*Media are the ways in which motivational impulses can appear. Positive ones include such things as challenging assignments, supportive statements, routine reports, tie pins, certificates, etc. Negative ones are reprimands, reject notices, mistakes, etc.

**Form is the style that influences the impact of the motivational impulse. It can be the way the award is presented, the words which are said during the telephone call, or facial expression, place, timing, etc.

Figure 8.7. A Representation of the Three Strategies Used by Management for Improving the Motivational Climate for Employees (Copyright © 1974 by Recognition Systems, Inc., Cranford, N.J. All rights reserved. Reprinted by permission; artwork courtesy NFPA.)

nition that few managers or officers commend their people for as many actions as they could. Apparently, managers rarely see the picture from the point of view of their subordinates. Even though they themselves feel the large number of negative and unpleasant impulses that reach every person in today's complex world, they rarely give much thought to any responsibilities they might have to do something about them. The increasing complexity of the world with which it is so difficult to cope sometimes, the reports that are becoming more detailed, the many different ways in which machinery or gadgets can fail to operate properly, the large amount of routine paperwork—all these contribute to unpleasant moments or unpleasant sensations. Several unpleasant minor incidents can fully offset some important matter that is proceeding smoothly.

If there were less tension and frustration, people could easily accept their work environments with only few pleasant events. Managers have a responsibility to balance the negative impulses employees receive, at least to some extent, by providing satisfying moments or pleasant impulses. People can provide some positive input to help balance the environment, but much of the positive imput must come from the work itself—from success, from doing things well, from pride in accomplishment.

The first or short-run strategy for improving motivational climate concerns the steps a manager can take directly by spending a few minutes several times each week just thinking about and listing the actions for which subordinates can receive recognition and the ways in which recognition can be given. Managers who have tried this have found that lists get longer and longer with practice and experience. It turns out that there are many ways in which a manager can say thanks for a job well done and that it can be said sincerely to every employee, not only the outstanding ones. For instance, a manager can commend *individual* staff *members*: for each job done well, for helping others, for making some arrangements, for taking initiative with something that needs to be done, and so forth.

It is important, however, that recognition be given not only to the few outstanding people but also to others. It is really not difficult to find pertinent things to say to the star performer or to the most highly motivated person. But such persons possibly need commendation less than the others do. What is important is that everyone on the team finds pleasant moments that are related to the work. (For more on providing recognition, see Appendix C.)

The short-run strategy is based solely on the manager personally providing more recognition and other pleasant work related events. The emphasis here is on "work related" because compliments or other nonwork-related friendly words are not likely to have the same impact on the motivational climate.

They lead more to a "Country Club" atmosphere than to the desire to achieve.

The diagram of the strategies in Figure 8.7 indicates that a manager who wishes to take full advantage of the opportunities which the short-run strategy can give should begin to use more media (newspapers, bulletins, letters, informal notes, various verbal forms, etc.) to bring more frequent instances of pleasant experiences to staff members. This action in turn may lead to higher job interest and greater esprit-de-corps. There is no assurance of this, however, because there is a limit to the effect which the short-term strategy can have. There are just so many times in the course of a week or month that a manager can directly give recognition to a staff member. This is why there is a break in the diagram in Figure 8.7 in the line between "Higher frequency of positive impulses" and "Higher esprit-de-corps" and again before "Higher levels of motivation."

More is needed to increase pleasant work-related occurrences than just a short-term strategy. The intermediate and long-run strategies can bring the additional positive impulses that are needed. To carry out the intermediate strategies, the manager must involve other managers at his or her level and at higher levels, suppliers, and maybe even customers or the public to provide pleasant work-related experiences. To implement these strategies, the manager can, among other things, send a reminder to the next higher level manager to commend someone for something that has occurred recently. Or the manager can commend people in other departments or on other shifts, whose managers might respond in kind. Steps taken to anticipate and prevent friction and differences between members of the team and with other teams can also help create a more pleasant job-related environment by increasing the satisfaction of social needs or, at least, by preventing them from being decreased. Anything that brings recognition or other positive impulses and does not come directly from the immediate superior is part of the intermediate strategy.

As long as all of the pleasant experiences come from people, they must, of necessity, be greatly limited. The average person will not receive too many in any time period. To greatly increase motivation, a long-run strategy is needed. The long-run strategy is the most likely to help a person reach the higher levels of motivation since positive impulses come directly from the job itself and reinforce its positive aspects without dependence on other people. It is for this reason that Herzberg recommended what he called Job Enrichment as a major strategy for improving motivation.

Herzberg was certainly right. If jobs can be shifted or changed in such a way that the job itself provides satisfying sensations, then there is a much more continuous flow of pleasant experiences; and from these will undoubtedly come a higher motivation to achieve job-related goals. As you will note in the diagram, there is no longer a broken connection between action and result. If the job provides the satisfaction directly, then there is little question about the job's potential impact on motivation.

This is where the three strategies for climate improvement come together with goals reviews and performance appraisals in helping to improve the overall motivational climate. If a manager keeps in mind the list of things which will bring more fulfilling jobs (see page 162), then he or she can easily practice job enrichment. By trying to develop a satisfying work atmosphere, the manager reinforces directly the other actions he or she must take to guarantee a smoothly operating goals program, one that makes goal achievement a way of life.

The Role of Goals Reviews and the Planning Process

Linking Elements, as has been pointed out before, do not exist in a vacuum, nor are they independent entities. They support and reinforce each other extensively, as is illustrated by the connection between goals reviews and performance evaluations.

Evaluation has been discussed extensively in previous chapters, both in terms of accountabilities and in terms of the role of performance appraisal in a goals program. The review step has also been discussed, but the significance of the review step in helping to create a more positive climate in which people can find higher levels of motivation has not been stressed. Therefore, at this point the total planning process, from the situation analysis through plan revisions to meet the changing situation, needs to be analyzed in the light of the satisfaction of psychological needs which it can provide.

Comprehensive planning, whether for the total organization or for a specific project, involves the following steps:

1. Defining the mission of the organization or the project
2. Conducting a situation analysis:
    a. to determine what events led to the current situation
    b. to collect data which describes current status

     c. to analyze the data to define strengths (resources) and weaknesses (relative to the mission)
3. Establishing goals (strategic goals)
4. Developing strategies and action plans (operational goals and action steps)
5. Implementing strategies and action steps
6. Evaluating progress (regular goals reviews and annual performance evaluations)
7. Repeating steps (2) through (6) or (1) through (6) as indicated by the situation and developments if the evaluation indicates that strategic goals may not be achieved.

Each of these steps can bring psychological rewards to subordinates, as the following paragraphs discuss.

Involvement in Mission Statement and Situation Analysis

Involvement in the mission statement and the situation analysis, even if it only amounts to hearing reports, satisfies much of the desire for knowing "what is going on". If the involvement is more extensive, it brings some of the stronger satisfactions that stem from participation in decisions affecting the work environment. Working on the situation analysis, furthermore, provides greater knowledge and broader perspective; and this makes more successful participation in other decisions possible, bringing many of the other good things that successful decisions, jointly made, can bring.

Establishing Goals and Action Steps

When someone participates appropriately in the establishment of goals and action steps, that person obtains an even greater feeling of having some influence over environment and future than he or she does from participation in the situation analysis alone. This is true even if the involvement is not extensive and if the influence on decisions is not great. The mere fact that the person has been consulted and has had an opportunity to voice an opinion about directions that are being taken is important in itself. With more sophisticated, more knowledgeable, more experienced individuals, of course, a higher level of participation is both possible and necessary in many goal decisions, though by no means in all of them.

Establishing goals and allowing an individual to set action steps to the extent to which that person's experience permits gives the individual the freedom to do the job the way he or she thinks it should be done, again within the widest range that the individual's level of experience, knowledge, skills, and maturity permit.

Implementation and Evaluation

In the implementation step of the plan, there are many opportunities for *successful* completion of tasks which, like any other form of success, provides warm and pleasant feelings. Finally, the evaluation process, if it is conducted as suggested in the previous chapter, can strengthen trust and provide further assurance that the manager wants to help the subordinate develop to the maximum of his or her ability. All in all, this spells confidence in two directions. It tells subordinates that the manager has confidence in them and that, in turn, gives them an opportunity to increase their confidence in the manager.

Reviewing the Plan

The reviewing step provides many of the satisfactions that people consider ingredients of higher levels of self-realization:

A regular review, whether it is conducted once every month, once every two months, or even, sometimes, once every three months, will certainly provide much more information about what is going on if the manager knows how to communicate with subordinates. Open, two-way discussions are essential to good reviews. (This will be discussed in greater detail in Chapter 10).

Formal goals reviews also reinforce the fact that the manager wants staff members to take the initiative in setting action steps and wants them to have increasingly greater freedom to do their jobs the way they feel the jobs should be done. At the same time the manager reaffirms that he or she wants to help subordinates gain the competence which will allow them even greater influence in decisions affecting their jobs.

When you regularly review progress toward goals with subordinates, particularly when you discuss what help you can provide, you give considerably more guidance than you do when your reviews are sporadic. In a review, the opportunity to provide guidance is often greater than in a day-to-day contact, and the help given can be more thorough and meaningful. When people list the need for guidance as one of the items which they feel their bosses should provide, to some extent, they are speaking of guidance in their career and in their self-development; and little of this can occur during specific, project-oriented, day-to-day contacts.

A periodic goals review also gives you many chances to provide recognition and to tell your staff members in what ways you are satisfied with their work. You are providing factual feedback on planned action steps. If you are careful to stress that you are not evaluating performance during goals reviews and if you remain fully supportive, you will be giving the factual feedback that can tell your people where they stand. Even if you show them what could be done better during a discussion of a particularly difficult goal, in most instances, you are also assuring them that they have done as well as you feel could have been done.

If you hold regular goals reviews, you will without a doubt know more about what individual subordinates are doing and what they are thinking. Subordinates can provide you with insights about what they consider interesting assignments, and you can help them develop the skills and knowledge to perform those assignments successfully. And, without question, properly conducted goals reviews provide subordinates with frequent evidence that you stand ready to back them up with the support they need when they need it.

In view of all the benefits that regular goals reviews provide in addition to the thorough review of priorities, the selection of new goals, and the greater chance for progress on existing goals, it is rather surprising that only few organizations help and encourage their managers to hold these formal reviews on a regular basis.

This chapter has covered the important Linking Element dealing with the many ways a manager can help lower level managers and employees come closer to achieving their personal goals. Now you may want to compare the notes you made at the beginning of the chapter with what has been covered. Do you feel that the three climate improvement strategies discussed above, coupled with competently managed goals programs—grounded on thorough, regular goals reviews—would be a good way to complete the box between the arrows on page 145?

Chapter 9

Human Resource Development

RATIONALE FOR DEVELOPMENT PROGRAMS

Development of human resources* is one of the most important tasks of a manager, if not *the* most important task. The linking element aligning the technical competence requirements of the organizational unit with the technical competence that people bring to the organization is concerned with human resource development. If you have the time, you should write out, either in Figure 9.1 below or on a separate sheet of paper, the skills you believe important in aligning the technical competence requirements of the organizational unit with the technical competencies or knowledge/skill deficiencies of the people in the unit.

Behavioral scientists and managers often speak of aligning goals of people and goals of the organization. Though this may appear to be achievable, the Linking Elements concept quickly shows that it is not. The goals of an organizational unit are aimed primarily at improving control—for example, the achieving of higher production goals, better coordination, and better adherence to rules—as well as at developing higher levels of technical competence. The goals of individuals, on the other hand, are aimed at achieving higher levels of satisfaction for the time and effort spent at work. Trade-offs do exist, of course, between the organization and the individual: In effect, the organization provides higher levels of satisfaction for employees directly through its people and policies and indirectly through the work itself; in exchange it receives greater em-

---

*Dr. Leonard Nadler, in his book DEVELOPING HUMAN RESOURCES (Houston, Texas: Gulf Publishing Company, 1970), defines human resources development (HRD) as: (1) A series of organized activities (2) conducted within a specified time (3) designed to produce behavioral change. He distinguishes three major segments of HRD: *training* for the job; *education* for the individual; *development* for the organization. He points out that these three segments apply to other types of organizations, whose human resources are just as much employees as are the resources of associations, community organizations, and organizations using volunteer help.

171

ployee acceptance of organizational goals and a greater desire
to achieve them.

Figure 9.1. Segment of Linking Elements Diagram

One place where the requirements of individuals and
those of the organizational unit are directly connected is in the
Linking Element pertaining to development of adequate competence. This is especially true for people who have accepted
specific positions because they are interested in acquiring experience and the knowledge and skills required for the positions.
The achievement and development of the skills and knowledge
provides great personal satisfaction, while at the same time assuring a higher level of performance for the organizational
unit.

While most managers recognize that employee development is one of their most important responsibilities, in the
course of day-to-day operations it is often not given the priority

it deserves. Competent managers recognize that they must keep the process of developing their people constantly in mind if they do not want it to be managed haphazardly. This means regular reviews to see what each person needs in order to become more competent in the current job and to develop knowledge and skills for other jobs along the career path. While opportunities for diagnosing specific development needs occur regularly, there are several formal occasions when managers can obtain a more comprehensive insight into the development needs of the people reporting to them. These formal occasions include goals reviews and, especially, performance appraisals.

Because of the pressures of daily business, managers tend to avoid the detailed diagnosis necessary to attack a specific knowledge or skill deficiency directly. Emergencies often bring needs to their attention. When they do attempt to deal with development needs, they often use a buckshot approach. Employees are sent off to enroll in a course, or the personnel department is called in to develop a program to deal with a problem on a general basis. A systematic approach to development is required, and development must be carried on in an environment that supports what is learned. It must be based on individual needs, capabilities, the job, and the atmosphere in the department or section. Outside training can rarely cope with these influences.

Prerequisites for an Effective Program

In order to assure effective education and training, several basic conditions must be satisfied:
- Individual deficiencies must be correctly identified.
- A program to eliminate deficiencies must consider the relative importance of the individual's shortcomings.
- Provisions must exist for continued surveillance of learning.
- Learning goals must be revised regularly to reflect changing conditions.
- Study materials and expected level of achievement must be geared to the individual so that they are neither too easy nor too difficult.
- As much as possible, learning should be immediately applied on the job.

These objectives can best be satisfied with individualized knowledge/skill analyses and then with study and practice assignments geared to the specific situation. A needs analysis, to be of most value, must be very specific in identifying for each individual those knowledge areas and skills which will help improve performance.

The two people who can best develop such a needs analysis are the individual and his or her direct superior. A joint effort involving both supervisor and subordinate is therefore desirable in the production of an accurate analysis with priorities based on the expected effects or benefits to the organizational unit and to the individual. People must assume responsibility for their own education and training, but managers must be thoroughly involved and supportive for full effectiveness.

OVERVIEW

Development activities will bring much better results if the people in the organizational unit are capable of learning and have the desire to perform well in their jobs. Elimination of deficiencies in knowledge and skills therefore starts with the *selection* of new employees. It continues with appropriate *position management* so that people will be in jobs which make best use of their abilities and where they will find the greatest amount of personal satisfaction in their work.

Selection, position management, training, and education and development are so intertwined and dependent on each other that they really should almost be seen as one function. While on the one hand the way you structure the positions in your organizational unit has a lot to do with the way you look at candidates (What skills and knowledge do you need to make your unit functional?), on the other hand, the people you get often determines how you will shape the work into specific positions to gain the greatest benefit, for both your employees and for your unit, from the mixture of people and jobs. Training, education, and development depend entirely on that mixture of people and jobs which you create and they must be handled well if they are to support the motivational climate you want to achieve.

The bulk of this chapter covers the developmental responsibilities of managers. First, though, to provide perspective, selection, position management and analysis of performance problems are discussed to uncover specific areas where training and education are most likely to be beneficial.

Selection

The road to higher levels of technical competence starts with the selection of new employees and with careful decisions when people are chosen for promotion. Ability to learn and interest in learning the whole job should be an important selection criterion. When people lack these characteristics, it is difficult, if not impossible, for them to develop high technical competence. This applies whether their skills are highly specialized, as in engineering, or of a more general nature, as in many areas of management.

Many managers, in looking at qualifications of applicants, look primarily at past experience and accomplishments. These *can* be excellent indicators of success, of ability to adapt to a new environment, and of motivation to gain additional knowledge and skills; but frequently they are not. Many people who are highly motivated to achieve success on their current jobs just will not devote the additional effort that would properly prepare them for advancement. The result is described in the *Peter Principle*, by Dr. Lawrence Peter, which says, in effect, that people usually get promoted to a job they are no longer able to do right. That's why there is so much incompetence, claims Dr. Peter. The Peter Principle is a tongue-in-cheek argument, but there is considerable truth to it. Few people will devote the effort to self-development, once they have received the degrees they sought, to thoroughly prepare them for the more demanding positions they often achieve. Many do not even put enough effort into learning what they need to know to keep up with the changes in their own jobs.

Careful initial selection and equally careful observation of new or recently promoted employees during their probational periods will therefore do more good than training, and other developmental efforts at a later time. While discussion of specific selection techniques is somewhat beyond the scope of this chapter, a checklist of interviewing techniques, which may be adapted to individual needs, is provided below.

AN INTERVIEWER'S CHECKLIST

Prior to the Interview
1. Know what you are looking for. This means you must *know the job* and know what skills are needed before you begin the search.

2. Set reasonable standards. Too much education for the job, for instance, will not make for a satisfied employee.
3. *Plan* your strategy and the timing of your search.
4. Determine what personality traits are desirable for the job. If the new employee will not work directly for you, think of the person for whom he or she will be working. Will they be able to work smoothly with each other?
5. Get the FACTS about the job that you may not readily remember—exact salary range, special benefits, overtime hours expected; get both the pleasant and the unpleasant facts so that you can inform the applicant about the problems and opportunities in a realistic way.
6. Review available applications for candidates who may be well qualified.
7. Read the application carefully *before* you see the candidate. This will help you plan your interview.
8. *Plan your interviews* to get information either not covered at all on the application or not covered as fully as you wish. Prepare a list of questions.

During the Interview
1. Make applicant feel comfortable.
2. Explain the requirements, difficulties, and opportunities of the position for which the applicant is applying.
3. Give the applicant the chance to ask questions.
4. Review the application and probe to check the accuracy of each item, particularly the reasons for leaving each position.
5. Probe for applicant's knowledge of facts and skills that are needed for the job he or she is to assume.
6. Get information on specialized knowledge the applicant may have.
7. Try to determine some of the applicant's personal characteristics such as interest in learning, aspirations, motivation, emotional stability, willingness to accept responsibility, etc.
8. Discuss the applicant's financial needs and the financial rewards of the position.
9. Probe for the applicant's attitude towards the posi-

tion—what he or she sees as its advantages and disadvantages and/or strengths and weaknesses.
10. Record all pertinent information.

After the Interview
1. Check references.
2. Decide which applicants to call for repeat interviews.
3. Hold repeat interviews with applicants who seem interesting.
4. Decide whether to continue looking, transfer or promote within your organization, or offer the position to one of the applicants you interviewed.

Position Management

Once new employees have been on the job long enough so that it has become clear what their strengths and weaknesses are, the manager's attention can turn to exploring the ways in which strengths can best be used to improve the entire team's effectiveness and how weaknesses can be corrected. Work arrangements or techniques may have to be changed. Some work changes occur naturally from the way the new person approaches the job. Other changes occur as team members adjust to him or her. Still other changes are initiated deliberately by the manager. These changes may simply concern minor rearrangements, or they may be more extensive and involve several members of the department. Changes can occur gradually as people discuss with each other the adjustments they would prefer, or they can come through carefully planned steps.

Changes in positions are not only the result of adaptation to new people but are often brought about by changes in work load or work composition. In either case, an awareness of position management concepts can be useful. The best way to understand position management is to look at a brand new organization and at the work that the manager would have to do before instructing the new employees in their jobs. The manager, either alone or jointly with the people who will become the members of the organization, has to:
1. Analyze the work that has to be done and break it into clearly definable tasks.
2. Arrange these tasks into positions that fit the capabilities and interests of the people who will have to follow them.

3. Try this arrangement so that all can see whether it leads to:
   a. high productivity
   b. good quality work
   c. ability of the organization to quickly and effectively respond to changing demands of clients, customers, or the public
   d. the highest possible level of needs satisfaction for the organization's members
4. Rearrange the tasks to achieve improved performance as specified in (a) through (d) above.

In an existing organization, steps 1 and 2 are or should be already completed. Step 3, however, is continuous and is especially important whenever a new person joins the organization. A competent manager always looks at the positions of the organization the way a football coach looks at the players on the field and on the bench to decide who should do what during the next play: The coach rearranges the tasks and assigns the players accordingly. The same thing occurs in any organization. The manager assigns the tasks on the basis of the capabilities of the individuals.

Obviously the organization must have back-up people capable of handling each task that may come along. This requires cross-training so that most people can do more than one job. Nevertheless, when the organizational unit is faced with situations that must be handled expediently, it is best to use people in positions which will take advantage of their greatest strengths.

The appropriate selection of people for tasks and assignments in keeping with their strengths can go a long way to improve the technical competence of the organization, but only for the moment. For the long run it is an error to use individuals over and over again only on those tasks which they can do best. That would make the organization heavily dependent on each individual and inflexible, or even impotent, in many situations. Good technical competence means flexibility and the ability to adapt to many different environments. Therefore, for every task several people should be available; and analyzing deficiencies in knowledge and skills and taking appropriate steps to eliminate them must be continuous.

Careful selection of people and assignment of functions in keeping with their interests as well as with their knowledge and skills is as important in the selection of outside candidates as it is in the selection of current employees for vacant positions. In selecting from current employees, the manager usually has access to the employment records and can get additional information from the people with whom the employee has worked in the past. This information can help to plan the way the organizational unit might adapt to the new member.

If the person who is to be selected for the job is a competent employee, it would seem wise, in the interest of the unit's technical competency and its ability to achieve a high level of performance, to rearrange positions. If this is done jointly with the members of the unit, an arrangement can usually be found that leaves everyone at least as satisfied with their respective jobs as they were before, and some no doubt will be more satisfied.

Training and Development

Good selection and position management are not enough to bring high technical competence in an organization. Continuing training and development is essential even if experienced, competent people are selected and job assignments take full advantage of their strengths. There are many reasons why this is necessary, among them:

1. Continuing changes in technology bring the need for frequent updating of knowledge and skills.
2. Employees and their managers usually can achieve smoother communications with other departments from learning more about the work of the departments with whom they are in contact.
3. All employees and managers are more knowledgeable and skilled in some areas than in others. Considerable education and training is needed to eliminate or at least reduce deficiencies as much as possible.
4. Career development for those who aspire to higher level or more specialized jobs requires continuous developmental activities.
5. Knowledge and skills which are not in continuous use begin to fade; refreshers from time to time help to avoid surprises when knowledge or skills are suddenly needed.

Before deciding on training as a way to resolve a knowledge or skill deficiency, it is worthwhile to look at whether a training need really exists or whether other problems stand in the way of a particular achievement. The diagram on page 181 can be used to help identify whether training is really the solution, or even part of the solution.

Analyzing Performance Problems

Training time should be devoted to those matters which deserve highest priority at the moment. It is therefore important to distinguish between those performance problems which can be rectified by training and those which are the result of causes other than lack of knowledge and skill.

Following the diagram in Figure 9.2 down from the top, if an employee has a performance problem and it is an important one, then the first question that a manager should ask is whether or not a knowledge/skill deficiency is involved. If this appears to be the case, then the next question is whether the employee used to be able to do the work involved. If the answer is no, then training should definitely be arranged.

If, on the other hand, the employee was able to perform the task in the past, then it is more likely that a knowledge/skill deficiency is not the primary problem but may contribute to it. Retraining should be arranged to see whether it can solve the problem or whether other causes requiring other corrective measures must be found.

If in Figure 9.2 the manager must answer the question "Knowledge/skill deficiency?" with a *No* because the employee knows how to do the task, then the problem is not one that can be solved by training. Following the line labeled *No* down from the box labeled *Knowledge/skill deficiency* leads to four other causes that could be the source of the performance problem. (1) Performance may be punishing. (2) Nonperformance may be rewarding. (3) Performance may not appear to matter. (4) Other obstacles to performance besides skill deficiencies may exist.

Punishing Performance

Performance may be punishing in many ways. For instance, inventory taking may be performed poorly in an organization. This could, of course, be due to inadequate training. But it could be due to the fact that inventories are not announced sufficiently far in advance, and employees are told at the last minute that they have to have their records in order.

PERFORMANCE ANALYSIS MODEL

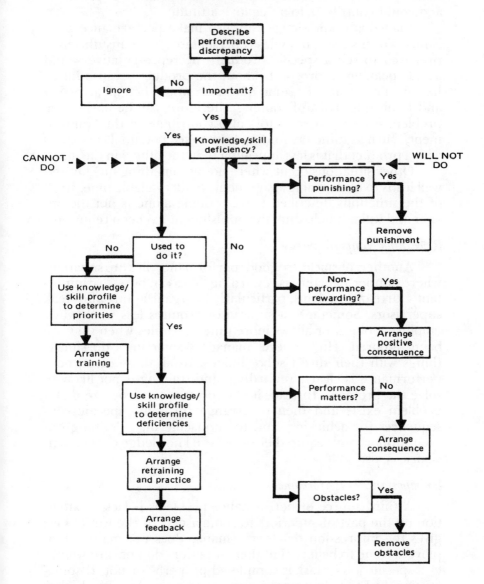

Figure 9.2. Performance Analysis Model That Aids a Manager in Determining Whether an Individual's Lack of Performance Is Related to Training or to Performance Problems (Adapted from ANALYZING PERFORMANCE PROBLEMS; OR, YOU REALLY OUGHTA WANNA, by Robert F. Mager and Peter Pipe. Fearon Publishers, Inc., Belmont, California, Copyright © 1970. Reprinted by permission; artwork courtesy NFPA.)

Lack of notification could thus be the major cause of problems and could contribute to a negative attitude.

Inadequate knowledge can also make performance punishing. For instance, if a sales representative were insufficiently prepared to sell a specific product, the representative would avoid speaking to prospects about the product because his or her inability to answer some questions would be embarrassing and punishing. Lack of training, therefore, can be part of the problem even if other factors also contribute to the "punishment," such as difficulty finding time to see potential customers with a product that is less appealing than the others in the line.

Other situations occur where doing something quickly and well leads to undesirable assignments to fill available time. In all of the situations described here, training alone is not the answer and will not help until the punishment has been removed.

Rewarding Nonperformance

Another obstacle to good performance lies in situations where nonperformance is rewarding. This can be a very important source of problems, particularly in organizations with weak supervisors. Sometimes a supervisor requires less work when employees object or allows more time for duties when they are being ignored. Higher level managers sometimes do similar things with their direct subordinates. In all these cases, nonperformance is clearly rewarding, and training is not likely to solve the problem. Instead, it is important to recognize that a problem exists and then to arrange for some specific consequences for achieving, and for nonachieving. Training can then support any required effort where knowledge or skill deficiencies exist.

Unimportance of Performance

A third source of performance problems is lack of attention on the part of superiors to some aspect of the work. This gives the impression that performance does not matter. Employees come to believe that their superiors do not care whether a specific job or task is completed properly, or not. If someone is asked to help prepare a report and no one asks whether that report has been prepared, or if a goal is to conduct a certain number of reviews and no one ever checks whether they have indeed been made, then subordinates may ignore parts or all of the assignment. The message from above appears to be that it really does not make any difference whether the task is performed or is avoided. More training will not solve this problem either; managers must provide evidence that performance is, indeed, important.

Other Obstacles to Performance

Obstacles to performance can take many forms, such as physical illness, inadequate funding, improper or insufficient tools or materials, inadequate instructions, and so forth. Obviously, to make training sessions count, all these obstacles have to be removed beforehand.

Summary

Achieving highest possible technical competence in an organizational unit involves several skills and activities which the competent manager constantly strives to improve. They include:

1. Good selection of new staff members.
2. Careful monitoring of positions to assure that they constitute the best arrangement for achieving high levels of productivity, quality of service, response flexibility, and needs satisfaction.
3. Review of performance problems to assure that all obstacles to improved performance are removed.
4. Appropriate education, training, and development.

The last item on the above list requires that managers have a general understanding of the principles of learning, which is the subject of the next section.

PRINCIPLES OF LEARNING AND PROGRAM DESIGN

The Learning Process

The traditional conception of an instructor is that of a person who dispenses information. Perhaps this is true because most people spend a significant portion of their early years in formal classroom settings where learning traditionally involves the presentation of information. In this "learning" process there is some give-and-take between instructor and class when class size and instructor temperament permit questions during the lecture; but usually only a very few learners avail themselves of the opportunity to question. In a one-on-one situation where a manager is the instructor who coaches a subordinate, the same can be true. Sometimes subordinates will freely ask questions. In many cases, though, subordinates are reluctant to ask questions for fear of showing ignorance or because they are apprehensive about taking up more of the boss' time than necessary.

This role of the instructor as a dispenser of information is changing to one in which the instructor is expected to pay as much attention to the *process* of learning as to the topic *content* with which learners should become familiar. Process refers to the particular steps which are necessary to assure that the learners will gain the greatest benefits from the learning experiences to which they are exposed. The likelihood that learning will occur is greatest if the instructor strives to be a manager of the learning process and works to shift the responsibility for the achievement of learning to the learner. To do this one must understand the entire learning process, which is often described as the learning cycle. This cycle consists of:

- Analysis of knowledge/skill deficiencies
- Setting of learning goals and priorities
- Preparation or design of learning experiences
- Implementation of the learning program
- Analysis of knowledge/skill deficiencies (those that remain)
- Etc.

An instructor* concerned with the process of learning does not concentrate on the topic and how it can best be presented in logical fashion but instead asks, "What do my students know now, before I work with them in this session? What is it that is more important for them to learn next, and how can I best help them learn it?" These questions are especially important in situations where learners are adults and may have had one or several exposures to the topic which their instructor is covering.

To dramatize the importance of this approach to the task of instructing, three diagrams can be useful. The first one, Figure 9.3, emphasizes how terribly self-defeating a good lecture can be, at least for those learners who do

---

*It is important to recognize that most of the principles discussed here apply to managers when they help subordinates acquire new knowledge or skill in informal circumstances as well as in formal on-the-job or classroom instruction.

not seek complete understanding themselves. It would seem that a clear, logical presentation would help students learn a topic by leading them from the fundamentals, step-by-step, to a thorough picture of the topic. To a limited extent, this is correct. But the educator who strives for *real* quality must also consider trade-offs between clear and logical presentation of the material on one hand and optimum student comprehension on the other.

Figure 9.3. Two Types of Learning Experiences.
A depicts a learning experience in which learners, having little contact with the unknown that surrounds the small island of knowledge gained and having developed a seemingly adequate picture of the subject, are not likely to probe beyond the circle of knowledge for more information. B depicts a learning experience in which only sufficient explanation is offered to give learners a basis for exploration. In learning experience B, the rugged, uneven format affords the learners the opportunity to probe for further understanding in terms most meaningful to each individual. (Artwork courtesy NFPA.)

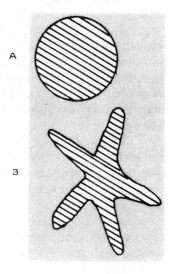

It seems odd, when stated this way, that logical subject explanation and learner understanding should be in conflict, yet this can well be the case. The well-organized learning experience often provides the learners with little awareness of the limits of their new knowledge. Because they follow the presentation, they assume they understand the message fully. Few questions come to their minds and, even though they have mastered some difficult thoughts, they leave the training environment with only a shallow comprehension of the subject, inadequate for application to complex, real-life situations.

The circle (A) in Figure 9.3 depicts the kind of learning experience where learners have little contact with the unknown which surrounds the small island of knowledge gained, where they have developed what seems to them an adequate picture of the subject, and where they are therefore not likely to probe for more information. At some later time, when they attempt to apply what they have learned to the solution of a problem, they discover their lack of understanding. By then the educator is no longer readily available to supply guidance, and the learner must either devote much more effort to learning the necessary material or forego a clear picture of the subject.

The star-shaped figure (B) depicts the presentation of information in a rugged, uneven format, far less satisfying to instructors schooled in the more orthodox methods. In presenting material this way, only enough is explained to give the learners a basis for exploration. Here they probe for understanding in terms that they find most meaningful. If such a learning experience is carefully designed, it involves some form of problem solving and provides for answers to questions which arise in the process—as they are needed, and asked for, by the learner.

The second diagram, Figure 9.4, illustrates why an instructor should be concerned with the level of difficulty which the topic or learning goal presents to the learner. The diagram compares the level of aspirations (how strongly the learner wants to achieve) with the task level (how difficult the learning experience is for that particular learner) to define the zone of ego involvement where the learner can devote maximum attention to the task of learning.

CHALLENGE AND LEARNING TASKS

```
Level of
Aspiration  |                Task Level           |
---------   |                --------             |
   ---      | Extremely difficult   Never         |
    H       |                       attempted     |
    I       |                                     |
    G       | Very difficult   --------------------!----------------
    H  ___  |                                     | Zone of Ego
            | Difficult        Experience         | Involvement
   ___      |                  of                 | (Shifts up
    M       | Medium           success            | or down some-
    E       |                  or                 | what to accom-
    D  ___  | Easy             failure            | modate changes in
   ___      |                                     | levels of aspiration)
    L       | Very easy        --------------------T----------------
    O       |                                     |
    W       | Extremely easy   Routine,           |
            |                  always             |
   ___      |                  successful         |
```

Figure 9.4. Comparison of the Level of Aspiration With the Task Level (Based on work by Wallace Wohlking, New York State School of Industrial and Labor Relations, Cornell University, New York. Artwork courtesy NFPA.)

As Figure 9.4 shows, there are three factors involved in learning: level of aspiration, complexity of the task level, and ego involvement. These suggest that high motivation is likely only if the task level is set so that it is *perceived* to be within the experience and competence of the individual (even if some failures are expected). Aspirations, of course, will influence the way a task is seen and the attitudes with which it is approached.

If a task is perceived as *much too difficult* and has never been attempted, it is outside the Zone of Ego Involvement. A Russian literacy test would fall into this category for most people. At the other extreme, any task which is immediately recognized as *much too easy* also does not bring ego involvement and therefore presents little challenge. It will quickly be considered a waste of time. Most satisfying are those experiences which are achieved by a narrow margin; failure is a constant threat and challenge is highest. Here, of course, the payoff in satisfaction of accomplishment is high and motivation to tackle the task is greatest.

The person upon whose work Figure 9.4 is based reports on research with children which shows that those who have a history of success will usually set realistic goals, while those who fail regularly tend to set unrealistic goals—either too high or too low. Those who set goals too high seem to do so because they are usually rewarded for trying, while those who set them too low do so as defense against possible failure. The conclusions for training design are fairly obvious.

1. For all complex tasks, the designer of a training experience must set *subgoals*.
2. Subgoals must be attainable so that successful experiences are developed.
3. A specific effort must be made to teach toleration of failure.

The third diagram, Figure 9.5, emphasizes the importance of motivation and shows the limits of lecture-type presentations

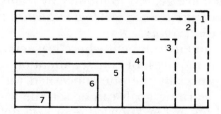

Figure 9.5. The Limits of Lecture-Type Presentations (Artwork courtesy NFPA)

from still another perspective. If the large rectangle (no. 1) in Figure 9.5 can be considered to contain completely the currently available knowledge about a specific subject, then it can reasonably be assumed that an instructor will know, at best, only a proportion, as indicated by rectangle no. 2.

The instructor, faced with limited class time, prepares a presentation dealing with that portion of his or her own knowledge considered most important (rectangle no. 3). Often various delays are encountered so that usually less is covered than anticipated. What is actually discussed is represented by rectangle no. 4.

The communications process being what it is, different people assign different meanings to words and phrases; there are lapses of student attention, screens of personal biases, misunderstandings and false impressions of concept clarity; all in all, what reaches the students is far less than that to which they were exposed. What they remember a few weeks, months, or even years later is still another matter. The three smallest rectangles can be considered to represent what the students actually hear (no. 5), what penetrates their consciousness (no. 6), and what they remember at some later date (no. 7).

What is the moral here? The futility of conscientious effort? Probably not. While there may be some exaggeration in this analogy, the point is a familiar one: *How* the subject is presented is far more important than how *much* is explained to the class. The curiosity of learners can be aroused by presenting only that portion of the material that they can absorb readily. If this material is presented in an interesting, stimulating format, then they will reach out for more information. More will be absorbed, much more will be retained, and the ability to apply new knowledge will be enhanced substantially.

But as with significant concepts in any field, presenting material in an interesting manner is more easily said than done. To change emphasis, instructors must make use of all available techniques which are geared to inquiry by trainees in order to *create a climate in which trainees will find motivation to accept responsibility for their own learning.*

To achieve an environment where learners will find maximum motivation requires, of course, attention to all the Linking Elements, especially the one concerned with goal setting. But before any learning goals can be set, the learner's current knowledge and his or her knowledge or skill deficiencies must be analyzed.

Learning Needs Analysis

Before a manager can determine in what sequence topics should be covered and what specific subtopics are most important for a particular person, the manager must review what the subordinate should know and be able to do to be more effective on the job.

Analyzing Individual Learning Needs

Often new employees know little or nothing about a job. Classroom sessions or on-the-job training can be planned by looking at the topics the learner must master and at the learner's characteristics so that the topics can be presented in the most stimulating way. The situation is more complicated when planning for on-going development. Not only must the instructor be concerned with the logical sequence of topic segments and with presenting them enticingly, but the teaching plan must concentrate on those subtopics (knowledge or skill areas) for which additional learning is desirable.

For this purpose a needs analysis is required. Such an analysis attempts to obtain answers to the following two questions: (1) What do learners need to know or be able to do? (2) What do learners know now, or what are they able to do now? Based on the answers to these two questions, a specific learning program can then be prepared and scheduled.

The tool with which a needs analysis can best be conducted is a knowledge/skill list that shows all the things which the learner should know or be able to do. Such a list, incidentally, can also be helpful in hiring because it spells out the knowledge or skills which an applicant should possess or be able to learn quickly.

An abbreviated sample of a knowledge/skill list for a product manager is given below:

SAMPLE KNOWLEDGE/SKILL PROFILE
(for product managers)

Knowledge
- Basic marketing concepts
- Product knowledge
- Market knowledge
  —Where to obtain data about various segments
  —People and organizations in the market segments
- Profitability statements for products
- Components of a technical proposal
- Technical literature pertaining to the trade, etc.

Skills
- Proposal writing and presentation
- Goal setting for product sales
- Analysis of financial statements
- Forecasting and estimating
- Planning and laying out programs for achieving objectives
- Conduct of meetings, etc.

There are many ways in which a list can be constructed. It is important, when preparing one, not to get too involved in the distinction between knowledge and skills. Many skills imply the knowledge requirement so that there is little need to spell it out separately. Similarly, the knowledge of something can often assure that the skill exists. If the distinction is difficult, any item can usually be placed into either segment of the list, without causing any problems. Here are some suggestions for developing a knowledge/skill list.

1. If a detailed job description exists, the list can be based on that, though it usually cannot match the job description exactly. For instance, two lines on the job description for a product manager may read: "Analyze competitive moves to determine probable market impact" and "Develop and evaluate alternative market strategies." Similar knowledge and skills are needed for analysis of competition as for evaluating marketing strategies. Analyzing competition and strategies covers many things a product manager must know or be able to do, from marketing through estimating and forecasting. On the other hand, a job-description line which reads, "Must be thoroughly familiar with the assigned products," could also be part of a knowledge/skill profile since it concerns a single topic which the product manager must know.

2. A knowledge/skill list can also be constructed from the goals which apply to a particular position. Goals provide a good basis for knowledge/skills lists and job descriptions.

3. A list can be developed by the manager alone or by the manager and the subordinate jointly. In the latter instance, both subordinate and manager prepare separate lists and then, through discussion, create a common one. Such a jointly developed list is often most likely to provide a basis for learning goals which are challenging and which the subordinate would really attempt to achieve.

Once the knowledge/skill list has been completed, manager and subordinate can review the subordinate's strengths and weaknesses and thus develop a profile that can be used to set learning goals and priorities.

Analyzing Team Learning Needs

An analysis of learning needs cannot concentrate exclusively on the knowledge and skills which individuals must acquire. There are team needs which go beyond those of the individual members of the team. Even if every person has the necessary knowledge for performing specific tasks, if the team has not learned how to coordinate its members' knowledge and skills, many problems can occur. These can be prevented only through joint team practice that gradually develops the necessary skills. For example, in a sales meeting, every participant must understand how to support the other participants and what his or her respective role is in contributing to the success of that meeting. Or if a task involving all team members must be done on a regular basis, there must be joint practice sections. A good example of this is an assembly line operation in which people must not only be able to perform their own job, but must also know what to do to support the next worker. Another job in which coordinated team effort is required is firefighting. Each firefighter in a company must not only have a clear knowledge of the standard method of attacking a fire, but must also be able to perform smoothly in coordination with other team members. Joint drills are therefore necessary to prevent snags in critical operations, which could turn out to be very serious indeed.

Joint team practice is needed for responding to any emergency, whether the emergency is a car crash or meeting end-of-the-month deadlines. This also holds for nonemergency situations requiring considerable coordination, such as preparation of complex plans, budgets, or schedules.

Setting Learning Goals

The end result of new learning is usually a change in behavior. Goals, when properly set, represent a contract to oneself or to others to achieve such change. For that reason, educators sometimes speak of a learning contract when they refer to goals which learners have agreed to achieve.

After the knowledge and skill needs of a person or a team have been identified, goals are set so that developmental expe-

riences can be planned to stimulate the greatest desire to
achieve them. To achieve the goals of a learning contract, the
segments of a successful learning experience should be considered, and how they lead, in a spiral fashion, to the goal.

As discussed in other chapters, joint goal setting defines
what is expected of the subordinate, but also what support the
manager is expected to provide. Similarly, a learning contract
defines the goals and the responsibilities of learner and instructor and thereby places these responsibilities clearly where they
belong.

The Goal Achievement Spiral

A complete learning experience consists of three stages,
acquisition, demonstration (vicarious application), and personal application (see Figure 9.6).

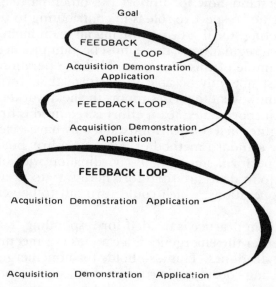

Figure 9.6. Basis of the Continuing Process for Achieving Learning Objectives (Artwork courtesy NFPA)

- During *acquisition* new knowledge is obtained through
  the written word, from live presentations, in group discussion, etc.
- During *demonstration* the new material is made more
  meaningful or more explicit with demonstrations of the
  practical application of new data, principles, or concepts.

These can take the form of dramatic presentations, films, slides, audio or video tapes, actual illustration with models, etc.

• During *personal application* the learner comes face-to-face with his or her ability to use the material in various situations. If experiences in this stage are designed properly, they will be quite similar to those which the learner normally faces in the real environment.

Instructors who work with simulations and other participative learning experiences know that the third stage is really the most important one. In this stage there exists an opportunity for both the learner and the instructor to check how well the picture which has built up in the learner's mind meets the needs of reality. In the checking process, two feedback loops immediately come into being, one for the instructor, who can observe the progress of the learner or the group of learners in meaningful terms, and one for the learner, who can diagnose his or her own knowledge deficiencies. The three stages with their built-in feedback mechanism thus become the basis for a continuing process that can be used to achieve any learning objective which is not blocked by attitudinal or emotional obstacles. As depicted in Figure 9.6, learning involves a spiral-type repetition of the three stages and the feedback loops; less and less new knowledge has to be acquired in each turn. This becomes especially apparent to instructors when they experiment with various types of simulated experiences. Serious learners inevitably ask more precise and penetrating questions during and after personal application than they do—or are able to do—beforehand.

It must be remembered that for new knowledge to be meaningful, it must be explored in the learner's own terms. Although perhaps obvious, this point cannot be overemphasized. For every person, words and images have personal meaning. Therefore, application of new knowledge in the classroom or coaching session must be to situations similar to those which the learner normally experiences in the work environment. There is another requirement: Learning must proceed at the learner's own pace and must be adapted to personal ability and related previous experience. Thus, development programs must make use of flexible techniques and permit adaptation to the individual needs if they are to achieve learning goals with the least possible effort from the instructor as well as the learner.

Identifying and Overcoming Obstacles to Learning

The learning spiral just described can be used to help learners overcome any knowledge/skill deficiency only if learning is not subject to some blockage. Some external obstacles have already been discussed in the beginning of this chapter. In addition to these, all of which are under the control of managers, there are those which are peculiar to each learner. The latter are based primarily on the attitudes, emotions, and physical limitations of learners. Sometimes learners are opposed to training. At other times the subject is so complex that understanding is not gained easily. Then there are times when both these obstacles are in the way of achieving learning goals.

There is usually little negative attitude towards learning in general in organizations in which employees know that learning is essential to effective performance. Still, the learning process can be obstructed by physical or emotional obstacles and by negative attitudes with respect to specific topics or instructions. These obstacles can be referred to as blockages.

Figure 9.7 illustrates most of the possible blockages and thereby highlights the many ways in which learning can be obstructed, even if the instructor is highly knowledgeable and can present the subject in a fairly interesting light.

Acquisition of New Knowledge and/or Skills

If no blockages exist or blockages have been eliminated, learning can proceed and the learning cycle takes over, starting with the analysis of knowledge and skill deficiencies, the setting of learning goals and priorities, and the implementation of a learning program.

There are primarily three major areas of blockage, as shown in Figure 9.7.

1. Attitudes toward learning in general
2. Attitudes toward a subject
3. Other blockages that are not attitudinal.

For instance, in regard to attitudes toward learning in general, many people either never liked school or lacked interest in learning at any time during their lives. Some of these people can, nevertheless, learn subjects quite well, particularly those that they see as relevant to their career objectives or their work needs.

Attitudes towards a subject, such as apprehension of a particular subject, cause other possible blockages to learning. As

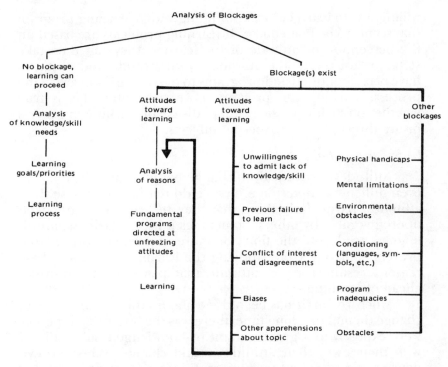

Figure 9.7. Acquisition of New Knowledge and/or Skill

Figure 9.7 illustrates, unwillingness to admit lack of a knowledge/skill can be one of these. An attempt to find out the real reasons why a person may not want to learn something can sometimes uncover interesting information about the person that can help in gradually overcoming his or her resistance to learning. People often are ashamed to admit that after having been exposed to a subject they still do not understand an idea, principle, or procedure that others seem to understand. Similarly, previous failure to learn a topic can result in the feeling that the topic is "too difficult" and in the failure to devote the effort necessary to master it. At the other extreme, if learners believe that something is simply "common sense," they will sometimes tune out in the erroneous belief that the message does not contain anything of value to them. If, on the other hand, the topic is perceived to be too "theoretical" or not relevant, learners may not pay adequate attention.

In view of the many possible obstacles to learning, managers must first determine the real reasons for inability or unwillingness to learn before continuing with a learning program that seems to be inadequate. If learning problems are based on the perception or attitude of the learner, they can then take steps to "unfreeze" the attitude. Once attitude and obstacles have been identified and programs to overcome them are in the process, learning can proceed more smoothly. This is true whether obstacles are the result of dislike of learning in general or are directed against specific subjects.

Unfreezing Attitudes

Attitudes are difficult to change; very frequently, they are even difficult to determine. People do not like to expose their attitudes, particularly those that they feel may not be looked upon favorably by others. Sometimes it is only laziness, unwillingness to devote the time, or more important projects that prevent someone from studying the learning. But even these reasons result from an attitude that places many priorities ahead of learning.

Much research has been done about attitudes and how to change them. For a long time, there was the belief that if people were exposed to a great amount of knowledge that conflicted with their own, their attitudes would change. When no evidence could be found to support this view, it was thought that possibly training was not intensive enough, did not involve people sufficiently. More intensive training experiences were designed, the most famous of which were the sensitivity training programs that flourished during the late 50's and early 60's. Sensitivity training was intended to help participants gain a clearer view of themselves, of their attitudes, and particularly of their impact on others. During an intensive four or five day session, participants were encouraged, and gradually forced, to open up so that they could express their feelings and opinions more freely, especially in regard to their relationships with other people. It was found, however, that even sensitivity training rarely had significant impact on attitudes. Although it did bring some behavior change, research showed that it had little documentable effect on attitudes.

If such intensive training would not change attitudes, then what would? Researchers investigating this question came to the conclusion that more fundamental steps than sensitivity training were necessary to bring about changes in attitudes. They identified several possible steps, the most important of which involved "structure changes." They determined that the change proved that attitudes would change when people were required by their jobs or situations to behave in a manner contrary to their attitudes and, at the same time, were given training that exposed the problems which their attitudes created for them and for others. Behavioral scientists supporting this view claimed that training could not be effective against strong attitudes unless there was first an organizational (structural) requirement which people had to follow. Training could help people satisfy such a requirement more easily and thus help them change their attitudes. An example was the unwillingness of whites in certain parts of the country to work with blacks in the same organization. When they were forced to do so and, at the same time, received training in interracial relations, their attitudes began to change.

Another important factor in attitude change is evidence of group disapproval of an attitude. When an individual is exposed to the fact that peers, and particularly friends or the group with which he or she identifies, do not approve of a certain attitude, that attitude will be questioned and probably will change. And if learners find that acting on their own views and attitudes will actually hurt team effort, then it is likely that they will question and modify their views. Here, too, training can support change or hasten it and make it easier for the individual involved.

The views of respected and successful people in the field also can have great influence on learner attitudes. When an individual finds that his or her attitudes are in conflict with the attitudes of respected people, attitudes are likely to be questioned. Presenting irrefutable evidence of the attitude of successful professionals in the field (through guest appearances or through testimonials) can help a manager lead the group toward desirable attitude changes.

Finally, activities that force people with biases to come face to face with the detrimental impact that these biases can have on their career, their future, or their style of life can bring about attitude change. In this situation as in others, training can assist in the process of attitude change.

In each of the instances above, what happens is that first an individual begins to question a certain attitude, possibly not in a fully conscious way. This is akin to an unfreezing process which allows the individual greater freedom than theretofore to shape his or her opinions. Once attitudes are partially or fully unfrozen, the process of change can begin, and that is when training can make its greatest contribution.

Other Blockages

The extreme right side of the diagram in Figure 9.7 depicts blockages to learning that result from limitations and are not based on attitudes or emotions. The instructor must be aware of physical handicaps and mental limitations. Learners may be ashamed of physical handicaps and unaware of mental deficiencies. For instance, a firefighter may be aware that an old knee injury makes it increasingly difficult for him to climb a ladder, but he may have successfully hidden this minor handicap during the physical examination and during the probationary period. This firefighter will resist training sessions involving ladder work. If an instructor is not aware of the handicap, considerable effort can be wasted in misdirected attempts to achieve learning.

Common examples of physical limitations are hearing and sight defects. Often people with these deficiencies are reluctant to obtain hearing aids or glasses. The obvious obstacles to learning which these defects present cannot be resolved until the manager becomes aware of them.

Mental limitations are of a more serious nature, yet once they are recognized, they too can be overcome. Like many physical disorders, learners may be reluctant to face them objectively. Once the manager is aware of them, however, then the learning program can be adjusted to take them into account. Usually only a slower pace and some personal help are needed so that subordinates can achieve essential learning goals.

Environmental obstacles also can block effective learning. These include noises and other distractions which interrupt the thought processes of instructor and learners alike. Finally, illogical presentation of topics and other instructor deficiencies such as talking over the heads of learners, talking down to them, or using visuals poorly seriously detract from a learning experience. Such deficiencies, of course, apply primarily to lectures and demonstrations. The participative learning experiences which provide personal application are usually so involving that interruptions and distractions have relatively little effect on them.

SPECIFIC LEARNING PRINCIPLES

There are several major and minor principles which must be considered by a manager of the learning process in addition to those already discussed. The first of these—that *learners who are motivated will learn to master a subject faster and more thoroughly than learners who are not motivated or who have less motivation*—has already been referred to in various ways on previous pages.

Motivation is achieved only if the climate is such that learners can find sufficient benefits in the learning experience. The pleasure of gaining new, useful information or desirable skills can be one of the strongest of psychological satisfactions. Interesting, varied presentations that hold attention can help people experience more of that pleasure than dull or monotonous instruction.

Learning can be akin to entertainment if it is appropriate to the learner's interests and capabilities. Varied use of techniques to involve learners, together with good selection of media and topic sequence, can go a long way to achieve learning sessions which come close to the goal of holding full learner attention.

Evidence of rewards—that is, achieving a sense of greater professionalism or better self-protection, winning in a competition, or achieving something the learner wants to achieve— can contribute to providing the satisfaction of psychological needs which is so essential to motivation. In addition, of course, the other Linking Elements must be satisfied:

- As previously discussed, learning goals must be set properly. This means that attention must be given to satisfying the concepts expressed by EQIFAPPO (see page 50).
- Learning activities and learning needs must be coordinated through use of knowledge/skill profiles and the like in order to avoid the "demotivating" impact of confusion or lack of clear direction. The sequence of topics must be arranged carefully to assure that all new concepts are understood before they are used to explain other matters or to draw conclusions.
- Clearly communicated and enforced rules, if they are appropriate, will also contribute to a favorable motivational climate by reducing doubts, confusion, and distractions. Simple rules such as insistence on completion of learning assignments on time or on starting and stopping learning

sessions as scheduled (when emergencies do not interrupt) can give learners great confidence in the professionalism which lies behind the training program.

Motivation to learn for the sake of learning is different from motivation to work, though. How to establish a climate which motivates one to achieve on the current job has already been discussed at length. As Herzberg pointed out, managers at one time threatened people to "motivate" them.* When that did not work, incentives were given for performance. The incentives worked, especially when work was clearly defined and allowed pay for piece work.

While more output was achieved, with it came more games. Employees attempted to get higher piece rates without working harder. Employers redesigned the operations so they could set lower rates whenever employees earned more. With both sides playing games, trying to gain advantage rather than sharing the benefits of greater effort and thought, many financial benefits were thus lost and the psychological costs were high—in distrust and often, as a consequence, in strife. Managers spoke about "motivating" people to do more work but were really holding out candysticks and clubs, pushing and pulling people into turning out more work.

As the world became more complex and managers found they had to "motivate" the knowledge worker for whom piece rates could not be set, new ways had to be found for managers to achieve their goals. From the work of the behavioral scientists, a greater awareness of the manager's role in developing a better motivational climate has emerged. However, there is still some question as to whether the same practices that promise to motivate one to achieve more on the job will also translate into higher motivation to learn.

There is another level of complexity involved in helping people develop. It seems that even when people have been aided in gaining higher levels of self-realization and more satisfaction from their work, there remains the difficulty of helping them motivate themselves to become learners. Many see themselves as learned; they enjoy their current work and do not prepare for the future.

---

*Frederick Herzberg, *One more time: How do you Motivate employees.* Harvard Business Review. Jan./Feb. 1968. Copyright © 1967 by the President and Fellows of Harvard College; all rights reserved. Reprinted by permission.

The environment in which people find motivation for their current jobs may not be stimulating enough to get them to think about the future. It appears that the overwhelming majority of people are "today-oriented," rather than "future-oriented." A future orientation requires some sacrifice of enjoyment today in return for a possibly higher level of enjoyment in the future. Establishment of a climate that is future-oriented obviously calls for more work on the part of the manager. He or she must help people find the interest to learn more about things beyond their immediate tasks so that they gain a broader view, so they see their work and themselves in better perspective, so they appreciate more what the organizational unit is trying to achieve, and so they can see their own career opportunities more realistically.

Another principle with which managers should be familiar is conditioning. *Conditioning (stimulus-response) can enhance learning of simple tasks.* While studying automatic reflexes associated with digestion around the turn of the century, Ivan Pavlov, the Russian physiologist, noted that:

> "When meat powder is placed in a dog's mouth, salivation takes place; the food is the unconditioned stimulus and the salivation the unconditioned reflex. Then some arbitrary stimulus, such as light, is combined with the presentation of the food. Eventually, after repetition and if time relationships are right, the light will evoke salivation independent of the food; the light is the conditioned stimulus and the response to it is the conditioned response."*

Conditioning is important in many operations because certain tasks must be performed almost instinctively in the prescribed way to assure that they are done as naturally as possible and in the shortest possible time. Tasks such as those carried out in certain types of emergencies require extensive practice so that they can be performed with precision. For example, police, rescue squad, and fire services need practice sessions and drills to assure that the mental processes involved in certain operations are firmly fixed in mind. Other operations needing much practice for high-quality performance are typing, using adding machines, and using calculators. Even writing letters and preparing reports can become almost instinctive after a

---

*Ernest R. Hilgard and Gordon H. Bower, THEORIES OF LEARNING (3rd ed.; New York: Appleton-Century Crofts, 1966), p. 48. Reprinted by permission of Prentice-Hall, Inc., Englewood Cliffs, N.J.

great deal of practice. A manager can practice giving recognition until it becomes second nature. The same is true of analyzing reports that are issued at regular intervals. And with adequate practice, even subtle personnel and other types of problems can be spotted easily. Repeated practice that makes performance of a task akin to a conditioned reflex can lead to a high degree of effectiveness.

One important principle concerns the speed with which new concepts are presented to learners. *Learning pace must be adapted to the learner's ability to absorb new material if the learning process is to proceed without interruption.* All learners have different learning capabilities. Some have quick understandings; others have good memory; still others have a good attention span. A lecture that is fairly fast paced can lose some learners at various points, and a slow-paced lecture has difficulty holding the attention of all but the least capable learners.

Learning will be absorbed better and retained longer if it is directly work-related and can be applied on the job. Even when all subjects in training are work related, some of them are rarely applied. If a task is important, then regular practice or drills in a simulated environment may be necessary to assure adequate skills to perform the task properly.

Things that are learned and understood tend to be better retained than things learned by rote. This principle suggests that adequate testing should be done to assure that a subject is thoroughly understood—even if the tests are self-tests to avoid giving the impression of lack of confidence in the learner.

Practice distributed over several periods is more economical in learning than the same amount of practice concentrated into a single period. If an important skill has to be practiced extensively to assure full mastery, initial practice sessions need not continue until the skill has been mastered. Pauses of several days between relatively short sessions will help to bring better retention.

The order of presentation of materials to be learned is very important. This principle appears to be obvious, yet many learning programs attempt to present complex topics first, before adequate foundation exists in the minds of learners.

It is easier to recognize something than it is to recall it. This principle is of greatest importance in selecting ways to test knowledge of learners. Testing should emphasize recall, not recognition.

Learning something new can interfere with remembering something learned earlier. This is often overlooked by instructors who fail to reinforce subject matter or skills learned earlier when helping learners acquire new skills or new knowledge. Taking this principle into consideration is especially important when a new topic overlaps a previous one or is similar to it. At first it is difficult to believe that new knowledge or skill in, say, receiving procedures would have any effect on shipping procedures, yet there is some effect. Learning a new set of requirements and forms clearly can have strong impact on the retention of other procedures.

Knowledge of results helps learners maintain motivation to continue learning effort. Obviously, if learners do not know whether they are acquiring knowledge correctly or whether they are possibly learning things which are incorrect, they will be hesitant to devote full effort until they can be certain. Testing or participative activities in which learners can receive feedback on the correctness of the knowledge or skills they are acquiring are therefore important segments of satisfactory learning experiences.

The principles discussed above are not the only ones that can be considered when planning learning experiences, but they are the more important ones. A manager who keeps these principles constantly in mind will truly "manage" learning experiences and is not likely to rely excessively on talking and explaining.

INSTRUCTIONAL STRATEGY

Once learning needs have been identified and goals set, the instructor can plan the instructional strategy. This strategy consists of two major segments: (a) topic sequence (content) and (b) processes to be used for each topic segment. As previously discussed, these two are closely interlinked. Topics must be presented in a logical order. Simple concepts or skills which form the foundations for later ones should be presented first; and the more complex ones or those using some fundamental skills or concepts should follow.

Each topic segment, however, must be presented as part of a satisfying learning experience consisting of the three steps of acquisition, demonstration and personal application (see Figure 9.6). The techniques which can be used for these steps will first be discussed, and then their application to the two major learning environments—the classroom and the actual work-place—will be explored.

In preparing an instructional strategy, a planning table can be most useful since it can help to assure that:

1. Topic segments are arranged in logical sequence.
2. Appropriate techniques will be used for each topic segment.
3. Acquisition, demonstration, and personal application will have been considered for each topic segment.
4. There is sufficient variety in techniques to present the most stimulating environment to the learners.

Such a table could look like Table 9.1 which has been prepared for a segment of a course in retail selling. The more techniques an instructor can use effectively, the more varied the program which can be prepared. While Table 9.1 is for a classroom with several learners, a similar one could be prepared for individual instruction.

TOPICS	Acquisition	Demonstration	Personal Application	Correction of Deficiencies
Greeting customers	plenary group discussion	film	small group analysis of actual conversations with customers	small group discussion, role play, on-the-job coaching
Initiating conversations	discussion, presentation	demonstration role play	simulation exercise	small group role play, on-the-job coaching
Dealing with several customers simultaneously	programmed instruction	audio-tape demonstration	simulation exercise	plenary and small group analysis of simulation exercise
Responding to questions and handling objections	text reading	demonstration role play	role play	simulation exercise
Concluding conversations	plenary group discussion	audio-tape demonstration	simulation exercise	role play, small group discussion
Product information	product literature	demonstration film	simulation exercise	written and verbal tests
Etc.				

Table 9.1. Program Design Matrix

Techniques for Acquisition of New Knowledge or Skills

Correction of deficiencies will involve a manager or an instructor in various assignments. Managers should therefore constantly strive to become more familiar with a wide range of possible techniques and experiment with them in helping their people learn.

First exposure to unknown subjects—acquisition—may come from, among others:(1) lectures; (2) reading from straight text or programmed instructional materials; (3) audiotapes; (4) films, filmstrips, or videotapes.

Lectures and Verbal Explanations

Lectures (used here to mean any verbal explanation) have advantages and disadvantages. They are the most widely used method of transmitting information. On the surface the lecture is the easiest, the least expensive, and the most readily available acquisition technique. Lectures are flexible; they can be changed on the spot by the instructor who perceives a previously hidden learning need; they can be used with one person or with many.

Lectures can be given by one person alone, or variety can be introduced by using several people as lecturers. But, according to one source,

"a lecture generally consists of a one-way communication. The instructor presents information to a group of passive learners. Thus, little or no opportunity exists to clarify meanings, to check on whether trainees really understand the lecture materials, or to handle the wide diversity of ability, attitude and interest that may prevail among the trainees. Also, there is little or no opportunity for practice, reinforcement or knowledge of results."*

Some of the disadvantages of lectures can be reduced through good practices in handling questions. This is practical only with small groups; and those who encourage all learners to ask questions can overcome most of the disadvantages of straight lectures.

One pitfall which managers have to watch is frequently encountered when the group contains several highly motivated learners who give the impression of heavy participation. In such a situation it may seem to the manager that all the learners are exploring the subject to gain thorough understanding. In reality only a small percentage may be doing so while the other learners may be seriously confused by the topic but reluctant to speak.

---

*Bernard M. Bass, et. al. TRAINING IN INDUSTRY (Belmont, California: Brooks-Cole Publishing Company, 1966), p. 94.

Use of audiovisual aids is generally considered an excellent way to enhance the ability of a lecture to transmit knowledge. The 3M Company's booklet entitled *A Guide to More Effective Meetings* states:

"People are Visual-minded: We are visually-oriented from birth. People grow up surrounded by the visual influences of television, movies, books, school blackboards and projectors, road signs, advertising signs, all kinds of visual stimulation. People *expect* visuals in meetings. And visuals help the presenter control the meeting and maintain the group's attention.

"Retention Is Increased: Speeches may motivate, but what about retention? When relying on verbalization alone to communicate, an estimated 90% of a message is misinterpreted or forgotten entirely. We retain only 10% of what we hear! But consider this: Adding appropriate visual aids to verbalization increases retention to approximately 50%.

"Visualization Encourages Organization: Visualizing forces a presenter to organize thoughts in an orderly fashion that will lead to a conclusion. In so doing, he or she learns to simplify and condense the message into a concise, understandable story, which saves both time and expense.

"Misunderstandings Are Less Likely To Occur: By both seeing and hearing the message simultaneously, meeting participants can understand the presenter's intent easier and quicker. Misinformation can be effectively avoided."

Some of the most common lecture aids are blackboards, overhead transparencies, and slides and filmstrips. These are quite versatile, and a good manager will make wide use of all of them.

Reading

Independent study through reading of text or programmed instruction is an alternative to the lecture method of acquisition. Reading affords the learner the opportunity to stop when necessary, take notes, clarify meaning by referring back to earlier material, and consult various sources for more detailed information.

Obtaining answers to questions that come up in reading is, however, usually more difficult than obtaining answers to questions during lectures since lecture questions can be explored immediately with an instructor.

Programmed learning is a special form of instruction which involves learners by quizzing them on material covered in one section before allowing them to proceed to the next.

The advantages of programmed learning are that:

1. The learner can move at his or her own pace.
2. The learner follows a logical sequence of thought.
3. The learner must actively respond to questions asked by the presentation.
4. A wide variety of media, such as audiotapes, filmstrips, pictures, etc., can be employed to enliven programmed instruction.
5. Programmed instruction is self-administered and may be used whenever the learner is ready to learn.

Programmed materials are, however, somewhat tedious. Moreover, the selection of programmed materials is limited; materials are not available for all topics.

Conference Technique

A conference is a "pooling of knowledge, experiences, and opinions among a group of people who have something to contribute toward achieving specified objectives, or among people who are capable of analyzing information relevant to these objectives."* The conference technique is especially useful with small groups and can be used with brief lectures to provide a mixture of acquisition, demonstration, and personal application techniques on a somewhat superficial level.

Group discussion offers some immediate reinforcement to newly acquired knowledge. For this reason group discussion often follows a lecture. During conferences, unlike lectures, discussion affords the learner the opportunity to compare personal reactions to subject matter with reactions of other learners as well as with the views of the manager.

A conference, therefore, is a planned learning experience where the manager's role is not one of lecturer but rather one of "facilitator." The manager encourages group thinking and provides background information as necessary to enable all learners to take part in discussion. The manager also summarizes, at the end of each discussion, what conferees should have learned.

Advantages of the conference technique are many. It tends to get learners or trainees to give more thought to subject matter. It helps to show each conferee how others think about a subject or problem. It adapts the presentation of the subject matter to the needs of the group and, by exposing group opinions, helps to change those attitudes which are detrimental.

---

*CONFERENCE LEADERSHIP (New York: American Management Association, 1974), p. 5.

One major disadvantage of the conference technique is that it requires a skillful leader—one who can carefully plan for a variety of eventualities that could occur during the conference program. Another disadvantage is that it has limited usefulness since it lends itself only to those topics about which the conferees, together, have adequate knowledge.

Techniques for Demonstration

Demonstration is the step in a learning experience in which learners are shown how the information, concepts, or materials discussed during the acquisition phase can be applied to their respective situations. Showing how to use a piece of equipment or a product is a demonstration. But a role-play in which the manager takes the role of a customer and a learner shows how to deal with customer objections is also a good demonstration.

Demonstrations include most of the techniques available to a manager (lecture, by itself or supported by props, in classroom or on-site; slides or filmstrips; audio- or videotapes) as well as some forms of the participative techniques which are discussed more fully later on in this chapter (case studies, simulation, role play).

The important point to note about demonstration is that it constitutes an important step in the learning process. It is often overlooked and the resulting gap in the learning process may take considerably more effort to close later than would have been needed immediately after initial acquisition of knowledge.

Techniques for Personal Application

All personal application techniques are based in one way or another on case studies.

Case Studies or Case Method

Case studies vary greatly. They are descriptions of real or imaginary situations ranging in length from single paragraphs or brief verbal statements to small books with great detail about the organization which serves as the subject of the study.

Uses of the case-study method of instruction vary as widely as do case studies themselves. Cases may serve as foundations for simulations and role-plays. They also may be used:

- As simple descriptions. Learners are expected to review the case, decide what issues it raises, and then draw conclusions about these issues. For instance, a case-study session could start by presenting learners with certain marketing data and with instructions to review the data and to comment on it in light of their own products.

- As part of a more structured inquiry. Specific questions on the case are asked at the end of the case.
- As part of an in-depth exploration. Learners are asked very detailed questions on the case.
- As material for the "Incident Process" method of instruction. In this use of a case study, learners are provided with only part of the information that is necessary for thorough analysis. They must first decide what additional information is needed to work on the case. After they have asked for and received the additional information, they can begin to analyze the case. For instance, in a case dealing with the financial situation of a company, the net worth, retained earnings, and so forth may have been omitted in the description though they are important to the case.
- As material for single learners, for small or large groups of learners, or for large classes broken into small teams.

Cases stimulate creative thinking because learners are asked to ferret out what is essential about the situation and then decide what actions, if any, should be considered. They are easy to use because much data available to managers—records of sales, operational costs, inventory, schedules, etc., as well as articles from trade magazines, newspaper stories, and text books—can form the basis for cases.

Cases can be used spontaneously when it becomes clear that learners need to explore certain issues after a lecture where many questions indicated inadequate comprehension, or when the learning process clearly needs a change of pace to maintain learner interest.

Simulations

If learners are asked to make believe that they are some of the people described in a case study, they begin to participate in a simulation. Invariably learners are asked to solve specific problems in a case study when they are working on it as a simulation.

Simulations, like case studies, can involve elaborate descriptions of a situation with detailed data, pictures, charts, graphs, or floorplans. They can be supported with transparencies or can be worked on paper. Some can be programmed for use with computers; some can be expanded into field work and, in certain cases such as sales presentations, can turn into role-plays. Simulations can also be simple verbal descriptions used spontaneously just as case studies are used and for the same purposes. All the learners can assume that they are the same person or they can take on different roles in the situation.

Simulations are an ideal vehicle for learning. They can dramatically enhance interest in training sessions and contribute greatly to awareness of the crucial features relevant to the organization. In addition, they can help to make valuable use of existing plans and, coincidentally, can serve as a basis for continual improvement in these plans.

A manager or instructor who decides to build most instruction around exploration of strategies and tactics for promotion of products can expand them into simulations. These can concentrate on advertising and promotion plans, as well as specific sales tactics and strategies based on various assumptions about the market and the people who may be interested in the particular product. The inevitable outcome of such job-related simulations is greater interest in learning, greater knowledge of market conditions, and enhanced interest in improvement of sales plans and presentations.

Simulations are usually far more involving than case studies; they therefore can be more enjoyable and hold attention even better. But they can also be threatening to learners who are inadequately prepared—in knowledge or experience. Thus, they should be chosen and used only after learners have had exposure to the subject.

Role-Plays

If at issue in a simulation is not only what should be done in a particular situation but also exactly what words should be used, then the simulation is likely to become a role-play. Role plays are applicable primarily to situations in which learning objectives involve communications between individuals or groups. However, the word "role-play" does not have precisely the same meaning to all instructors. Sometimes simulations in which learners assume different roles are referred to as role-plays. More commonly, though, "role-play" is applied to those activities in which learners act out the specific roles assigned to them.

Even though the most common form of role-play is a live demonstration in which only a few learners take part while the remainder act as observers, this is rarely the most effective form. Much more effective for skill development is the type of role-play technique which involves all the members of the group simultaneously. The group is broken down into small teams, and team members take turns playing various roles. Those not involved critique the players at the end of the role-play session. Role-play sessions conducted this way are usually both stimulating and interesting to the participants.

APPLYING LEARNING PRINCIPLES AND TECHNIQUES TO COACHING

Classroom training and drills can provide much of the knowledge and skills which employees and supervisors need for their jobs. Since classes can be used only when there are a number of people who must be trained in the same skills and since individuals vary in the way they perceive their jobs and in the amount of learning they obtain from classes and drills, there is considerable need for individual coaching by superiors. Coaching can take two forms. A manager can either (a) suggest self-study goals to eliminate deficiencies and prepare the subordinate for advancement and can help with any difficulties the subordinate may encounter or he or she can (b) provide on-the-job training in those skills and areas of knowledge which require individualized attention.

Self-Study

Self-study recommendations and help in achieving study goals are effective coaching methods for professionals. They are, or can be, easily geared to the needs and aspirations, as well as the knowledge and skill level, of the individual.

On-The-Job Training

Many topics, especially skills, are so important that they cannot be left to the more leisurely self-study approach and require the more intense activity of on-the-job training.

The U.S. Army uses a comprehensive chart describing the four steps in OJT to guide on-the-job training of civilian employees. The chart is reproduced in Table 9.2.

It is interesting to note how the steps in Table 9.2 parallel the steps of a complete and satisfying learning experience.

Step	Purpose	How accomplished
1. Prepare the learner.	A. To relieve tension. B. To establish training base. C. To arouse interest. D. To give him confidence.	A. Put him at ease. B. Find out what he already knows about task. C. Tell relation of task to mission. D. Tie task to his experience. E. Insure that he is in a comfortable position to see you perform the task clearly.
2. Present the task.	A. To make sure he understands what to do and why. B. To insure retention. C. To avoid giving him more than he can grasp.	A. Tell, show, illustrate, question, carefully and patiently, use task analysis. B. Stress key points. C. Instruct clearly, completely, one step at a time. D. Keep your words to a minimum. Stress action words.
3. Try out learner's performance.	A. To be sure he has right method. B. To prevent wrong habit forming. C. To be sure he knows what he is doing and why. D. To test his knowledge. E. To avoid putting him on the job prematurely.	A. Have him perform the task and do not require that he explain what he is doing the first time through. If he makes a major error, assume the blame yourself and repeat as much of step 2 as is necessary. B. Once he has performed the task correctly have him do it again and this time have him explain the steps and key points as he does the task. C. Ask questions to insure that key points are understood. D. Continue until you know that he knows.
4. Followup.	A. To give him confidence. B. To be sure he takes no chances, and knows he is not left alone. C. To be sure he stays on the beam. D. To show your confidence in him.	A. Put him on his own; praise as fitting. B. Encourage questions; tell him where he can get help. C. Check frequently at first. D. Gradually reduce amount of checking.

Table 9.2. The Four Steps of On-The-Job Training

Acquisition is covered by step 1, learner preparation, and the first items of step 2, task presentation. *Demonstration* is covered by the remaining items of task presentation. *Personal application* occurs in step 3 where the learner practices the task until he or she has mastered it. *Follow-up* assures correction of any remaining deficiencies.

This four-step process also satisfies some of the learning principles discussed earlier in this chapter.

- *Motivation* is enhanced through the careful attention to the learner's personal needs in step 1 and through the thoroughness with which the learner is helped to master the task.
- *Blockages* are recognized and overcome during step 3 when the learner begins to try the task.
- *Conditioning* occurs during repeated trials.
- *Understanding* is assured when the learner explains the task.

- Subtasks are presented in logical *order* since they are practiced exactly the way they are demonstrated.
- *Knowledge of results* is immediately available since the learner's performance is checked several times as the total task is learned.

On-the-job training can or does employ several of the techniques discussed previously.

- *Lectures* are used during the explanation of the task.
- *Simulation* is used during the first trials of the task by the learner if either danger, inconvenience, or considerable costs are involved. For instance, operating highly complex processing machinery or using dangerous chemicals may be practiced in simulated fashion before on-the-job training actually takes place.
- *Role-plays* can be useful, even before more thorough simulation practices, when the learner explains in detail how tasks involving other people will be performed.

Classroom Instruction

Unlike on-the-job training, which is structured by the job itself, classroom instruction is, or can be, quite varied. However, if the principles discussed in this chapter are to be honored, some pattern of instruction still should be followed in the classroom.

1. Lectures should be of limited duration. Many educators feel that serious, uninterrupted lectures which last more than 20 minutes are unlikely to hold audience attention very well.
2. Instructors should closely adhere to the sequence of acquisition, demonstration, personal application, and correction of deficiencies. One way to achieve this almost invariably is to follow a simple sequence of four steps:
   a. A lecture to explain concepts, supported with visuals, if possible; as much opportunity for learners to ask questions as the environment permits; and a concluding demonstration.
   b. An appropriate activity such as a problem, a case study, simulation or role-play, which is worked individually by the learners or, preferably, by small teams.
   c. A review of the activity through reports and discussion of the reports.

    d. An opportunity for learners to ask any questions which may not have been clarified.

3. As much as possible, the atmosphere should be informal and relaxed so that learners feel free to ask questions and to explore points in language most familiar to them. Lectures should allow for interruptions for questions almost continuously, and instructors should answer questions without condescending or belittling the questioners if the atmosphere is to be an informal one. At the same time, instructors must be careful not to allow questions to draw the lecture away from the logical sequence of thoughts that is necessary for an orderly presentation.

    Furthermore; the instructor must be honest and open with learners. While most instructors will more than likely be highly knowledgeable, that still does not mean that they know everything. An instructor who cannot answer a question should frankly admit it and immediately either offer to obtain an answer, if it is important, or assign one of the learners to research it.

4. There must be opportunities for slower learners (or those whose attention had strayed) to catch up with the class and for fast learners (or those who are more familiar with the subject) to find challenge in the learning process. Problems, case studies, simulations, and the activities suggested in role-plays can provide such opportunities if they are worked in small teams since the slower learners or those whose attention has lapsed feel freer to ask questions in the more comfortable environment of the small group. At the same time, those who understand the topic better can verify their command of it by explaining it to the others. Such explanations serve to further strengthen understanding and help to achieve full mastery since few things are as thoroughly understood as those that have been explained to other people who are free to question extensively.

5. There must be effective but polite discipline. This helps learners pay greater attention to the subject matter. Instructors who have difficulty maintaining orderly progress can find help in any of the books on conference leadership or classroom discipline.

It is obvious that a classroom that satisfies the guidelines above is one that also conforms with most of the principles discussed in this chapter. To follow them, however, requires a willingness to experiment with different ways of managing learning experiences and thoroughness in keeping the learning process in mind.

It is most important for instructors to feel comfortable when learners take an active role in the classroom. Much can be gained from allowing employees to take turns in leading the discussion of various case studies. Assignments of discussion leaders should be made at sessions prior to discussions so that learners can prepare themselves appropriately. Rotation of discussion leadership on team or class activities can be especially valuable if, as has been suggested, work-related examples and cases are used as foundations for the activities in the training sessions.

Summary

This chapter has covered the important Linking Element of how a manager can improve technical competence of employees and help them become better trained and more competent in their jobs. At this point, you may want to compare your notes from the beginning of this chapter with the thoughts expressed in the chapter. Do you feel that careful selection, good position management, and training and development based on the training cycle would be a good way to complete the box between the arrows on page 172? If you have not already listed them for this Linking Element, you might add to your box on that page analyzing learning needs through knowledge/skill profiles, setting learning goals through learning contracts, and identifying and overcoming obstacles to learning through analysis of blockages.

Chapter 10

Coordination, Cooperation, Rules, and Tangible Rewards

A manager who understands and uses a goals program to its maximum capability, who understands how to satisfy the psychological needs of staff members, and who considers development of people a major responsibility and acts accordingly will create a healthy climate for all employees. Such a climate allows staff members to enjoy their work and find self-motivation for achieving the objectives of the organizational unit.

The three linking elements discussed up to this point in the book require the most effort on the part of the manager, who must reconcile the contradictions currently existing between theory and practice or between the various aspects of existing theories. The three linking elements still to be discussed require less initiative on the part of the manager. But before they can be developed most fully, a manager must understand goals programs, psychological needs, and development needs so that actions can be avoided that would seriously injure the overall management program.

The remaining linking elements are:

1. The skills and actions necessary to align the organization's need for good coordination and the willingness of individuals to cooperate with any coordination procedures or with each other

2. The skills and actions necessary to align the rules of the organizational unit and the philosophy, morality, and personal behavior of the unit's members so that rules and behavior beneficial to the organization can contribute to the total climate

3. The skills and actions needed to align the tangible rewards an organization can offer with the desire of people for the satisfaction of tangible needs.

ACHIEVING IMPROVED COORDINATION AND COOPERATION

As the Linking Elements diagram in Figure 10.1 shows, the manager has two primary responsibilities in the area of coordination: setting up coordination procedures and making them work. It may be useful for you to think about the necessary skills and tasks which are required of a manager for the best alignment of the arrows in the diagram and to write them down before you read this segment of the chapter. This will give you a chance to compare your present thoughts on coordination with the ideas presented in the summary provided later on.

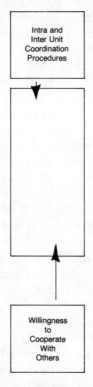

Figure 10.1. Segment of Linking Elements Diagram

An urgent project may require that several teams, units, departments, or what have you, complete their respective assignments on time and have them in the proper place in the form most useful for the next activity. This involves coordination procedures and illustrates the three elements of coordination: time, place, and form. An item presented in proper form but submitted to the wrong place may cause as much delay as an item submitted in the wrong form to the right place. Coordination therefore requires many skills. You have to schedule carefully yourself, and you have to see to it that others who participate in the creation of schedules are equally proficient and communicate them well.*

Good coordination procedures, however, also require cooperation from all your people, not only those concerned with scheduling. A somewhat extreme but obvious example illustrates this point. If you were to move a very heavy and tall object with the aid of just enough people to lift it, you would need the cooperation of every person to bring it across an obstruction such as a change in floor level. Coordination is, of course, necessary so people will all move in the same direction at the same time.

You therefore have to keep an ear carefully tuned to any indications that there may be problems with cooperation. Unhealthy friction between your team and other teams, and between the various member of the team is such a signal. Once you find evidence of a potentially troublesome conflict, you have to decide whether the conflict is healthy or not. It is not always easy to distinguish problems from healthy conflict. Competition is a form of conflict, yet it stimulates performance. Most would consider competition desirable, except when it becomes so intense that persons or teams obstruct one another's work rather than concentrating on perfecting their own activities. It has always been said that a griping army—or organization—is a healthy one (because there are outlets for airing dissatisfactions) and that real trouble exists only when there are no complaints. When you hear two people commiserate about delays from another section or department and about the problem these delays cause them, it is not easy to recognize whether you have overheard a gripe. Such gripes often resolve themselves. Sometimes they are merely the reflections of frustrations about conditions which the gripers accept as inevitable. It is im-

---

*Coordination procedures require proper goal setting, but they also require good scheduling. Scheduling, like financial analysis or EDP flowcharting or programming, involves specific technical knowledge and skills which a manager may need to function efficiently in certain situations. Since this book concentrates on the management of people, scheduling procedures such as Network diagrams (PERT and CPM), or Gantt charts are beyond its scope.

portant, however, to distinguish these minor complaints from the more serious indications of conflict with other people or other units that may lead to detrimental actions such as open or hidden refusals to cooperate.

Managers who wish to improve coordination have to work on their ability to distinguish between major and minor complaints. Along with this, they must develop the counseling skills that are needed to resolve serious conflict.

Most managers have not had training in counseling and therefore may be reluctant to start a private discussion with a staff member in an attempt to resolve a conflict. Some managers may step in too quickly—or speak too bluntly—and thereby possibly do more damage than good.

To acquire counseling skills adequate for the purposes of achieving coordination one does not need extensive training in psychology, only good communication skills and sensitivity to the feelings of others. Good communication depends on a number of factors, among them:

- Creating an open climate in which participants feel free to express themselves.
- Providing feedback (information on how you interpret the other person's statements or how you feel about them).
- Listening therapeutically (i.e., listening in a manner that helps the other person "get things off the chest" and thereby relieves burdensome feelings so that the discussion about a problem can proceed with fewer emotional interferences).
- Listening empathetically (i.e., listening with understanding for the other person's point of view). Empathetic listening shows the other person that there is a genuine desire to understand that person's point of view and therefore encourages full explanation. Empathy can be combined with a sympathetic attitude towards the other person's point of view but does not require it. One can be empathetic and wish to fully understand the other person without agreeing.
- Using concepts of transactional analysis to help control one's own emotions during discussion. Such concepts can provide greater insight into the psychology of communications.
- Using questions intelligently.

Creating an Open Communications Climate

The so-called Johari Window is pictured in Figure 10.2. The name of this diagram comes from its developers, Joseph Luft and Harry Ingham. The concepts embodied in the Johari Window can help improve those skills that lead to more open communications.

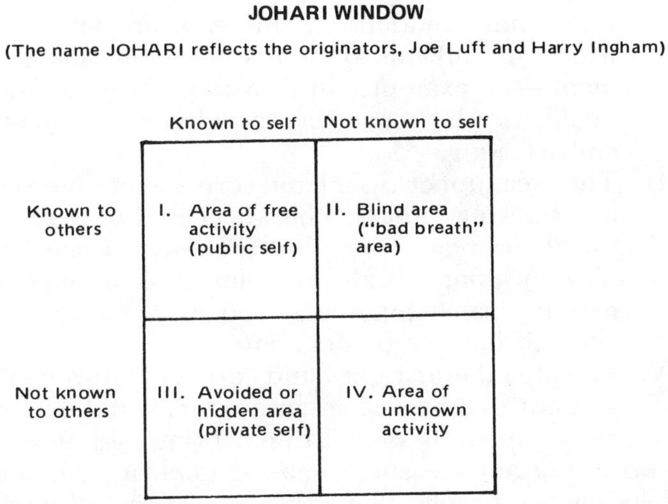

JOHARI WINDOW

(The name JOHARI reflects the originators, Joe Luft and Harry Ingham)

	Known to self	Not known to self
Known to others	I. Area of free activity (public self)	II. Blind area ("bad breath" area)
Not known to others	III. Avoided or hidden area (private self)	IV. Area of unknown activity

Figure 10.2. The Johari Window (From GROUP PROCESSES: AN INTRODUCTION TO GROUP DYNAMICS, by Joseph Luft. Mayfield Publishing Company. Copyright © 1963, 1970. Reprinted by permission; artwork courtesy NFPA.)

Figure 10.2 shows the four areas which are created if you consider that (a) there are some things that you know about yourself, and some things that you do not know about yourself; (b) there are things that other people know about you, and there are things that other people do not know. The four areas of the diagram in Figure 10.2 therefore are:

I. The area of free activity representing those subjects, topics, and characteristics known to you and to others. Since you usually know when one of your people is knowledgeable on a specific topic and the staff member likewise is aware of knowledge, then you can discuss the topic with the staff member freely. The same is true when both you and a staff member know that the staff member must learn about a particular subject. You can then talk openly about how he or she can learn that subject and how you can help.

II. The area (lower left-hand corner) known to you but not to others. For instance, John, a staff member, may know that he is unhappy with some of the assignments he has received from his manager but may feel that he would have difficulties with the manager if he told the manager about his unhappiness. He therefore keeps his feelings hidden. In this area are all the topics which are difficult to discuss in the existing environment—for example, information about fellow staff members which may be considered confidential or embarrassing.

III. The area (upper right hand corner) not known to you but known to others. This area could be described as the "bad breath" area, but it is not restricted to unpleasant things. It also contains pleasant ones. There may be many things that you may not know about yourself but that others know.

IV. The area (lower right-hand corner) known neither to you nor to others. This area is totally hidden and becomes apparent only if events bring new awareness.

Two important measures help to open up communications between two people. These are engaging in self-disclosure and providing feedback. How these measures affect the Johari window is shown in the diagrams in Figure 10.3.

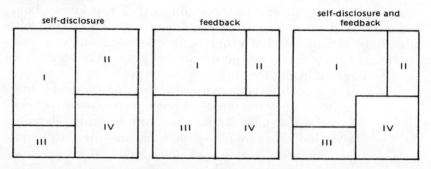

Figure 10.3. The Johari Window (From GROUP PROCESSES: AN INTRODUCTION TO GROUP DYNAMICS, by Joseph Luft. Mayfield Publishing Company. Copyright © 1963, 1970. Reprinted by permission; artwork courtesy NFPA.)

Self-Disclosure

Self-disclosure concerns talking about things that the other person does not know. If an employee is willing to disclose feelings or views about assignments, then these become part of the open area and can be discussed freely. Similarly, if the employee's manager provides feedback by pointing out that the employee needs these assignments to improve certain skills, then this, too, will help to open up a discussion and, at the same time, reduce or eliminate any tensions that may be building up.

Feedback can sometimes lead to self-disclosure. For example, an employee may not want to initiate a discussion and the manager may have to begin. The manager may want to find an appropriate moment to point out to the employee that he or she appears unhappy about something, which may lead the employee to respond with self-disclosure that he/she is indeed unhappy, thus opening up the possibility of freely discussing the dissatisfaction with assignments.

The three diagrams in Figure 10.3 show that self-disclosure and feedback used together bring the largest area of free activity that can be achieved. When both parties practice self disclosure and provide feedback, then discussion can come rapidly and effectively to a conclusion which will be as satisfactory to both sides as it can possibly be. But even if only one person consciously employs the communication techniques of self-disclosure and feedback, discussion will be more open than if neither party does.

Many managers are apprehensive about providing even limited self-disclosure because they are concerned that it may weaken their leadership position. Generally, this is not true. If a manager expects subordinates to speak openly of their own feelings, the manager also has to be prepared to share his or her own with them.

Providing Feedback

Providing feedback is not easy. If it is too abrupt or too blunt it will not achieve its purpose because it intimidates or hurts the other person. If it is too subtle it may be unclear and easily misunderstood.

Here are some useful rules on providing feedback:
1. Feedback should be as factual as possible. This means that it should be based on specific occurrences.

2. Feedback should be timely. It is not much good to say to somebody, "Three months ago you did such and such, and that was not the best way to go about this thing." Feedback should, if possible, be given immediately since then it will have more impact and more meaning to the person receiving it.

3. Feedback should concern only those things that are under the control of the other person. Telling a young man that he is not smart enough is not going to help him very much. On the other hand, suggesting that he study some specific subjects or specific chapters in a book or practice a specific way of doing something could be very helpful to him.

4. Feedback should be given calmly. Feedback given in an excited way is usually perceived as reprimand or criticism. In a discussion, criticism may put one of the parties on the defensive, thus making the person less willing to share thoughts or feelings.

Transactional Analysis

Another concept useful in counseling is transactional analysis. The term comes from the work of Eric Berne, the psychiatrist who wrote the book entitled *Games People Play.** Transactional analysis is a technique for analyzing human behavior and communications. It is an excellent way to see emotional involvement in the transmittal of messages. Transactional analysis says that within you there are three ego states which constantly vary in strength. These three ego states are:

- The parent ego state, which is made up of all the things that you have been taught by your parents, teachers, and others you have encountered in life. The parent is the righteous segment of your personality. It tells you to work hard, to stay pure, to follow the rules. The parent is usually stuffy, self-righteous, and has an answer for everything.
- The child ego state is the emotional, happy-go-lucky, rebellious part in you. It is almost the opposite of the parent. It rushes into things. It likes to play, to explore and create, to enjoy life, to be happy; but it also feels free to

---

*Eric Berne, *Games People Play: The Psychology of Human Relationships* (New York: Grove, 1964).

express anger and other emotions. The child in you is relatively weak and insecure, but it is also stubborn and often unreasonable.

- Finally, the adult ego state is the rational person, the factual part in you. The adult ego state makes decisions based on information it receives from the child and the parent and the world in general. The adult is logical, reasoning, helpful, understanding, responsive, and so on.

These three ego states are often depicted as in Figure 10.4. Though the adult state appears to be, and is, the more appropriate one for most work-related situations, to be "adult" at all times is not necessarily a desirable goal. A natural, open individual often displays the child, and even the parent, in his or her personality—because to be natural means to be one's self, and a complete self contains all three ego states.

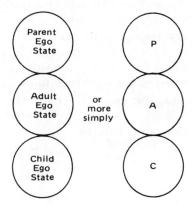

Figure 10.4. A Representation of Transactional Analysis Ego States (Artwork courtesy NFPA)

Transactional analysis starts by defining each communication between people as a transaction. If one person says hello to another person, that is a transaction. If the other person answers, that is another transaction. If the other person does not respond, that is also a transaction, though of an entirely different kind. The friendly greeting is a positive transaction; a refusal to return the greeting is a negative transaction.

Transactions have to start from some ego state. If at any one moment the parent ego state is dominant in you, then when you speak, it is the parent ego state that other people hear; or, if the child ego state is dominant at the moment, it is the child that is speaking when you say something.

Sets of transactions can come in three different ways: A set can be complementary or it can be crossed. There can also be a double set, with one set hidden.

Complementary Transactions

Complementary transactions occur when a message from an ego state of one person is responded to by a message from the ego state which it addressed in the other person. An example of this transaction is shown in Figure 10.5. It could depict a manager saying, jokingly, to someone who is struggling with a specific task: "Hey, why don't you stop playing with that thing and get started on the project you should be working on?" (Parent-Child statement [P-C]) The reply might be, "But that wouldn't be as much fun." (Child-Parent statement [C-P])

Complementary transactions are usually quite satisfying. They need not be between different ego states. "Come on, let's go out and have some fun. What do you say?" and "OK, that sounds super" are complementary Child-Child transactions, for instance. At work, the most effective transactions are complementary Adult-Adult ones, though there are appropriate times when it is desirable for the Child or the Parent to be dominant.

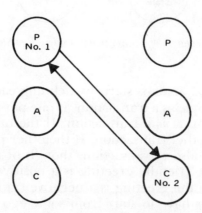

Figure 10.5. A Representation of a Complementary Transaction (Artwork courtesy NFPA)

Crossed Transactions

Crossed transactions are the result of an unexpected response made to a statement. Take, for example, the following exchange, represented by Figure 10.6.

> Manager: "What did you do with that report?" (Adult addressing adult)
>
> Staff member: "I gave it to you. Did you lose it?" (Parent addressing child)

It is obvious that a crossed transaction does not lead to easier and friendlier communications. At the extreme, this kind of transaction (Figure 10.7) could almost immediately lead to a heated exchange, as in the example below.

> Person A to Person B: "You are doing this all wrong. Let me show you how to do it." (Parent-Child)
>
> Person B to Person A: "When I need someone to show me how to do it, I'll call you. Otherwise, mind your own business." (Parent-Child)

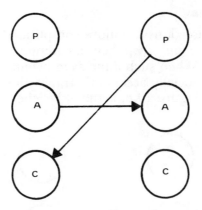

Figure 10.6. A Representation of a Crossed Transaction (Artwork courtesy NFPA)

Crossed transactions can occur easily because often either the child or parent ego state is dominant in a person. The manager who must get something done starts a conversation from the adult state and receives a reply from either the child or the parent in the other person. The result is a minor crossing of transactions; and if this is recognized, it is generally not difficult to switch to complementary transaction. Obviously, the most work can be done if complementary transactions are adult to adult because then the facts of the situation can be reviewed and the actions that should be taken can be discussed in a calm and factual way.

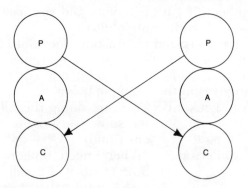

Figure 10.7. Another Type of Crossed Transaction

Hidden Transactions

Hidden transactions are more complicated than the other types. They have an unspoken meaning, somewhat like a double message. When such a message is sent, it is usually disguised behind a socially acceptable transaction. A well-known one, depicted in Figure 10.8, is the old cliche, "Would you like

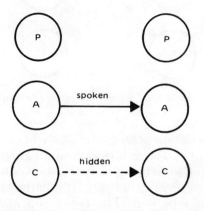

Figure 10.8. A Representation of a Hidden Transaction (Artwork courtesy NFPA)

to come up and see my etchings?" Obviously, the person is speaking out loud from the adult ego state. The purpose of the invitation, however, is not to see etchings. If no etchings exist, then it is really the child inviting the other person's child; and the response can be, "Yes, I would love to see your etchings, but let's have dinner first." Or it could be a cold, "No, thank you."

In the first example of a complementary transaction (Figure 10.5) there may also be a hidden meaning if the manager feels that the employee has taken too long to finish. The hidden meaning (Adult-Adult) might be, "When you have problems, please let me know so I can arrange for help, and that way we can stay on schedule."

Recognizing ego states and understanding transactions are the most important aspects of transactional analysis and can help you maintain calmness when another person is temporarily dominated by the child or parent. Remaining in the adult state is the more mature course of action, and the satisfaction of knowing this can help you to maintain your own equilibrium and thus help you to gradually bring the other person to the same adult ego state.

In addition to the ideas just discussed, there are three other ideas in transactional analysis that are useful to managers and deserve a brief discussion here. They are: (1) "life positions," (2) "strokes," and (3) "stamp collecting."

Life Positions

The four life positions come from Dr. Thomas A. Harris' book, *I'm O-K, You're O-K.** They are:

1. I'm O-K, you're not O-K. In a general way this is the position of the parent who has to tell the child what is right and what is wrong.
2. I'm not O-K, you are O-K. This characterizes the child who has not yet reached full maturity and recognizes it, or a person who feels a little guilty about what he or she is doing. This position, however, can also indicate a mental health problem that is more serious than just a temporary child ego state.
3. I'm not O-K, you're not O-K. This position is definitely one that is assumed by people who have moderate to serious mental health problems.

---

*Thomas A. Harris, I'M OK, YOU'RE OK (Boston: G. K. Hall and Co., 1974).

4. I'm O-K, you're O-K. This is the position which the adult person assumes. The adult views every individual as having both strengths and weaknesses but as being fundamentally sound. The I'm O-K, you're O-K position is that people have three ego states and that any of these ego states can be dominant at any moment but that in every person there is a strong adult. Everybody does, and should, enjoy the child state; from time to time they give in to the parent when it is appropriate; otherwise, they allow the adult to be in control.

Strokes

In every transaction there is a stroke. If what is said or done gives the other person a pleasant feeling, then the stroke is positive. If what happens gives a negative feeling, then it is negative. A friendly greeting is a positive stroke; an unfriendly greeting is a negative stroke. A failure to return a greeting is a negative stroke; unfair criticism is a negative stroke. Commendation or praise is a positive stroke. In general, those things discussed above as positive impulses in the section dealing with climate improvement strategies (see page 163) are positive strokes when they come from people or even when they come from the work. Strokes are, of course, very important for job satisfaction.

Stamp Collecting

Stamp collecting is based on strokes. In a relationship between two people, or possibly between a person and work, if the positive and negative strokes are balanced, then no stamps are collected. If, however, one person provides a series of positive strokes to the other person, that person is collecting positive stamps and sooner or later will cash them in—that is, respond to the other person in a pleasant manner. On the other hand, if one person collects many negative strokes from another person, sooner or later, some explosion will take place.

Empathetic and Therapeutic Listening

During effective counseling sessions the counselor listens a lot and says very little. Good counseling requires that the person being counseled be made to see clearly the advantages of looking at the situation from a different perspective. The person being counseled must have an opportunity to talk about feelings to someone who is willing to, and can, understand them, not to someone who is openly and visibly opposed to them or who wants to do a lot of talking.

Hence, good counselors must keep tight control over their own expressions or feelings, at least until the people they are counseling have fully expressed themselves. And, then, good questioning, with few direct statements, will usually be far more effective than "telling" the other person what to do. Positive or thoughtful listening is a skill that can be practiced.

The Use of Questions

Questions can be excellent tools in helping to achieve agreement on one issue when they are used properly and in moderation. Most managers who have attended seminars on nondirective counseling feel that they have greatly improved their ability to solve people problems just from the use of the nondirective questioning technique. They also find that as they apply the technique to the various situations they encounter they get to know a lot more about their people.

For obtaining information, three types of questions and statements are most useful: (1) open questions, (2) reflective questions and statements, and (3) directive questions. None of these questions can easily be answered with "yes" or "no" or other short replies. *Open* questions are intended to start the other person talking and generally begin with phrases like, "How do you feel about . . .?" "What do you think of . . .?"

Reflective questions and statements, on the other hand, merely repeat the last point which the other person has made without adding anything significant. They reflect what has been said in different words. These statements and questions are intended to encourage further explanation and very often, thereby, lead to new information. *Directive* questions are a third way to expand the area of agreement by leading to further explanation of a particular point. Directive questions could start with phrases like, "May I ask why you like . . .?" "To what extent would you agree . . .?"

There are many benefits which good questioning and listening skills can bring to the counselor, among them:
- More accurate knowledge about the other person's needs
- More information about the problem
- Greater opportunity to recognize potential areas of agreement

- Greater confidence that the situation is being handled correctly.

It is important to recognize the inappropriate use of questions. For example, there is a difference between the good use of questions and an interrogation. An uninterrupted series of good questions (including reflective statements which are often viewed as questions) from the counselor can turn into an interrogation. It is essential that this impression be avoided. One good way to prevent an interrogation is to allow enough time between questions for the other person to answer at length and also to restate or summarize, from time to time, in order to show that the other person's position has been understood. Thus, a steady stream of questions can be interrupted and more meaningful two-way communications can be established.

Manipulative questions are also inappropriate. Inexperienced managers sometimes use these in the erroneous belief that they are allowing their subordinates to express opinions freely. Take this exchange, for example:

Manager: Good morning, John. Do you know what time it is?

John: Yes, Bill, it's 9:15, and I am afraid I'm late.

Manager: That's correct John, and do you know how important it is to us that everyone comes in on time?

John: Yes I do.

Manager: Do you know, John, how often you have been late during the last week?

John: Yes, about four times.

Manager: What would happen if everyone were late that often?

John: I guess that would disturb the work quite badly.

Manager: Well, if you know that, why don't you do something about your own lateness?

Summary

To align the coordination requirements of the organization with the willingness of people to cooperate a manager should continue to develop technical skills such as scheduling, programming, and flow charting. These are needed to assure that good coordination procedures exist and are appropriately communicated, thus allowing people to work as smoothly with each other as they are willing to. A manager should also: (1)

Monitor procedures to assure that they are adequate for the required level of coordination. (2) Be alert to signs of cooperation problems. (3) Intervene when necessary, but not at the first sign of minor complaints. (4) Counsel, open up communications by applying techniques such as those described in the Johari window concept, by applying transactional analysis, or by using feedback and questions properly.

Before reading on, you might compare your thoughts at the beginning of this segment with this summary to see what new insights, if any, you have gained.

ALIGNING RULES AND PERSONAL BEHAVIOR CODES

Here again, before you read on, it might be worthwhile to give some thought to the skills and tasks which are part of the Linking Element on rules and write them in the appropriate box in Figure 10.9.

Figure 10.9. Segment of Linking Elements Diagram

A manager's responsibilities with respect to rules fall into five categories:

1. Communicating the rules and making sure that everyone clearly understands them
2. Assuring that all necessary rules are in writing but that the "rule book" does not grow to unwieldy proportions
3. Enforcing rules with compassion for the needs of individuals but at all times keeping in mind that every privilege granted can become a precedent other people may demand as a matter of right
4. Reviewing rules regularly to see whether the rules are right for the organizational unit, changing those which can be changed directly, and working towards changing those which require the agreement of higher levels of management.
5. Maintaining a balanced view on rule enforcement and on granting privileges during periods of organizational stress.

Communicating Rules

Rules exist so that every person in an organization knows what behaviors are detrimental to the organization and therefore cannot be permitted. If the purpose of rules is to tell people what they may not do, then the manager's first role is to assure that rules are appropriately communicated. If people are not aware of rules or do not understand them clearly, they cannot abide by them.

Written Rules

Some organizations attempt to achieve wide understanding of rules by issuing detailed rule books. This practice can create more problems than it solves. The more rules there are, the more likely it is that people will perceive the rule book as the complete set of requirements. Anything not spelled out in the rule book, therefore, is open to individual interpretation. People feel that they can do as they believe is right because if there were a rule, undoubtedly it would be in the rule book. Attempting to obtain control with tight sets of rules is, therefore, a futile effort, at least in part.

Having a small number of written rules is highly desirable for the most important issues since rules allow everyone to see what is basically reasonable or acceptable behavior. Beyond this basic set of rules what is needed is an open climate in which problems can be discussed and decisions made in fairness to all concerned. In this instance as in many others, the manager sets the climate by the way in which he or she expects adherence to the rules.

Enforcing Rules

As every manager knows, privileges once granted are difficult to take away. And if one person receives a privilege, others expect it. By granting privileges to one person but not others, a manager can quickly achieve the reputation of playing favorites or of discriminating against some people. Similarly, failure to enforce rules which a majority of the members of the team consider appropriate can bring a manager the reputation of softheartedness or, worse, lack of backbone and lack of ability to make difficult decisions. When employees are unionized, evenhandedness in enforcing rules becomes even more important because privileges extended by management in one department can be demanded by the union for all employees in other departments as well. Still, rules cannot be enforced rigidly since there are an infinite number of circumstances when exceptions should be considered to respond to the special needs of an individual.

When granting a privilege on a matter of great importance to an individual, it may be possible to make the privilege dependent on some sacrifice. This may allow the organization to offer the same privilege to others who request it, provided they are willing to make the same sacrifice.*

The maintenance of constructive discipline is therefore of prime importance and requires creative but consistent adherence to principles. Many managers do not realize how wide a range of choices is available to them for resolving rule problems or problems related to requests for privileges. Since requests primarily involve saying yes or no, it appears as though there is little to consider. In reality, however, a manager can say yes to a request in such a way that it clearly makes it very difficult or impossible for the person making the request to ask for another favor in the foreseeable future. Or, a manager can deny a request in such a way that the person requesting the privilege

---

*A more detailed discussion of the influence of rules and privileges on morale and discipline may be found in Appendix D.

feels that the manager has been very fair and has given the request the most favorable consideration but has had no choice but to deny it. The point is that before making the decision on a request, a manager can carefully analyze the choices that are available and make a decision accordingly, always keeping in mind that privileges once granted are very difficult to take away.

Regular Review of Rules

A manager who wishes to create the positive motivational climate which the Linking Elements foster must keep in mind that rules considered unreasonable or arbitrary do not enlist support. It is the manager's duty therefore to keep an eye on existing rules and to watch for those that may no longer be relevant. There are innumerable instances of unreasonable or obsolete rules either being ignored or enforced at high cost to an organization's chance to heighten the esprit de corps of its employees. The alert manager changes poor rules as soon as possible or works to have them changed. Appropriate participation of team members is essential in any rules changes. Such changes require a high degree of acceptance (See Chapter 6).

Rules in Times of Stress

One frequently recurring problem with respect to rules and the granting of privileges lies in the lack of flexibility with which managers adapt to changing situations. During times of stress even managers who normally are people oriented will frequently become more autocratic or less gentle in their relationships with their people. Managers commonly pass on to their people any pressures that they receive from above.

When production demands are high, rarely will managers be as free with granting privileges as they are when production demands are low. They may enforce rules more rigidly than at other times and in general pass along the tension that the work pressures impose on them. Usually this is just the reverse of the type of behavior that is needed for the situation. When there is considerable pressure in an organization because of the demands which quotas, schedules, or problems place on it, people usually sense the pressure. For managers to increase the pressure through their own behavior will often fluster people and lead to less careful work. If managers become less willing to grant privileges at the same time or become more inclined to demand strict adherence to existing rules, the work climate can rapidly deteriorate, and efforts in other areas to improve the motivational climate will be hurt.

When the work pressures are high or problems exist, managers should not change their normal behavior. (See Appendix D for a discussion of the Morale-Discipline Continuum.) The extent to which they grant privileges or insist on adherence to rules should remain consistent with their actions in the past. If anything, to the extent possible rules should be relaxed slightly to compensate for the extra pressure that the work schedules or work problems have created.

Summary

Several things have to be done in order to align organization rules with the behavior of staff members:

1. Rules must be clearly communicated.
2. Written rule books must be limited in size in order not to be self-defeating.
3. Rules must be enforced to avoid precedents, but enforced with compassion in special situations.
4. Rules must be reviewed regularly to assure that they are appropriate to changing situations.
5. Rules that are no longer appropriate should be changed as quickly as possible.
6. Team members should have as much of a voice as possible in deciding on rule changes.
7. During times of stress, enforcement of rules and granting of privileges require even more careful thought to avoid damage to the motivational climate.

Stop here for a moment, if you wish, to compare your thoughts at the beginning of this section with this summary. Did you gain any new insights? Did the section help organize the subject better for you?

SATISFYING TANGIBLE NEEDS OF EMPLOYEES

The final linking element shown in the Linking Elements diagram concerns tangible rewards. As has previously been discussed, these rewards include not only salary, bonuses, and incentive payments but also fringe benefits, which do so much to add to the tangible feeling of safety and security, and promotions, which have wider implications.

Most managers have very little opportunity to influence the extent to which their organization satisfies some of the tangible needs of employees and subordinate managers. Decisions about overall pay and benefit levels are usually made only at the highest level.

There are basically three ways in which a manager can help to support the climate that is created through the other linking elements. These are

1. Administering salaries, commissions, bonuses, and incentives equitably
2. Obtaining maximum advantage from the fringes that are available, and
3. Helping employees reach the highest income level of which they are capable and attain more rewarding positions through appropriate career guidance and promotion management.

The linking element dealing with tangible rewards is very important even though, as Herzberg notes, most tangible rewards are hygiene factors. Tangible rewards are likely to be dissatisfying when they are inadequate. However, when they are adequate they are rarely satisfying or stimulating. People work harder when they know they are going to get an increase, but that usually does not mean that the pay raise has given them a higher level of motivation. Several factors contribute to their higher enthusiasm for their work. If a merit increase is involved, the recognition it brings frequently acts as a temporary motivator. Even if the reward is more of a routine adjustment, the anticipation can reflect favorably on performance. More importantly, the promise of a raise tied to a specific performance improvement can exert a strong influence on most people. During the time that people are being observed to determine whether or not they will receive the increase, work performance usually is superior to the normal level. Shortly after they have received the increase, however, there often is a gradual return to old ways.

What is true of salary is even more applicable to fringe benefits. A highly adequate fringe package rarely stimulates people to work harder or better or pay more serious attention to important aspects of their work. On the other hand, the failure of an organization to provide adequate fringes does have a negative impact that helps people justify to themselves why they don't care, why they don't do their work the way they themselves are sometimes aware it should be done. Because pay and fringe benefits do not affect motivation directly, the manager's work in administration of pay and fringe benefits involves a rather passive role. The opportunities in career guidance and promotion management are more extensive.

Before reading on, give some thought to the skills and tasks which align the arrows in Figure 10.10.

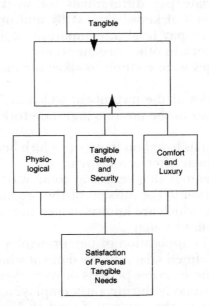

Figure 10.10. Segment of Linking Elements Diagram

Administration of Salaries and Other Payments

The functions of managers, except those who determine salary structure, lie in three areas: pay administration, administration of fringes, and promotion management. Most managers have tightly prescribed rules governing the increases or bonuses they can pay. Very often their task mainly concerns distributing a specific allowance among staff members in an equitable way which gives due consideration to merit, longevity, and the potentially unfavorable impact of increases that are considered to be inadequate. So that the distribution of pay raises has as much positive effect as possible, a manager should be articulate in explaining the reasons for the size of the increase to each staff member. This requires an understanding of the principles of pay administration.

Pay administration demands balancing the following considerations, some of which clearly contradict each other.

- Pay increases which reflect the performance record of the individual
- Equal pay for equal work
- Appropriate pay differentials for work requiring different levels of knowledge, skills, and physical exertion
- Reasonable pay level in comparison with pay levels for similar work in other organizations
- Pay ranges wide enough to allow for differentials based on merit
- Capabilities of the incumbent which are beyond the requirements of the position and therefore not given great weight
- Differentials based on longevity which become very small or disappear after several years
- Total earnings that reflect in some way the individual's contribution to the mission of the organization
- Pay scales which are known to members of the organization and not hidden
- Fairness in application of pay principles
- Clearly defined salary review dates at which increases are given (These review periods or increments should occur more frequently during early employment).

In addition to the conflicts found in the foregoing list, there are many problems of definition. For example,

1. What are factors involved in aligning compensation to performance evaluations (see Chapter 7).
2. When is work equal? While it is possible to rank positions in a general way and various systems exist for doing so, there is little that is factually comparable in the criteria which the ranking systems use. For instance, how can one make a factual comparison between the value of costly decisions required in one position and the value of extensive travel required in another.
3. Inasmuch as it is so difficult to establish when work is equal, how can pay differences be established factually for different kinds of work?
4. Because of the uniqueness of most jobs, pay differentials in one organization are difficult to compare in all classifications with those in other organizations.
5. Pay ranges wide enough to allow for differentials based on merit are also difficult to set up so that they satisfy

everyone because if they are too wide, a person in a "lower" job (one that requires less knowledge/skill and/ or physical exertion) might earn considerably more than somebody in a much higher job who is either relatively new or who is not performing as well.

It is usually quite difficult to determine exactly how well a person is performing. In most organizations managers therefore try to encourage their people to do better work by giving them pay increases until they come close to the top of the range. Only then do managers really take the difficult step of refusing the merit increment to people whose work is only average or below average.

As a result, people who are neither performing well nor have highly demanding positions often earn more if they stay with an organization a long time than do competent people in more qualified positions who are there a shorter period of time.

6. Wide pay ranges are in conflict with the principle that differentials based on longevity should become very small or disappear after several years.

For all these reasons, many organizations do not provide wide pay ranges at each level, allow even people who are doing only an average job to come close to the top of the pay ranges, and use the opportunity for promotion as the incentive to performance on the job.

Some organizations, in addition to salary increases, offer at least one other form of payment such as bonuses, commissions, or incentive payments. Where these exist, managers have a somewhat greater opportunity to satisfy the conflicting requirements listed above. Nevertheless, the ability of organizations to provide high incomes to their people is greatly limited. This is not as tragic as it may seem. High pay is not necessarily an impetus to serious effort, and it may not contribute to a motivational climate at all. Exceptionally great effort, for instance, is rarely an outstanding characteristic of sales representatives who receive large incomes. Many become what others in the organization call fat cats, and resist new policies which either require new learning or additional effort during the initial period.

Economists have always spoken of the "backward bending supply curve of labor," which means that at substantially higher levels of pay employees will often work fewer hours and turn out less work than at more moderate levels. Though this is far from universally true, there is a certain amount of validity to the principle. The highly paid employee whose physiological and security needs are met often will turn his or her attention to gaining greater satisfaction of those aspects of psychological needs which may not be satisfied on the job.

The unfortunate conclusion from this is that organizations gain very little from paying exceptionally high wages far in excess of those being paid in other organizations for similar work, even if they are financially in a position to do so. The well-managed organization, for this reason and for purely economic ones, does not attempt to set wage scales much higher than those offered by other organizations. It is, however, wise to provide incomes somewhat higher than those of other organizations in the area or industry to give an organization the best pick from the available people.

Of course, no employees should be expected to subsidize an organization by accepting below-average wages. It is clear that a motivated employee will expect to receive a fair salary or wage. If the employee perceives that the financial rewards offered by the organization are less than those offered elsewhere, the motivated, competent employee will leave to perform the same work elsewhere. It is only the less motivated employees who will stay to work for what others consider to be inadequate financial rewards.

On the other hand, high incomes will not hold those capable people to whom the work does not appeal. Though they are well paid, they will leave to find satisfying work even if they must take a cut in their pay.

The Manager's Role

The competent manager will make certain that his or her unit has the budget to pay the people in the unit as well as, or somewhat better than, other units. The next higher level manager, therefore, has the responsibility to see to it that salary increases of different units are compared carefully.

Not keeping salaries more secret than is absolutely essential can help prevent the development of unnecessary dissatisfaction since pay levels can be discussed more openly when they are not treated as overly confidential (see Johari Window, page 221).

People rarely perceive the salary they are being paid relative to other people in the same perspective as their manager. If managers can openly discuss with their respective subordinates why salaries are what they are, then the managers can satisfy their staff members as well as can possibly be done. This means that a manager should be prepared to justify income differentials for different people on the basis of the salary principles and individual performance whenever challenged to do so. At the same time, however, every manager should strive to establish a climate of trust and confidence so that each staff member is certain that the manager is indeed doing his or her best to provide the greatest tangible benefits that are available.

A healthy climate requires absolute fairness in income decisions, both for people who have a tendency to exert great pressure on the manager for higher salary increases and for those who are reticent to discuss salary and who feel that it is the manager's job to do the best that he or she can do. This is difficult to do with competent employees who are outspoken and to whom the tangible benefits of the job are very important. In an earlier chapter, Maslow's Hierarchy of Needs was discussed, as well as the different weight that people give to comfort and luxury as sources of satisfaction for esteem and social needs. Individuals who gain most of their satisfaction from the ownership of things, if they are highly articulate, are likely to be much more demanding than those people to whom the material things are of lesser importance. This is true even though money may be equally important to the latter group because of security needs. No matter how money is viewed, fair treatment is still important for self-esteem and is perhaps the most essential element in good pay administration.

Good communication on salary matters is also important for a healthy climate. It is necessary for staff members to understand the difficulty in setting salaries equally and fairly. Employees often say to the manager, "Don't tell me what others are earning or how they are paid. Let's discuss me in relation to my job and what I contribute." But the same employees are not loath to mention the salaries of others when they feel they are being treated unfairly.

To obtain the greatest positive impact on the motivational climate from salary decisions, managers have to communicate very clearly the reason for increases by assuring employees that careful comparisons are being made with other organizations, with other organizational units, and between people within the units. It is necessary to do this regularly because staff members may not be aware of how much effort goes into these decisions.

Such discussions at salary reviews can dispel the common belief that pay is based much more on the personal preferences of the manager than it really is.

Administration of Fringe Benefits

In administering the fringe-benefit program within their respective areas of responsibility, managers have three primary principles to keep in mind. Fringes will be least likely to lead to dissatisfaction if the manager:

1. Makes sure that employees clearly understand their fringe benefits
2. Shows a sincere interest in helping employees gain all the fringe benefits to which they are entitled
3. Devotes the necessary effort, when required, to help overcome any problems that staff members encounter in promptly obtaining any of the fringe benefits due them.

Managers who can influence fringe-benefit packages must see to it that benefits are equivalent to those offered by other organizations in the community and in the industry. Some fringes concern time off such as vacations and holidays. Here the manager's role is an obvious one—to plan and arrange schedules in such a way that they will satisfy the special needs of staff members as much as the demands of the job permit.

Career Guidance and Promotion Management

Career guidance and promotion management is linked to the manager's responsibilities for satisfying both the tangible and psychological needs of employees. In one sense, the manager's objective is to help the employee gain the greatest possible satisfaction from work and career and at the same time gain greater financial rewards.

Among the manager's responsibilities in career guidance are the following:

1. Providing help in defining possible career paths
2. Making realistic evaluations of the strengths and weaknesses of the individual in relation to positions along these paths
3. Helping the individual set developmental goals that are challenging, but still achievable in light of the individual's capabilities
4. Providing fair performance evaluations so that the individual will receive proper consideration in the selection

of the candidates for a position that has either opened up or that is otherwise available
5. Adhering to an openly communicated system that helps to assure fairness in selection of individuals for promotion.

Defining Possible Career Paths

The manager must do the very best that can possibly be done to help staff members reach those positions to which they aspire and in which the manager believes they can perform effectively. This means shooting for a moving target, of course, since people often change their views on the work they would like to do. Furthermore, to predict what someone else will be able to do is a treacherous task and must be approached with great care.

There are many ways to help people find out what type of work they might enjoy. Yet it is unwise to discuss directly with an individual preparation for positions that are substantially above the level currently occupied. If someone wants to be president of the organization, the manager could discuss a series of positions in the management hierarchy and then point out specific steps that would help an individual prepare for one or several of the positions which would most likely be next in the career path.

One obstacle to open discussion and sincere career guidance from managers is the possibility that younger and highly educated, possibly more competent subordinates might replace them when they are adequately trained. Managers who think of subordinates as competition are likely to abort their own chances for advancement. For competent managers it is more important to have appropriate and adequate back up than it is to be without competition. The manager who has someone else available to fill his or her place is more likely to be selected for promotion when an opportunity arises than an equally competent manager without a well-trained subordinate capable of taking over.

Detailed Analysis

Detailed analysis of the strengths and the weaknesses of a subordinate is a normal and logical part of the annual or semi-annual performance appraisal. To conduct the appraisal in conjunction with the performance evaluation can be very useful because it can add a highly positive aspect to evaluation.

At the same time, it is important to make clear the distinction between the performance evaluation and the assessment of strengths and deficiencies relative to several positions on the possible career path.

Performance evaluation applies performance criteria (see discussion of the eight criteria, pages 86–92) to the work of the past year or half-year. Analysis of strengths and weaknesses uses knowledge/skill profiles (see Chapter 9) as the major tool for developing greater competence. For career purposes, however, the knowledge/skill lists are based on the requirements of future positions rather than on requirements of the present one.

Actual performance has a great deal to do with the positions for which an individual can be considered. During performance evaluations this is always stressed. Besides performance, strengths and weaknesses in knowledge and skills determine the extent to which an individual is capable of assuming the responsibilities of a desired position. It is a manager's responsibility to make certain that every subordinate is clearly aware of how performance and knowledge and skills interrelate and how they jointly prepare one for a promotion.

Helping to Choose Realistic Career Goals

Some people, although competent, do not believe that they have the qualifications to rise several levels in an organization. Others, on the other hand, think that within a few years they should seriously be considered for very high positions. In both cases the manager can do much to support individual development. The more timid people need support and encouragement in order to gain greater confidence in themselves and in their capabilities. People who have excessively high expectations require counseling to understand what they can realistically expect and what would be meaningful for them. Without discouraging such people, a manager can lay out the possible steps in the career path and thus bring a more factual view of the situation. A detailed analysis of positions immediately within reach can then help subordinates to plan meaningfully for the next achievable career step or possibly for several such steps.

Setting goals to eliminate any knowledge/skill deficiencies for one or several of the possible next positions on the career path requires the same outlook on goal setting as was discussed in Chapters 5 through 7 and demands attention to seven out of the eight potential problems in EQUIFAPPO. The eighth problem, assuring that developmental goals are part of the goals program, would, of course, not be involved.

Some decisions are easier, however. For instance, with respect to involvement on the part of the manager and participation by the subordinate, the choices are far fewer. Since the goals which are involved are the individual's and not the organization's, it is obvious that the primary responsibility for making decisions lies with the subordinate. These are goals which very often should permit the manager to provide advice and guidance but also to say to subordinates that they can and possibly should set goals any way they wish and support will still be forthcoming no matter what the goals may be, that is, within the range of job-related goals possible.

Since this was discussed in great detail in Chapter 7, there is little that needs to be added here. The importance of fair evaluations in satisfying the aspirations of individuals should be noted, though. Since people generally seek to satisfy their own tangible and psychological needs rather than organization goals, commitment to organization goals can be engendered only by serious management effort to help employees achieve their own goals.

The direction which an organization takes may, to some extent, help an individual achieve his or her goals; but, then again, it may not. It is therefore not fully accurate to speak of aligning organizational goals and people goals because they do not fall in the same areas. An organization has an obligation to help people achieve their goals, and people have an obligation to help the organization achieve its goals. Clear awareness of this mutual responsibility helps to foster achievement.

Fair Performance Evaluation

It is important for managers to remember that fairness is a *subjective concept*. No matter how fair a manager actually is in evaluating performance, unless the people being evaluated understand his or her criteria, they may not put credence in the evaluation. People have to be aware of the way the manager measures performance. This requires time and effort in communications; fortunately, it is the same time and effort required to review goals and to make performance evaluations.

Letting people evaluate themselves on the basis of factual data jointly collected over a long period of time can be an excellent means of achieving good communications. Employees will accept evaluations even if they are not as favorable as they wish them to be if the evaluations are properly supported with data.

Furthermore, fair evaluations, when they are less than laudatory, can be used to set goals and develop programs to achieve better evaluations in the future. If this is done, then the entire system takes on a far more positive aspect than it would have otherwise.

What we have discussed so far in this section provides compelling reasons for frequent goal reviews and performance evaluations in addition to the normal annual or semi-annual reviews. Semi-annual performance evaluations have the enormous advantage of providing a dry-run evaluation in which subordinates gain a clearer picture of how their performance is seen and what their strengths and weaknesses are. It allows them time to remedy any deficiencies that exist and to show how seriously they want to eliminate or reduce them.

Fair Selection Systems

Job selection systems must be clearly communicated and give an equal chance to all who are qualified. Discussion of such systems are beyond the scope of this book. It is sufficient to say here that most good systems provide for posting job openings and for factual discussion of why specific individuals either were not considered or not selected.

Summary

Among the skills which a manager must exercise in aligning the tangible needs of people with the rewards which an organizational unit can provide are:

1. Distributing increases fairly and equitably, in keeping with salary administration principles, budget, the relationship of salaries and jobs, and especially the performance record
2. Distributing incentives and bonuses available to the organizational unit fairly and equitably, on the basis of contributions to the unit's performance
3. Obtaining the greatest benefits for the staff members from available fringes
4. Providing career guidance and help in career development
5. Selecting candidates for promotions fairly

6. Maintaining open communications to assure that members of the unit can express concerns and dissatisfactions so that they become aware of the realities of the situation and to develop or maintain confidence that the manager is doing the best that the environment permits.

Stop here for a moment to compare what you have written in the blank Linking Elements boxes placed at the beginning of this section of the chapter with this summary. If you think of additional skills and tasks, add them now. It is hoped that this summary and the discussion that preceded it will have helped you to organize your thinking about the kinds of skills and actions necessary to bring about the best possible alignments.

CONCLUSION: LINKS BETWEEN LINKING ELEMENTS

The discussion of the Linking Elements covering coordination, rules, and tangible rewards brings to a close the description of the Linking Elements concept. The remaining chapter in the book contains case studies involving the Linking Elements and practical suggestions on how the Linking Elements concept can be used for diagnosing problem areas and developing solutions. It also discusses, to a limited extent, how the concept can be used to ferret out opportunities for the organizational unit and what steps are needed to take advantage of them.

Before closing this chapter it would be beneficial to discuss the interrelationships of the Linking Elements. As was pointed out previously, the Linking Elements support each other in creating a climate in which people can find motivation not only to do better work but also to prepare themselves for greater achievement in the future. Most of the "linkages" between the Linking Elements are fairly obvious and do not require elaboration. A brief review of some might, however, be useful here.

Goals/Performance Standards and Coordination/Cooperation

1. Goals reviews provide considerable information about where coordination problems may exist.
2. When working to eliminate coordination/cooperation problems, goals may have to be set if important matters are involved.
3. Goals can be useful in the establishment of improved coordination procedures.

4. Self-development goals for staff members (in the areas of scheduling, planning, organizing, and coordinating) may have to be set to improve unit performance and cooperation.
5. Counseling skills are a necessary prerequisite for improvement.

Goals/Performance Standards and Rules

1. Goal reviews can provide information about rules that are, or are becoming, inappropriate.
2. Goals can be set pertaining to the way a staff member adheres to rules.
3. Goals can be set for changing rules that are no longer appropriate.

Goals/Performance Standards and Technical Competence

1. Goal reviews provide information about developmental needs of subordinates.
2. Performance evaluations also provide such information.
3. Goals should be set to eliminate deficiencies.

Goals/Performance Standards and Satisfaction of Tangible Needs

1. Career goals can lead to satisfying tangible needs.
2. Guidance in setting career goals occurs during goal reviews and performance evaluation.
3. Competent goal setting on the part of staff members can lead to greater respect by superiors and thus help with the achievement of career plans.

Goals/Performance Standards and Psychological Needs

1. In joint goal setting the subordinate, whether a line employee or a manager, has an opportunity to influence the shape of the work.
2. Through effective goal setting the subordinate gains information about what occurs in the organization.
3. The open communications which comes from meaningful joint goal setting leads to a much more open working climate in all areas.
4. Effective goal setting and performance evaluation provide several levels of meaningful factual feedback on performance.
5. When goal setting is done properly, the subordinate knows that superiors are aware of his or her contributions to the organization.

6. In goal setting the subordinate receives considerable guidance with career plans for personal development.
7. With proper goal setting, performance appraisals are factual and fair, and subordinates are not held responsible for matters over which they have little control.

Chapter 11

Applying Linking Elements: Problem Diagnosis, Opportunity Identification, and Performance Improvement

In previous chapters the Linking Elements concept has been described. As you can see, it is a rather comprehensive framework which sets management tasks and skills into perspective and thus provides a guide for achieving superior performance in an organizational unit.

IMPLICATIONS OF THE LINKING ELEMENTS CONCEPT FOR THE INDIVIDUAL

So far discussion has concerned the aligning of the characteristics and needs of your employees with those of your organizational unit. There is, of course, another side to the Linking Elements diagram, and that is the side that emerges when you consider yourself as an individual in the organizational unit headed by your boss. When viewed from this perspective, the Linking Elements concept describes the obligations which you as an individual have toward your boss and your organizational unit. A thorough understanding of this concept can therefore serve as a basic guide to the improvement of personal competence.

Most people do not give enough thought to determine what they could do to improve their own competence and their present performance. They seldom question their goals or assess their strengths and weaknesses realistically. They rarely inquire what work will provide them with greater satisfaction; and they do not, therefore, prepare themselves deliberately, in a planned program, for that work. Yet, there is probably very little that does as much to distinguish a highly competent manager or employee from all others as regular self-assessments. The person who steps back regularly from the demands of the daily tasks to achieve new perspective on the work he or she is doing is indeed unusual. To look for potential problems and also for opportunities that are not being considered because of the pressures of daily operations is not an easy task, nor is it one that rings a bell when it is neglected. But it is one of the potentially most rewarding tasks if it is done on some regular—even if infrequent—schedule.

The management tasks and the skills which lead to greater success for an organizational unit also can lead to greater success for the individual who understands them and knows how to apply them. A factual review of strengths and weaknesses and of personal work preferences can be used to search out the developmental activities most suitable for the individual. Such reviews, then, are crucial for effective career management and performance improvement in the organizational unit as well.

ORGANIZATIONAL USES OF THE LINKING ELEMENTS CONCEPT

The Linking Elements concept can be used for two purposes in addition to the primary one of management skill development. Once it is understood, it can serve (1) as a diagnostic tool to help ferret out problem areas in an organization and to identify opportunities for greater achievement and (2) as a guide for developing programs which will help improve performance.

The Linking Elements Concept as a Diagnostic Tool

As a diagnostic tool the Linking Elements concept can help identify problems and opportunities in the small team that reports directly to you. If you are at a high level in your organization, it can also help you to quickly identify the real sources of problems at lower levels, even if some are several levels removed from your position.

Diagnosing Problems and Identifying Opportunities in a Small Organizational Unit

From time to time it is worthwhile to review the actual diagram of the Linking Elements and, proceeding from left to right, to compare the way you work with your team of direct subordinates with the approaches described in this book.

Some of the questions you might ask in this comparison are listed below. They are by no means exhaustive, nor are they necessarily the specific questions that you would ask when you conduct your review. They are, however, representative of the kind of inquiries that can identify problems and opportunities.

SAMPLE QUESTIONS FOR DIAGNOSIS

1. How satisfactorily does our goals program operate?
   a. To what extent are our planning and goal setting processes and performance standards integrated to support each other?
   b. What about each of the segments in EQIFAPPO? How thoroughly is each considered by managers and supervisors in their work with their people?
      —Are we setting too many goals or too few with any individual?
      —Are our goals realistic yet challenging, and are the goals statements written so that they communicate clearly? Do we find that we disagree more often than we think we should about what our goal statements mean?
      —Do we make certain that at all times there is at least one developmental goal as part of the goals system?
      —Do our goals concern only problems, or are there goals to take advantage of existing opportunities or to define possible opportunities?
      —Are we sometimes too deeply involved with the way our subordinates work to achieve their goals? Do we delegate properly?
      —Do we conduct goals reviews frequently enough so that we have good communications with each of the people reporting to us? Do we maintain adequate records on each goals review so that we are developing a data base we can use to check our decisions and so that we develop a sound basis for performance reviews?
      —Do we adequately define our subordinates' responsibilities for them, and spell out our own too? Are we making use of the criteria for establishing responsibilities discussed in this book?
      —Do we make use of the full range of leadership styles available to us from tightly controlling to allowing full freedom of decision making to our subordinates? Do our subordinates perceive our leadership style the same as we do? Do we discuss leadership style with them from time to time?

—Do we hold at least one performance evaluation annually with each subordinate at which we review the goal
review sessions? Do we make it clear that we consider
the major outcome of the performance review to be a
set of developmental goals for our subordinates?

—Are subordinates given the opportunity to evaluate
themselves and to obtain a fair hearing when these
evaluations differ from ours?

—When we hold two performance appraisals annually,
do we provide an opportunity for improvement during the second period and give credit for it accordingly?

c. Do all members of the team understand the responsibilities which goal setting with its problems and opportunities (as embodied in the acronym EQIFAPPO) places on
them?

2. How are our coordination procedures working, and to what
extent are we getting cooperation from team members?

a. To what extent is our scheduling adequate?

b. Do people more frequently than necessary work at cross
purposes unintentionally?

c. Are there any indications of poor cooperation? When it
last appeared that there was a problem with cooperation,
did we have one or more open discussions with the
people involved and were we satisfied with our counseling skills?

d. Do all members of the team understand the concepts embodied in the Johari window and transactional analysis
concepts? Are they improving their counseling skills?

3. How well do the rules of our organizational unit suit our
needs? How carefully are they being followed?

a. What rules cause problems? What rules are not followed?

b. To what rules must we frequently grant special privileges
or exceptions?

c. Should rules which frequently require exceptions or
which are ignored be changed?

d. Do we communicate all rules clearly?

e. Are rules enforced consistently in each subunit of our
organizational unit?

f. Are we tougher on rules and privileges when we are under pressure?

g. Do all members of the team understand the Linking Elements tasks and skills required of supervisors and managers?

4. To what extent is the technical competence of our team members adequate for their current positions and for the positions next on their respective career paths?

   a. How satisfactory are our selection procedures?

   b. Do we evaluate the mix of people and jobs from time to time?

   c. Do we use goals reviews and performance evaluations from time to time to analyze knowledge/skill strengths and weaknesses?

   d. Do weaknesses, once identified, become the basis for developmental goals?

   e. Are analyses of knowledge/skill strengths and weaknesses conducted in such a way that it is clear that they are not performance evaluations? Are subordinates aware that these reviews are only for the purpose of helping them develop greater competence?

   f. Is it clear to everyone that managerial skills constitute a special technical skill and that managers must know how to manage as well as how to do their particular job?

   g. Are all members of the team aware of the responsibilities which the linking element on aligning technical competence places upon them?

5. How well does our organizational unit satisfy the tangible needs of its members? What, if anything, can the management team do to increase the satisfaction which the members of the team obtain from their compensation and other tangible rewards?

   a. Is the package of salaries (or wages), bonuses, incentives, and other payments in keeping with pay administration principles?

      —Are there ways to balance these principles to obtain greater satisfaction for staff members?

      —If the answer is *yes*, have plans been developed to gradually bring better balance?

   b. Are fringe benefits appropriate in light of conditions in the geographic area and in the industry? If not, what could we do to make them more adequate?

   c. Are pay-administration matters handled fairly and equitably, and is there an appeals procedure if someone feels unfairly treated?

    d. Do all team members understand the criteria upon which size of increases, bonuses, and other rewards are based?

    e. Do all members of the team clearly understand the responsibilities which the Linking Element on tangible rewards places on them?

6. Are we doing everything we can do to help members of the team and subordinates gain the highest possible level of job satisfaction?

    a. Do we have an approach to recognition of employee performance that involves all members of the team and uses many sources for providing positive impulses?

    b. Are we actively searching for ways to provide recognition for team members?

    c. Do we use goal review sessions and performance appraisals to help team members and employees gradually define what type of work would give them higher levels of satisfaction?

    d. Do we encourage social interaction between team members on the job?

As noted at the beginning of this chapter, this list of questions is by no means exhaustive, nor is it the only way a diagnostic analysis can be made. Nevertheless, asking questions such as these on some fairly regular schedule (for example, once every six months or once a year), either at a management meeting or by yourself, can undoubtedly lead to many ideas that are worth considering. It also can help to establish priorities on some of the on-going programs as well as to uncover new work needs.

Diagnosing Problems and Identifying Opportunities in the Large Organization

The discussion above deals primarily with small organizational units. Even in large organizations, top-level executives, as a group, form a "small organizational unit." When there are many levels below the top executive level, however, diagnosis of performance problems cannot be made only as suggested above. In addition to asking pertinent questions, responsible managers must make regular appraisals of the way the lower level organizational units approach their tasks and opportunities.

The high-level managers who sit astride a multi-level hierarchy usually cannot ask questions directly at substantially lower levels. But high-level managers can seek out opportunities to speak to people at lower levels and question them, diplomatically, of course, concerning the way goals are set and how the Linking Elements are approached at their levels.

The questions that are applicable to the small team are equally applicable when several levels are skipped by a high-level manager. Since not many questions can be asked before it appears that a high-level manager has lost confidence in a mid-level manager, answers have to be found through observation. Records of goal review sessions, evidence of recognition activities, indications of personal involvement by managers in the development process of the subordinates are all clear signs of the extent to which the Linking Elements concept is being applied practically and effectively.

To avoid the danger of undermining the authority and prestige of other managers, high-level managers have to rely on approaches such as the following for obtaining the data necessary to lead the entire organization toward higher levels of competence.

1. They can appoint an organizational audit committee whose members either already understand and can use the Linking Elements concept or who would be taught how to use the concept as a diagnostic tool. The committee could regularly audit organizational units.

2. They can establish monitors in every organizational unit of significant size to keep track of knowledge and skill needs for management with Linking Elements. One person can be assigned the full-time or part-time job of analyzing the data from all departments and providing a broad picture of organization needs. Monitors should have the opportunity to exchange ideas regularly so that they can coordinate their activities between the various components of the large organization.

To be really effective such audit committees, task forces, or monitors need access to the highest level in each division or department. Furthermore, they should be required to file regular, documented reports with top management on an annual or semiannual basis.

High-level executives can promote the use of the Linking Elements philosophy in the organization through personal involvement. But they must do more than pay lipservice to the concept, especially the principle that goal reviews and performance evaluations will not have detrimental effects for anyone.

They must provide evidence through personal actions that such reviews can only lead to better training and development and to decisions which bring higher levels of job satisfaction.

CASE STUDIES

The balance of this chapter is devoted to four case studies that offer some limited examples of practical applications of the Linking Elements concept. The four cases are described in the next section. The final section contain analyses of the cases and provides suggested approaches. In view of the limited scope of this chapter, only very brief descriptions have been provided. Similarly, the suggested approaches concern themselves only with major steps that can be taken.

Case 1: Establishing a Planning Program

A corporation operating several department stores employs approximately 4,000 people. Its management has decided to institute a comprehensive planning program in order to gain greater control over its destiny. It also hopes to reduce the number of unexpected crash programs which are frequently initiated to overcome unexpected problems. The president of the corporation feels that many of these problems could have been predicted and that good planning will reduce costly emergency programs.

The president is an astute and experienced manager who is aware that it will take considerable time to obtain a good understanding of the planning process throughout the organization and full cooperation with it. Since he himself is not experienced in the development of a planning program, he has appointed John Smith, the administrative vice president, who holds an MBA from Harvard and has attended many programs at the American Management Association. John has had some planning experience. In his previous position with a much smaller company he had developed a planning process, including a Management-by-Objectives program requiring submittal of annual goals. Smith's program was beginning to work at the time he left, about 10 years ago.

What do you think of the way the president is handling this situation? Is it likely that the approach will lead to a successful planning program? What Linking Elements are involved in a successful approach?

Case 2: Adherence to Personnel Policies

The Main Street General Hospital is an old established teaching hospital affiliated with the local University. Until about three years ago its employees had rejected union efforts several times. A change in management combined with a severe budget crunch brought concern about jobs and income stability, and all departments, even the residents, joined one of three different unions. The personnel director, who had been with the hospital for many years, grew progressively less able to cope with the job, which had expanded, and was given a less demanding position. His replacement, a highly experienced and energetic woman, noticed the following problems on a quick survey:

- When employees went on leaves of absence, their department failed to submit any forms.
- When employees were terminated, their supervisors failed to submit a termination form.
- Attempts were often made to violate seniority rights when hiring and promoting employees, which resulted in a larger number of grievances.
- Various incidents resulting in disciplinary action were not documented carefully.
- In several departments the affirmative action program fell far short of the plan.
- Applications were given out, open positions discussed, and people hired without involvement of the personnel department.
- Supervisors did not maintain accurate overtime records in their departments.
- Appointments scheduled by the personnel department often were not kept.
- Many grievances which could have been settled by supervisors were brought to the third step, which required involvement of the personnel department. By that time the issues were often much more difficult to resolve.
- There was considerable friction between the personnel department and several of the operating departments.

At the personnel director's request, the administrator of the hospital discussed these problems with her. They came to the conclusion that the core of the problem was inadequate knowledge of personnel procedures as well as of the union contract. It was decided that the best approach would be to conduct a series of meetings at which personnel procedures would be explained to all supervisory staff members and at which supervisors would be given an opportunity to ask questions.

The administrator, in a meeting with the executive committee, also emphasized how important it was to adhere to the personnel procedures. It was agreed at the meeting that the subject of personnel procedures would be discussed again in three months in order to see what progress had been achieved.

The hospital did not have an MbO program.

How effective do you consider this approach to be? To what extent do you think it will achieve its purpose?

Case 3: A Change in Department Management

When a capable and experienced female manager was appointed to head an established department in a governmental agency, she recognized that there were several considerations that she had to keep in mind, among them:

- The management change that had occurred could have an unsettling effect on office personnel.
- Her management style, which differed from her predecessor's, could further hinder a smooth transition.
- The "fresh, new look" at office problems that had been promised could be very threatening to the rest of the management team.

The department employs about 85 people. Reporting to the new chief are two managers. One of these has three supervisors, while the other one has four. Four of the supervisors are older people (within 10 years of retirement). All four have come up through the ranks without benefit of higher education. The other three are fairly energetic and are college educated.

The previous chief was an older man who had never been considered a strong manager by his superiors. During the last few years as he looked toward retirement, he had allowed his managers a fairly free hand within the limits imposed by the agency's policies and regulations. Generally, communications between sections were poor. Only essential information was passed down from the chief. Little information flowed up to him, and discussion between sections was limited to office routines.

There were other problems, some quite serious:
- Performance of some sections was less than satisfactory.
- Discipline and interpretation of agency rules varied from section to section, creating ill feelings.
- The appearance of the offices was generally below agency average.
- Problems were being studied superficially. Judgements and corrective actions were not founded on facts.

The new chief wondered how she could best proceed to raise the level of performance and job satisfaction. At the moment the agency has a superficial MBO program that requires all department heads to set a series of annual goals with the assistant administrator of the agency to whom they report. Accomplishment of these goals is one factor in the annual performance review but has had little effect on salaries or promotions.

What would you do if you were the Department Chief?

Case 4: An Organization Under Pressure

The organizational unit in this case is a 200-employee department in a manufacturing plant in an industry which has come under heavy competitive pressure during the last few years. In order to remain competitive, the company has reduced its prices. Profits have slipped sharply and management has instituted many cost reduction programs. This has involved new equipment, streamlining of methods, and reduction in staff wherever possible. Much of the work behind these changes has been performed by managers and supervisors in the plant because the engineering staff has been cut sharply.

One important element of the environment is the influence of competitive activities. In this industry marketing plans and especially new products are carefully guarded secrets to assure that the competition does not become aware of them until they are ready to be introduced. This makes it necessary for every organization to be ready to adapt to changes quickly, as the market situation changes.

As a result of the increased workload and the increased pace of change, work quality as well as the morale of employees, supervisors, and managers has suffered. The strain of long hours and the unrelenting pressure from their jobs has caused some managers and supervisors to be demanding without proper explanation and without consideration of the needs of their subordinates. This has caused additional resentment.

One department manager who was under pressure first concentrated on methods and production techniques so that the department could carry its workload within budgetary limitations. Once the new equipment and methods were in place, organizational problems assumed higher priority.

If you were the department manager, how would you proceed to gain the commitment of your people to improve quality and reduce costs?

ANALYSES OF CASES AND SUGGESTED APPROACHES

Each of the suggested approaches to the case studies is, of course, only one of the many possible solutions to the problems described above. Other approaches may work just as well or better.

The first step in approaching the case studies is to conduct a step-by-step Linking Elements analysis as outlined by the questions in the previous section of this chapter. This will highlight areas where action can be considered. The next step is to assign priorities to these areas and then to lay out a plan in each area where a problem or an opportunity deserves attention in the near future.

Since the suggested approaches are all based on the Linking Elements concept, they will have many common elements. All look first at the goals that could or should be set (even if that is not always the step that will receive highest priority). All tie performance evaluation to the goals program; all require careful, competent analysis of the knowledge and the skills of subordinates; and all strive to improve the amount of recognition which individuals receive. Where applicable, the approaches suggest a review of rules and coordination procedures and another look at compensation plans.

It might be worthwhile to reread each case, and before you read the suggested approach, write down several of the more important steps you think would do the most to improve the situation or to gain control over the problems and opportunities inherent in it.

Case 1: Establishing a Planning Program

The description of this case indicates that even though there are high costs in unexpected crash programs the corporation is operating satisfactorily. There obviously is no MBO program in operation because if there were an effective one, there would be no need for a separate planning program. In effect, MBO is a comprehensive planning program, but at the same time combines planning with implementation and performance evaluation.

Appointing John Smith to install a planning process is a useful step, of course. But, if the president lets John Smith make all the recommendations and lead the process, he is, in large measure, failing to meet his own responsibilities fully. A planning process, including the goal reviews and the performance appraisals, is not the type of responsibility that can be assigned to a subordinate. If the planning process is to be adhered to by all the managers in the corporation, then the president and his top-level executives must adhere to it as well.

John Smith, though a vice president, can implement on his own authority most of the steps that are required to gradually install the planning process. However, he is neither in a position to pass judgement on the quality aspects of the goals which the various managers set nor to conduct performance appraisals of people who do not report to him. In short, it is the president who has to take a firm and active role in starting this program. Total responsibility cannot be delegated to an administrative vice president.

Listed below are some of the steps the president could take to initiate the program:

1. Meet with the vice presidents and all others reporting directly to him to discuss plans for setting up a planning program.
2. Arrange to have the entire team learn at least those Linking Elements pertaining to aligning goals and performance standards and providing satisfaction of psychological needs. If possible, instruction should be given in development counseling as well.
3. Hold a planning session for those reporting directly to him to assure that the major planning elements are seen in the same light and to resolve such issues as the weight which good planning will be given in performance reviews and compensation decisions.
4. Establish regular goal reviews with each of these direct subordinates.
5. Establish semiannual performance reviews for each of these subordinates, one of which should review personal development plans.

6. Request that each immediate subordinate commit himself or herself to conducting similar goal and performance reviews with subordinates in his or her organizational unit.

7. Inform everyone that John Smith's role will be to assist in implementation and that he will monitor the process so that gradually a thoroughly integrated planning, goal setting, and performance evaluation program will be in effect.

Finally, the president has to review with John Smith the progress of the program and take corrective steps whenever it appears that intervention is necessary.

Case 2: Adherence to Personnel Policies

Even though the personnel director does not have authority over the various departments of this institution, almost all of the problems she is concerned with and has brought to the administrator deal with personnel matters. It therefore would be possible for her to work toward the resolution of the problems without discussing the situation with the administrator. Instead, she could lay out a program and submit it to the administrator for comments and approval. This would give her a stronger position since she would not depend as much on the administrator's thinking for any steps that might need to be taken.

While a series of meetings on personnel procedures would bring some relief—at least temporarily—such meetings in themselves would probably have only a limited impact. To obtain more thorough planning and more rapid progress, the personnel director should work with each of the department heads to gain a strong commitment for adherence to the personnel policies. Among other things, department heads might issue specific rules (procedures) and schedule review meetings with supervisors to achieve compliance throughout their respective departments.

The personnel director would greatly enhance her chances of cooperation if she offered specific assistance, such as preparation of outlines for training sessions and the loan of personnel staff members to conduct these sessions. If possible, she might even develop a brief manual highlighting the major procedures to be considered.

Her most important object is to obtain commitment to specific goals (for example, dates by which specific data collection or reporting will begin) from each of the department heads. Almost as necessary is planning with department heads how recognition can be provided for those supervisors who achieve the best record of adhering to the procedures and of reporting any problems that may exist with the procedures. The joint goal setting with each of the department heads should take into consideration the support that the personnel department would provide. Such an approach should guarantee maximum possible support from the administrator.

Case 3: A Change in Department Management

The department head in this situation has a very difficult task. Practices and habits that have been established for a long time have to be changed, and even the pace of operations will have to increase.

This particular case is a good example of the way Linking Elements can be applied at a relatively low organizational level. As the new chief clearly recognizes, changes should be scheduled very slowly. Setting only one or two goals with each manager would be an excellent way to start. This could be followed by asking managers to set one or two goals with each of their newer supervisors and only one loosely defined goal with each of their older ones. If these goals are carefully selected so that they pertain to things that the supervisors would themselves like to change and if the chief indicates strong support and provides help where needed, she would undoubtedly find ready acceptance.

It would probably be best if changes were made casually without letting people know that an MBO program was being started. In a situation such as this, to start on a more comprehensive program with great fanfare could easily do more damage than do good. The gradual approach is probably best since it allows the manager to shape developmental experiences through appropriate coaching.

There are many ways the chief can support these activities. She:

- Can set personal goals, communicate them, and encourage others to do likewise
- Can make it clear that she does not look to the actual

achievement of goals but rather to serious and competent effort toward reaching them
• Can give recognition to the managers and supervisors for their cooperation and help them give recognition to anyone taking a somewhat more energetic approach to their work.

These steps would very likely fall on fertile ground, especially with the newer, more ambitious staff members who would have to take the lead in bringing necessary changes. Initiating regular staff meetings with managers and encouraging them to hold similar meetings with their respective supervisors would greatly help to improve communications. At the same time, these meetings could help to establish over a period of time a reasonable set of rules to which everyone would have to adhere.

Such activities would provide much need satisfaction to managers, supervisors, and even employees. The chief could sit in on, or at least offer to join, manager staff meetings to help managers become comfortable with the approach. Managers may need some training, however; and their chief might want to conduct conference-leadership training sessions using any of the many conference leadership guides available.

As greater cooperation is achieved, the goals program could gradually be extended to cover all the problems that the chief has identified. Training, better communications, and appropriate recognition would help to bring active cooperation from all positive-thinking members of the department. After a few months, a positive momentum would begin to build, encouraging all to search for improvement.

Case 4: An Organization Under Pressure

Probably the most difficult situations for applying Linking Elements effectively are those in which pressures to complete routine tasks are very high; yet these are exactly the situations in which the Linking Elements concept is most needed by an organizational unit.

In the fourth case, in view of the heavy work load of the manufacturing plant and the unexpected changes that occur there from time to time, it is the first responsibility of the manager to do everything possible to break the tense atmosphere so that employees can get relief. In this case the need for social interaction is very high; and, therefore, stimulating social activity, providing a steady flow of recognition, and encouraging the acceptance of problems as challenges can help. At the same time the manager can attempt to reduce the emotional impact of the various changes. A joint manager-supervisor search for ideas to reduce tension and create a better atmosphere can do more than anything else to control the situation. Once there is even slight improvement in the climate, the manager can begin to introduce goal setting and goal reviews, which will gradually reduce the reliance on impulse management and bring a more coordinated approach to all the department's activities. Only then can the manager look more closely at training needs, cooperation problems, and rules.

Appendix A

Communications and Decision Making

If communications about job responsibilities are less than excellent—which is more the rule than the exception—then the picture you have developed of your own job may not correspond closely to that held by the people to whom you report. Unless your managers are unusually good communicators, they may not be spelling out regularly and clearly the priorities of your job, the areas to which you should devote heavy attention to achieve improvements, and those areas where normal attention is adequate to maintain your existing level of performance. It is unfortunate that higher-level managers frequently do not clarify these priorities.

If you are not certain that you understand the priorities of your job, it may be worthwhile to take the initiative and lay out a series of goals for an upcoming period. You can then go over this list of objectives with your boss to achieve a better understanding of what is expected of you.

Just as it is to your advantage to take the initiative in establishing good communications with your boss, so it is important that you establish good communications about job responsibilities with your subordinates. Once an open climate has been established, subordinates will feel free to come to you for clarification when doubts may arise or when they want to be sure that they see the situation in the same light as you.

The subject of communications is extremely complex and cannot be treated thoroughly in this book. However, those aspects of good communications that are relevant to the respective Linking Elements are discussed in the chapters. The brief overview provided in this Appendix may help you review your own practices and begin to eliminate any weaknesses.

COMMUNICATIONS SKILLS

When asked what skills are required for good communications, most people will immediately speak of the *ability to put thoughts into words as clearly and concisely as possible.* While many people consider this an innate talent, it has been shown that communication is a skill which can be improved with study and practice in both speaking and writing.

271

In order to be able to express yourself clearly either orally or in writing, you must be able to choose *words and word configurations that are appropriate to specific occasions.* Especially important is the ability to identify the points that shape the total presentation so that it can influence and persuade. This ability is especially valuable to those in managerial positions.

Another important skill for communicators is *listening.* First of all, it is necessary to identify the type of listening needed to understand a message. People who already have good comprehension of a topic often understand a message rather quickly; others must listen more attentively and hear more words before they achieve adequate understanding. Clearly, the sender must gear the speed of communication to the receiver's ability to accept, and the receiver must pay attention in proportion to the speed of transmission in order to understand the topic.

Levels of concentration must also be considered. For the morning news on the radio, the concentration needed may be minimal—possibly not much more than that used in listening to soothing music. However, when listening to instructions, attention to detail is crucial. For thorough learning concentration and attention to detail must obviously be very high.

Another dimension to listening concerns those things that are not actually said but only implied. Deeper meanings can be obtained by listening to emotional overtones as expressed by voice inflection and other signs.

In social and professional interactions, people often mean something other than what they say. Thus, the listener must pay close attention to the nonverbal signs which provide hints to that part of the message not contained in the words.

Not all communications use words; *some forms of communication are nonverbal.* Such secondary messages can be transmitted by themselves, or they can accompany verbal expressions. Nonverbal communication occurs through signals and the use of symbols. Facial expression, gestures, aural signs and symbols other than words, stance, clothing, the physical space between parties, the environment, all contribute to conveying messages. Some people estimate that less than half of the significance of a verbal message is transmitted through words. This is shown by the preference most people have for personal contact (rather than impersonal contact by telephone) on complex matters.

The use of properly worded questions to gradually achieve understanding and agreement is another good communications technique.

Especially important for managers is *knowing how to select appropriate visual aids and use them effectively.* Effective use of visual aids can add speed and clarity to the transmission of messages. Visual aids can be as simple as a small diagram drawn on a piece of paper for a one-on-one discussion or as elaborate as a multiscreen slide presentation for a large group.

The emotional impact of words and gestures cannot be ignored when communications are discussed. The ability to understand the reactions of others to certain words and phrases can be of great value to those in managerial positions.

DECISION MAKING

New managers usually need to practice the skills of decision making. If you have taken a course or attended a seminar in decision making, you probably have come to appreciate the importance of thorough analysis in decision making. Today, the decision making process is no longer the way it was when managers made most decisions unilaterally. Many people often have to be involved, and the skills you need to help a group arrive at good decision are sometimes more important than thorough knowledge of the decision-making process. However, if you never have had formal exposure to the decision-making process as a separate topic, the following explanation may prove useful.

Few people realize how significantly their lives can be affected by the application of good decision-making skills. Careful planning and well thought-out decisions can lead to better use of limited resources. The general application of management principles to one's personal life can also help to bring about more meaningful relationships with others.

Inexperienced decision makers often err by regarding decisions as a choice between two alternatives. Some decisions, of course, are that simple. For example, one either stays in bed or gets up. In most situations, however, there are a fairly large number of alternatives from which to select.

Granting a privilege, for instance, may seem at first to be a simple "yes" or "no" matter. But there are many ways to say "yes" or "no." An employee requesting a new uniform or a change in vacation may be told "yes," but in such a way that future requests are discouraged. Or "no" may be said in such a manner that the person making the request thoroughly understands the reasons behind the decision and feels no bitterness. Unskilled managers often say "no" in such a way that difficulties and hard feelings result.

Recognizing the possibilities that do exist is much easier when one follows a formal decision-making process. Therefore, it is appropriate to discuss decision making in the abstract—that is, as a process that helps one select those courses of action likely to be most successful.

A decision is usually not a single act. It involves chains of actions that are linked to each other, and it is in carrying out these actions that good skills in decision making are manifested. There are several decision chains:

- Chains for resolving problems
- Chains for performing routine duties

- Chains for achieving specific results, such as completing a project
- Most importantly, chains for seeking out opportunities.

This last chain receives least attention by most people, when it really deserves far higher priority. The difference between drifting and having some measure of control over one's destiny lies in the ability to select opportunities for improving one's future. These are the hard decisions that ultimately lead to better jobs and higher standards of living and lay the foundations for significant improvements in organizational performance and for a more profitable environment.

Problem-solving decision chains force themselves on you, as do those for routine duties. The numerous decisions involved in completing a project become necessary once you have decided the project needs doing. The only decisions for which there are no reminders or established discipline are those that concern planning and the seeking out of opportunities.

Many people never know how much they could have influenced their lives had they been aware that there were decision points for opportunities which required careful analysis of alternate routes. Other people see this only when their children blindly follow the most obvious but limiting path, or when they drift, unable either to analyze future possibilities or to accept some temporary inconvenience for the sake of future benefits.

All chains, of whatever type, are similar. Each consists of: definition decisions, analysis decisions, execution decisions, and follow-up decisions for correcting the course of action.

Definition decisions answer questions such as: What is the problem? Has the problem occurred in the past? How is it different from the previous problem? How important is this problem to the achievement of goals? For opportunities, the questions could be: What opportunities could be considered? Which of these are new opportunities and which have existed all along? What is different now that may make these opportunities more relevant today?

Analysis decisions concern the grouping of data, the selection of alternatives, the use of the data to determine which alternatives are most promising, and finally the selection of the best alternative.

Execution decisions involve questions such as: What resources will be needed for this task? In what sequence should the tasks be performed? Which people should be involved? Who should do what? In what way should each person be involved in making further decisions?

Follow-up decisions answer questions such as: Are there deviations from the plan? What should be done about deviations from expected results? This last question leads directly back into the initial chain. If there is a deviation from the plan, this, in effect, becomes a problem, and the problem-solving chain starts from the beginning. For other types of decision chains similar questions can be asked.

The second segment of the basic decision-making concept concerns the process for making each of the little decisions in each chain. It must be recognized that decisions come in all sizes. To lift one's finger involves, in effect, a decision—though it is one made almost totally subconsciously. On the other hand, the decision to get out of bed requires considerably more effort. Usually, it is a rather routine decision which requires very little analysis. Managers make many equally routine decisions; however, more complex decisions—which require more thought—make up the majority of a manager's responsibilities. The most complex decisions, of course, are no longer single decisions, but rather—as noted above—chains. As a matter of fact, most decisions that are of any consequence involve a series, and it is the entire series that is analyzed at one time.

In the formal analysis of a decision the following questions may be asked:

1. What data is required?
2. What alternatives should be considered?
3. When the initial alternatives have been determined, what additional data is required to evaluate them?
4. What additional alternatives are suggested by the collection of the data?
5. How can the data be used to evaluate the best alternative?
6. To what extent does this evaluation produce still additional alternatives?
7. What further data may be required to evaluate the additional alternatives?
8. When has sufficient data been gathered to support the selection of the best alternative? When is it more important to make a good decision now, rather than a better decision at a later date?
9. Which alternative is indeed best?

Keeping these steps in mind can help ensure that all important alternatives have been considered. Two other techniques helpful in decision making—decision trees and decision matrices—are briefly explained in the following paragraphs.

Decision Trees

Decision trees help to define and evaluate alternatives. A decision tree *depicts* the question that should be asked at every step in a decision chain: What alternatives are available at this point, and what consequences should be expected from each?

A decision tree starts by asking what alternatives exist at the moment. For example, a very simple tree could be built for a short trip from one town to the next. Assuming that three routes are available, that the trip must be made during rush hour, and that it is important to get to the next town by a specific time, the possible alternatives might be (1) a limited-access highway or (2) two major truck routes, each of which has some stretches containing traffic lights. These alternatives are depicted in Figure A.1.

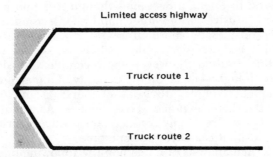

Limited access highway

Truck route 1

Truck route 2

Figure A.1. A Diagram of the Simple Decision Tree Described in the Text

Once the first branches of the tree have been drawn, the consequences for the end point of each branch need to be considered. The consequences, as depicted in Figure A.2, are:

1. For the limited access highway: (a) the possibility of heavy, slow-moving traffic—about 40 minutes, (b) the possibility of complete blockage due to an accident—maximum probable time two hours, (c) no obstruction, free traffic flow—15 minutes.
2. For truck route 1: (a) heavy traffic, slow moving—about 60 minutes, (b) total obstruction, good connection to limited access highway at four points—1¼ to 1½ hours, (c) normal traffic—35 minutes.
3. For truck route 2: (a) heavy traffic, slow moving—about 65 minutes, (b) total obstruction—good access to side streets that would require 95 minutes, (c) normal traffic—½ hour.

Some experts say that probability should be estimated for each branch of the tree. Others say that probabilities are not that practical and that decisions should be based on the decision maker's judgment about the value of the various alternatives without mathematical analysis. The important point about decision trees is that they help to identify alternatives which are not immediately apparent.

Decision trees need not be drawn for most situations since in most cases alternatives are quite obvious. Anyone who makes use of the decision-tree technique for complex decisions, however, finds that it can bring a certain discipline to analysis that is absent without it. One other advantage of the technique lies in its ability to clearly communicate alternatives when several people are involved in seeking out the best approach. However, the technique has one major disadvantage—it is cumbersome. Therefore, it should be used with dis-

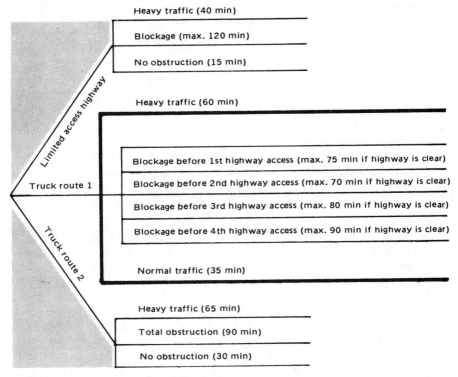

Heavy traffic (40 min)

Blockage (max. 120 min)

No obstruction (15 min)

Limited access highway

Heavy traffic (60 min)

Blockage before 1st highway access (max. 75 min if highway is clear)

Blockage before 2nd highway access (max. 70 min if highway is clear)

Truck route 1

Blockage before 3rd highway access (max. 80 min if highway is clear)

Blockage before 4th highway access (max. 90 min if highway is clear)

Normal traffic (35 min)

Truck route 2

Heavy traffic (65 min)

Total obstruction (90 min)

No obstruction (30 min)

Figure A.2. A Diagram Illustrating the Consequences for Each End Point of the First Set of Branches for the Simple Decision Tree Shown in Figure A.1.

cretion, and only for those decisions for which it can provide enough of an advantage to justify the effort.

Decision Matrices

Any decision that has at least two dimensions can be organized as a matrix which gives some insights into the relative advantages and disadvantages of the various alternatives. Tables A.1 and A.2 illustrate two matrices that lead to interesting insights. Both are simple tables containing only few boxes. The horizontal rows list all alternatives that are worth serious consideration; each vertical column then designates a criterion against which each alternative should be evaluated. For example, Table A.1 partially evaluates alternatives identified in the decision tree (Figure A.2), and Table A.2 compares the desirability of several pieces of equipment. (It is not necessary to construct a decision tree for each matrix, but only to identify alternatives.)

	Shortest possible time (Minutes)	Longest probable time (Minutes)	Reliability (Assurance that estimate is accurate)
Limited access highway	15	120	Low
Truck route 1	35	90	Medium
Truck route 2	30	95	High

Table A.1 Matrix for Route Selection

It is important to notice that in decision matrices, there are always tangible items such as initial cost and installation items and continuing expenditures. There are also intangible items that have to be evaluated subjectively by those making the decision. Because decision trees and decision matrices ultimately require judgment about intangibles, they do not give a precise result and no single answer emerges. For this reason, involving several knowledgeable people in decisions brings greater objectivity. Similarly, when considering the impact of a decision on people, a group is usually more accurate than an individual.

The value of matrices lies in the thorough analysis they require. Detailed analysis helps to assure that better decisions will be made more often. Strict adherence to the decision-making process and the

	Cost	Maximum Capacity	Operating Costs Per Hour	Special Advantages	Special Disadvantages	Operator Preferences
(Manufacturer A)	X dollars	R units	O dollars	Simplest to operate	Highest expected maintenance	High
(Manufacturer B)	Y dollars	S units	P dollars	Best controls and access for maintenance	Difficult to convert to other products	Medium
(Manufacturer C)	Z dollars	T units	Q dollars	Easiest to convert to other products	Uses most space	Medium

Table A.2. Matrix for Evaluation of a Machine Being Considered for Purchase

use of decision trees and decision matrices do not guarantee good decisions; but they do tie together to provide considerable support when a manager faces a difficult decision, and they assure that poor decisions will be made less frequently.

1. The *steps in the decision-making process* ensure an orderly and organized approach to the decision sequence.
2. The *decision tree* provides a framework for reviewing possible courses of action and helps stimulate creative thinking.
3. *Decision matrices* are useful in evaluating which alternative represents the best choice.

The following items might be listed among their purposes: (1) they provide a path and tools to help arrive at the best possible course of action when difficult decisions need be made; (2) they aid in forming a thought process that can guide decisions, thereby helping to bring about what is commonly called "good judgment"; and (3) they provide a shorthand record of the thinking that led to the decision.

Appendix B

The Foundations of Management Theory

To allow the discussion to quickly reach the central thesis of the book the treatment in Chapter 2 of some of the earlier contributions to management theory is very sketchy. To make up for this shortcoming, some important contributions are discussed in this appendix.

ADAM SMITH AND THE DIVISION OF LABOR

One of the first persons to record his thoughts about the way our work patterns affect our lives was the Scottish economist Adam Smith. In 1776, in his book titled *An Inquiry into the Nature and Causes of the Wealth of Nations*, Smith pointed out how the division of labor could help enrich a society. Smith believed that greater wealth could be derived from any system or method that helped produce more goods with the same amount of effort as required by previous methods. His famous example was that of a pin factory:*

> To take an example, therefore, from a trifling manufacture; but one in which the division of labour has been very often taken notice of, the trade of the pin-maker; a workman not educated to this business (which the division of labour has rendered a distinct trade), nor acquainted with the use of the machinery employed in it (to the invention of which the same division of labour has probably given occasion), could scarce, perhaps, with his utmost industry, make one pin in a day, and certainly could not make twenty. But in the way in which this business is now carried on, not only the whole work is a peculiar trade, but it is divided into a number of branches, of which the greater part are likewise peculiar trades. One man draws out the wire, another straights it, a third cuts it, a fourth points it, a fifth grinds it at the top for receiving the head; to make the head requires two or three distinct operations; to put it on is a peculiar business, to whiten the pins is another; it is even a trade by itself to put them into the paper; and the important business of making a pin is, in this manner, divided into about eighteen distinct operations, which, in some manufactories, are all performed by distinct hands, though in others the same man will sometimes perform two or three of them. I have seen a small manufactory of this kind where ten men only were employed, and where some of them consequently performed two or three distinct operations.

---

*Adam Smith, AN INQUIRY INTO THE NATURE AND CAUSES OF THE WEALTH OF NATIONS (London: W. Strahan and T. Cadell, 1776; reprinted as THE WEALTH OF NATIONS, New York: Modern Library Giants, 1937).

But though they were very poor, and therefore but indifferently accommodated with the necessary machinery, they could, when they exerted themselves, make among them about twelve pounds of pins in a day. There are in a pound upwards of four thousand pins of a middling size. Those ten persons, therefore, could make among them upwards of forty-eight thousand pins in a day.

Each person, therefore, making a tenth part of forty-eight thousand pins, might be considered as making four thousand eight hundred pins in a day. But if they had all wrought separately and independently, and without any of them having been educated to this peculiar business, they certainly could not each of them have made twenty, perhaps not one pin in a day; that is, certainly, not the two hundred and fortieth, perhaps not the four thousand eight hundredth part of what they are at present capable of performing, in consequence of a proper division and combination of their different operations.

It is important to note that the methods of production described by Smith came into being long before he wrote about them, and that they gave evidence of extensive application of management principles. Smith's example concentrated on explaining how division of labor brought about greater wealth.

FREDERICK WINSLOW TAYLOR, THE FATHER OF MANAGEMENT SCIENCE

One of the first to write about management concepts was Frederick Taylor. In the 1890's and the early 1900's Taylor, a Philadelphia steel mill superintendent who had developed a carefully thought-out system for managing work, saw around him a lack of detailed attention to the way work could best be organized. He saw wasted steps and wasted motions. He reasoned, quite correctly, that such waste required effort, and if that effort could be used to produce more, everyone would gain. Taylor was not working on a theory: he was working to produce more steel at less cost in order to increase profits for his company. A brilliant engineer, he approached the problem methodically.

Unlike many of the managers of his time, Taylor was interested in the well-being of his employees. Well-being, however, had a different meaning in those days. It was a paternalistic, benevolent outlook which placed on the employer some responsibility to help employees who suffered unusual hardship in their personal life—but this concern did not extend to the employees' psychological well-being on the job. The employer decided what was to be done and when and how, and the employee obeyed even if the work involved very unpleasant or unhealthy activities.

Workers accepted this role of the boss as the decision-maker, and regarded the shop or office as a place in which one was supposed to work. They accepted, without question, the right of employers to change the nature of the work environment without consulting them.

Of little concern was the modern expectation of employees for a voice in shaping their working conditions. However, some employees did believe that they should have such a voice; and that is evidenced by the rise of the trade unions around the turn of the 20th century.

Aside from those who spearheaded the trade unions, most of the people who worked in Taylor's time did not expect any greater reward for their work than to be paid for it. They worked for money. Although they expected to be treated decently, they did not expect their employers to care whether or not they liked their work, whether or not they were content in their work, or whether or not they were comfortable in their work. It is no wonder, then, that Taylor was not particularly concerned about the psychological needs of his workers. Instead, he was interested in how to increase the financial rewards that he considered to be the all-important element for leading employees to greater production and to greater efficiency. Though Taylor ignored them, managers were soon to become more aware that there were many other incentives that were even stronger than monetary rewards—that "Man does not live by bread alone."

Such was the environment for Taylor's work. Taylor observed that few people, if any, worked steadily and energetically all day. He reasoned that if he could somehow scientifically determine what constituted a day's work, he could better tell employees what he expected of them. He felt that if he were reasonable about it, he was bound to obtain a greatly improved output. Therefore, through experimentation, he set out to develop standards for a fair day's work. Following is an excerpt from one of his writings in which he discusses how measurement is easier if the work is analyzed one step at a time:*

The first impression is that this minute subdivision of the work into elements, neither of which takes more than five or six seconds to perform, is little short of preposterous; yet if a rapid and thorough time study of the art of shoveling is to be made, this subdivision simplifies the work, and makes the study quicker and more thorough.

The reasons for this are twofold:

First. In the art of shoveling dirt, for instance, the study of 50 or 60 small elements, like those referred to above, will enable one to fix the exact time for many thousands of complete jobs of shoveling, constituting a very considerable proportion of the entire art.

Second. The study of single small elements is simpler, quicker, and more certain to be successful than that of a large number of elements combined. The greater the length of time involved in a single item of time study, the greater will be the likelihood of interruptions or accidents, which will render the results obtained by the observer questionable or even useless. There is a considerable part of the work of most establishments that is not what may be called standard work, namely, that

---

*Frederick W. Taylor, *Time Study*, MANAGEMENT: ANALYSIS, CONCEPTS, CASES Englewood Cliffs, N.J.: Prentice-Hall, Inc., 1964), pp. 248–249.

which is repeated many times. Such jobs as this can be divided for time study into groups, each of which contains several rudimentary elements. . .

There is no class of work which cannot be profitably submitted to time study, by dividing it into its time elements, except such operations as take place in the head of the worker; and the writer has even seen a time study made of the speed of an average and first-class boy in solving problems in mathematics. Clerk work can well be submitted to time study, and a daily task assigned in work of this class which at first appears to be very miscellaneous in its character . . .

Taylor writes in his paper on "A Piece Rate System" written in 1895:*

Practically the greatest need felt in an establishment wishing to start a rate-fixing department is the lack of data as to the proper rate of speed at which work should be done. There are hundreds of operations which are common to most large establishments, yet each concern studies the speed problem for itself, and days of labor are wasted in what should be settled once and for all, and recorded in a form which is available to all manufacturers.

What is needed is a handbook on the speed with which work can be done similar to the elementary engineering handbooks.

Taylor correctly predicted that such a book would be forthcoming. It would describe the best method of making, recording, tabulating and indexing time observations since much time and effort are wasted by the adoption of inferior methods.

What was Taylor really doing? First, he analyzed the work to see what changes could be tried to find methods that would be most productive. Next, he taught these methods to employees. Finally, he timed the people doing the work to see what they could produce if they worked steadily without exerting themselves and set that as a standard on which their pay was based.

While Taylor was concerned with setting standards to determine what a fair day's work would be, he also recognized that people would have to share the benefits of any extra effort that would be required of them or the larger production that would result from their work. As he saw it, if more work was produced, employees could be paid higher wages and more would still be left for the firm. Thus, all would benefit—the employer, the employee, and society.

Taylor did not believe, however, in sharing on an equal basis with the employee, as a number of his examples showed. One of the most famous was his story of Schmidt, a laborer who worked at loading pig iron into railway box cars. Taylor described Schmidt as "a man of the type of the ox . . . a man so stupid that he was unfitted to do most kinds of laboring work." Part of Taylor's instructions to Schmidt were as follows:**

---

*Frederick W. Taylor, *A Piece Rate System*, SHOP MANAGEMENT (New York: Harper & Row, 1947), pp. 176–177.

**Frederick Taylor, THE PRINCIPLES OF SCIENTIFIC MANAGEMENT (New York: W. W. Norton & Co., Inc., 1911), p. 47.

Well, if you are a high-priced man, you will do exactly as this man tells you tomorrow, from morning till night. When he tells you to pick up a pig and walk, you pick it up and walk, and when he tells you to sit down and rest, you sit down. You do that right straight through the day. And what's more, no back talk. Now a high-priced man does just what he's told to do, and no back talk. Do you understand that? When this man tells you to walk, you walk; when he tells you to sit down, you sit down, and you don't talk back to him. Now you come to work here tomorrow morning and I'll know before night whether you are really a high-priced man or not . . .

Schmidt, according to Taylor's account, almost quadrupled his daily production (from 12-$\frac{1}{2}$ tons to 47-$\frac{1}{2}$ tons), and earned 60 percent higher wages (from \$1.15 a day to \$1.85 a day). This was small consolation to the labor leaders and social reformers who bitterly attacked Taylor's ideas.

Other employers even less generous than Taylor used methods and time study to increase profits, and they shared very little with employees. No wonder that there was considerable apprehension among employees that upon working harder and/or more efficiently, they would merely provide greater profits to their employers, or that by working more efficiently, fewer hours would be required and some would lose their jobs.

THE WORK OF HENRY GANTT

Like Taylor, Gantt's focus was on trying to improve the efficiency of work. The concerns of employees were not the only significant problems in Taylor's piece-rate system. When workers are paid by the piece and work is not available because other people have not completed their work or because machines are unavailable for any reason, then they have to be idle and lose pay until material or machines are ready. Gantt recognized some of the problems that Taylor had failed to solve and therefore concentrated on techniques for achieving better coordination between people, machines, and material.

The problems that resulted in slowing down the flow of work and production also caused financial drains on businesses and were constant sources of dissatisfaction to employees. Many of these problems contributed to the bitter struggles between management and labor that occurred from time to time. Gantt became involved in devising a system that he felt would harmonize the interests of both employers and employees. He believed there were two approaches to solving the problems of the slow-ups and losses in production time that resulted in lost revenue for employers and lost wages for employees. These approaches involved the use of so-called Gantt Charts and the Task and Bonus Plan.

The Gantt Charts

Gantt created in chart form detailed schedules of a type still in use today. Called Gantt Charts, these schedules indicate work to be done and when it is to be done. The schedules often show how the work is to be "routed," or where a semifinished batch of work is to be stored after a specific operation has been finished. The charts, in effect, force managers to do the detailed planning necessary for a smooth flow of work and to communicate these plans to all who are concerned with them.

The Task and Bonus Plan

Gantt was also concerned with the problem of employees who were unfairly penalized by loss of pay because things over which they had no control went wrong. To help solve this problem, Gantt devised a "Task and Bonus Plan." In simple terms, Gantt's plan meant that when an employee was assigned a "task" (based on a predetermined amount of piecework that could be used as a standard for a day's work or on a day's work as such), then he or she would be paid for that work even if, due to some uncontrollable circumstance, the standard could not be met. On the other hand, if the employee exceeded the set standard, an extra "bonus"—calculated at an even higher rate—would be paid for all that was accomplished above the standard. This gave the employee protection against undue loss of pay while still maintaining the incentive to do even better than the standard.

FRANK AND LILLIAN GILBRETH

Two other early management scientists whose work deserves mention here are Frank and Lillian Gilbreth. The Gilbreths improved time and motion study procedures by laying the foundation for the handbook of standards which Taylor had predicted. From their work come the minute, predetermined time standards that were used so widely in high production industries during the 1930's, 40's, and even 50's. These time values provide the ability to predict how long it should take to perform any operation by supplying standard increment times for such minute tasks as "grasp," "reach 6 inches," "reach 9 inches," "turn 90 degrees," "release part," etc.

The Gilbreths labeled seventeen basic elements of job motion with titles ranging from "search," "find," "select," and "grasp" through "wait-unavoidable," "wait-avoidable," and, finally, "rest" and "plan." Analyzing these steps in any task and adding the predetermined standards gives a fairly scientific standard for the entire task. For example, to find out how long it should take an employee to punch two holes in a piece of metal with a certain machine, one could look up the standard time for each of the motions required to accomplish such a function and merely add them up. The Gilbreths also began to use motion picture cameras to capture exact movements involved in a particular operation as it was being done. The pictures frequently used special clocks that made the determination of elapsed time very easy. The work done by the Gilbreths has, to some extent, lost its direct usefulness in highly automated, modern manufacturing processes in which most of the operations sufficiently repetitive to warrant such detailed studies are usually performed by machines.

Flow Process Charts

The Gilbreths also developed "Flow Process Charts." These charts provide a picture of the sequence of functions involved in a job so that wasted handling or backtracking can be identified and avoided. The sequence follows a product (or document) through all the steps that need to be performed on it before it can be completed.

A similar analysis could be made of the work of an individual performing a job function or a series of job functions. Entries under "details of method" in such a flow chart would be: waiting for assignment, receiving order, walking to storage, retrieving material, performing the operation, etc.

Symbols are used on the Gilbreth flow charts for the following:
1. Operation—where work is performed. Shaded circles represent work that changes the material worked upon (it includes entries on papers that are being processed). Empty circles stand for preparatory (make-ready or set-up) work and for cleaning up or putting away tools or other things that help with production.
2. Transportation—something is being moved from one place to another.
3. Storage—idle material waiting for the next step or operation.
4. Delay—idle time caused by a bottleneck; unplanned storage.
5. Inspection—proofreading, checking, or measuring, etc.

An activity not covered by any of the above symbols has its own symbol.

Methods, Motion, and Time Studies

Taylor, Gantt, and Gilbreth distinguished three basic elements in their work: (1) methods study, (2) motion study, and (3) time study. Methods study deals with how work can best be arranged and what portion of the work can be eliminated. Motion study concentrates on individual motions to see how they can be simplified or shortened. Finally, time study determines how long the improved methods should take and what, therefore, makes a reasonable performance standard; it analyzes how much time should be allowed for fatigue, how much for rest, how much for fumbling, etc. (i.e., how much time a particular job function should take considering all of the many factors involved.

In addition to the work of the management scientists, a few words should be said about another group of researchers and thinkers who contributed to the evolution of management theory. These are the educational psychologists.

EDUCATIONAL PSYCHOLOGISTS

One offshoot of the behavioral sciences, as applied to management skills, deals with theories on training and developing subordinates. HRD, as human resources development is called, has been defined by Leonard Nadler (see footnote, page 171) as consisting of training for the present job, education for future identifiable jobs, and development for future undefined jobs.

As more and more of the work in advanced societies has become "knowledge" work, continuous attention to HRD has become intimately related to success. The manager who claims that development of subordinates is the most important managerial function is no longer a rarity. HRD builds on educational psychology but shifts its focus from the formal education of children and preprofessional young people to adult learning.

One researcher who deserves mention in this discussion of foundations is B. F. Skinner. His ideas have reached beyond training into management practices; and though serious objections have been raised about the way Skinner's ideas are being applied, they nevertheless have had profound influence. Skinner's work* is based on that of the famous Russian psychologist Ivan Pavlov, who is noted for his studies of conditioned stimulus and response. Skinner used the concept of conditioning to develop the programmed instruction method in which a learner reads a few lines (a frame) and immediately has to answer a question about the content of the frame. If the answer is correct, the learner can proceed. If incorrect, the frame has to be repeated. Fairly spectacular successes have been obtained with this type of learning process, particularly on highly structured material. The method forces very attentive reading by involving the learner, and this brings reasonable assurance that the material being covered has been learned. As a result, programmed instruction has found wide application in skill training, but results in management development have been somewhat mixed. Management concepts are complex and broad; they therefore do not lend themselves as readily to a technique which depends heavily on simple responses.

In recent years, however, a modified form of conditioning has been applied somewhat more successfully to training in very specific supervisory skills such as interviewing of applicants for new positions, handling customer complaints, conducting performance appraisals, assigning work, delegating responsibility, etc. An attempt has also been made to apply the concept to provide what is called positive reinforcement for work well done. It is being suggested that supervisors and managers commend employees frequently, whenever someone

---

*See B. F. Skinner, SCIENCE AND HUMAN BEHAVIOR (New York: Free Press, 1965); see also I. P. Pavlov, CONDITIONED REFLEXES (trans. by G. V. Anrep; London: Oxford University Press, 1927).

does something well or better than in the past. Presumably, such positive reinforcement will bring greater desire on the part of the employee for still higher achievement. So far there is little evidence that these efforts are bringing significant results. On the other hand, the same technique applied during on-the-job training to reinforce a new learning experience or to increase confidence by learners undoubtedly serves a very useful purpose.

Appendix C

Providing Recognition

It is probably essential to point out that it would be unfortunate if a manager who is embarking on a recognition program sees it as an end in itself. To give praise more frequently or to provide more extensive recognition in some other way should not be the ultimate goal. Providing recognition is merely a step toward developing an environment which produces a more effective team and supports achievement orientation.

THE SPREADING PROBLEM OF NEGATIVE FEEDBACK

An important component of social and esteem needs is the need for greater recognition of one's contributions. Employees at all levels need to know that others—especially their bosses—are aware of the time, effort, and talent which they contribute. There is considerable evidence that such recognition helps to develop a stronger team and greater esprit de corps. Yet the modern management techniques which have done so much to increase effectiveness of organizations have also, on balance, greatly increased negative feedback.

Even though there is no intent to do so, computers, management by exception, network diagrams, budgetary reports, and even many MBO programs appear to provide much more negative than positive feedback. They seem constantly to highlight what has *not* been achieved, even if they present a complete and accurate picture of a particular situation. After all, the primary purpose of most routine reports is to show undesirable deviations from standard—to identify problem areas so that appropriate corrective action can be taken. Even if these deviations are not stressed, the reader usually looks for them; and somehow they seem to have greater emotional impact than the favorable comments.

Negative feedback, of course, is not all bad; it is a fairly good teacher; and, when not excessive, its detrimental impact can be very small. There is no reason why it should not be used to help individuals see errors and to identify and correct small problems before they become more significant.

People also must be stopped when they violate basic work rules or disregard safety regulations or when they otherwise fail to meet organization norms. But in an environment where social and esteem needs go undernourished, frequent criticism, even if only implied, often evokes hostility, which can have a strong detrimental impact on motivation.

Justified criticism, however, and realistic evaluation of performance against goals and standards are essential parts of work relationships. A well-planned program, specifically designed to offset the impact of discouraging information, brings balance and creates an atmosphere in which the entire environment—supervisors, managers, the work itself—provides emotional rewards to employees for their productive efforts and for qualities of character.

THE IMPORTANCE OF POSITIVE FEEDBACK

Unfortunately, attitude surveys consistently show that a large majority of employees feel inadequately recognized. They believe that their managers and supervisors are not aware of the complexity of their jobs and of the amount of effort, loyalty, and talent which they contribute. Many employees feel that they do not receive the credit they have earned by their labors. Interestingly, most surveys which cover several organizational levels find the same feelings exist as strongly among supervisors as among the people they supervise. The problem, it seems, appears at many levels in most organizations.

Managers who do not balance negative feedback sufficiently evoke in their people the feeling of discouragement, the belief that their efforts are not appreciated. And, conversely, the manager who knows how to use positive feedback to encourage people, without abandoning or even reducing negative feedback, invariably produces an enviable record of accomplishments.

It is interesting to note that most sales organizations are keenly aware of the value of motivation incentives. Besides monetary ones such as bonuses, commissions, and salary increases, there are plaques, certificates, desk stands, and clocks. Recognition is given to high performers with rewards such as Salesperson of the Month or Year or as membership in the Top Ten Club, the President's Club, or other elite performance groups. Many of these awards are conferred upon the recipients with a maximum of publicity, frequently at sales meetings in full view of management and the entire sales force. The recipients usually decorate their offices with the certificates or plaques. Rosters showing their names are often displayed prominently at company or divisional headquarters.

It is not surprising that recognition programs are so prevalent in sales organizations. Results of sales efforts are relatively easy to measure. Most of the time the salespeople are out in the field by themselves where managers cannot easily exert direct control. Furthermore, when a salesperson leaves, the loss of business often has an immediate effect on the organization. Direct cause-and-effect relationships are rarely evident in the office or the factory, and it is not clear that an organization depends for its success on the motivation of office or factory employees. Therefore, recognition programs similar to those of the sales organization are rare in the office. Nevertheless, it is in the office or the shop where the need for such programs is often greatest. This is true, in large part, because the individual employee has less direct evidence of the value of his or her contribution to the organization's accomplishments: There are fewer immediate positive impulses from the work itself.

When personnel people in business or government are asked what recognition programs exist, they may point to formal merit promotion procedures or in-grade performance bonuses. They may cite suggestion systems, attendance awards, bowling teams, and other athletic clubs and, of course, the quality of their managers and supervisors who "know that recognition is important." The striking fact in both the public and the private sectors is that apparently there are very few, if any, personnel departments that help managers develop the habits and skills which everyone agrees are so desirable. Frequently, even the newest supervisor is presumed to have the innate ability to provide recognition for moderate, steady, and reliable performance of an ongoing activity—not only for the exceptional accomplishment. Satisfaction of the fundamental psychological hunger is thus haphazard in the vast majority of organizational units.

To overcome the increasing apathy of employees and create improved esprit de corps, procedures must be developed to somehow assure all competent and loyal employees that they are not seen as pieces of equipment. People need to be told, over and over again, that management appreciates their efforts, is aware of their contributions, and wants them to be satisfied members of the total unit. It will, therefore, become increasingly necessary for organizations to provide regular recognition of all employees, regardless of whether they work for an enlightened manager or one who gives lower emphasis to important motivation factors.

Obstacles to Providing Positive Feedback

Most managers would very much like to see their people receive many pleasant experiences from their work environment. Due to real or imagined obstacles, though, they find it difficult to plan a cohesive program that would provide such experiences. First of all, they are usually not consciously aware of the almost infinite variety of events which provide opportunities for increasing an individual's job satisfaction. They thus feel their chances to provide recognition are limited. They have not been able to develop effective approaches which will make the employee feel wanted; they are unsure about how to give frequent sincere recognition without seeming insincere.

Managers are aware that sporadic, ritualistic attempts at praise or recognition, even when the sincerity is unquestioned, are perceived by the receiver as shallow and usually cause slight embarrassment rather than a true warm feeling. There are other major obstacles which managers have to overcome:

1. Like everyone else, managers are subject to the law of inertia, which is a natural obstacle to developing new habits. When managers are asked to prepare a list of things for which they could commend a particular employee they can think only of very few items. Only after considerable thought does the list begin to grow. A long list, of course, is necessary so that commendations from the managers are not seen as repetitious, one-sided, contrived, insincere, or—worst of all—clumsy.

2. Most managers are very busy with the technical parts of their jobs, including the traditional planning, organizing, and controlling functions. This leaves preciously little time to think about how, where, and when they could provide positive impulses for their employees. "I've got little enough time to do my own work," is a typical attitude.

3. Most organizations do not help managers plan recognition. They provide little or no encouragement such as suggestions on how to write letters of appreciation or active participation by higher echelons. Few have formal recognition programs. To the average manager it appears as though for providing positive feedback there are few alternatives other than words of appreciation. "I tell my people when they turn out good work" is a common statement. "What else can I do? And if I do that too often they'll think I am just buttering them up. On the other hand, if I do it only once in a while, they think I am doing it because I need a favor. You can't win no matter how hard you try."

4. Selecting appropriate employees to recognize appears to be difficult. Most managers believe that recognition has to be bestowed fairly. Otherwise, they will be accused of favoritism.

5. Many managers are seriously apprehensive that employees will respond to repeated praise or other commendations by requesting more tangible evidence of appreciation. They feel uncomfortable or are unwilling to expose themselves to such situations. Possibly they find it too difficult to tell employees that they are better off with their existing salaries and benefits *and* the pleasant feeling that comes from knowing that they are regarded highly than they would be if they had the same salary and benefits but not esteem. This is unfortunate because situations in which salaries cannot be increased represent excellent opportunities for a manager to show that he or she is doing the best that can be done with respect to income.

6. Finally, there is the $64,000 question: "How do I know that the effort and work I put into providing recognition will bring

beneficial results? After all, the happy crew is not necessarily the productive one. Don't I lose some control if I go for such a 'positive feedback program'?"

When some or all of these reasons combine with natural inertia and possibly with some lack of awareness of how much positive impulses can contribute to motivation, the result is apathy toward improvement in the way social and esteem needs are met.

One last word on the subject of obstacles: A program to provide greater job satisfaction must have its goals in proper order of priority—the satisfaction of social and esteem needs will not bring increased motivation overnight. If a program is started with the expectation that people will quickly respond with greater effort, then both long-run benefits and short-run hopes are likely to be frustrated. Employees quickly sense any manipulative attempt to influence them towards greater effort and output.

STARTING A POSITIVE FEEDBACK PROGRAM

Analyzing the Individual's and the Organization's Needs and Tasks

Despite the obstacles discussed above, a manager or supervisor at any organizational level can start a positive feedback program. There is only one requirement—a commitment. In the beginning, while foundations are being created, this commitment certainly demands considerable thought and some additional work. Once a manager has mastered the proper skills, however, and developed them into habits, then the maintenance and expansion of a positive, supportive atmosphere become part of the manager's style. Far from demanding extra effort, new skills make the manager more effective and are likely to reduce job pressures.

The most difficult part of a recognition program is its development. In searching for the positive impulses that support a recognition program, there are two things at which a manager should look, the job and its environment and the job holder.

Developing a Continuing Program

Impulses which come from the manager's personal behavior are only part of a short-run strategy. As such, they are a little like the medications which attack symptoms. Temporarily they achieve the same effect as a cure. But, for the long term, their primary benefit lies in the fact that they buy time, time in which long-run strategies can start to work.

Positive impulses raise the level of satisfaction for an employee and thus develop a sound foundation for "open" communications. This openness can bring several benefits:

- It can lead to more suggestions on how the work can be improved.

- It can give more information to the manager about the aspirations of individual employees and thus help in assigning more satisfying work.
- It can help identify ways in which jobs, procedures, and policies can be improved.
- It can help the manager diagnose capabilities of the team with greater accuracy so deficiencies can be corrected more easily and so that more information is available for selection of additional staff members.

Just as the benefit of a plan lies in the process of planning and not in the piece of paper that ultimately emerges, so the value in a continuing program lies in the better understanding that gradually develops between manager and managed. If recognition, praise, and commendation or even more tangible awards are seen as the objective of the program and the effort ends there, then they quickly become routine and insignificant. They are accepted simply as the friendly gestures which they are. They will certainly be appreciated as breaks in the discouraging wall of silence and negative feedback. But they quickly lose the little impact on the psychological climate which they can have because they seem out-of-place when they are not adequately based on sound, supportive relationships. If a manager sees these actions as steps toward fuller use of the talents of the team members, then the level of job satisfaction can improve and thus raise the desire to achieve.

Program continuity is essential, however, and it depends upon variety. Without use of a wide range of media to compliment the employee the well quickly runs dry. The manager must resort to repeating something that has been said or done in the recent past and the manager as well as the person receiving the positive impulse perceive it as either a little embarrassing or mechanistic. Without variety, commendations quickly turn into empty gestures. It is essential, therefore, that the program have variety if it is to progress steadily toward its objectives.

There are many ways to develop variety, but it is probably best to regularly set aside a few specific moments for planning where and how positive feedback can be provided to members of the staff. Praise can be given in any number of ways. Some managers review each of their employees every week to find a basis for positive impulses. Some even carry notes of their thoughts on the subject with them. Other managers reward for one group of activities at a time. Of course, in addition, they watch for instances of achievement that can be commended at the time they occur. All attempts to achieve continuity have one feature in common: They contain some activity which will assure that the program receives specific attention on a regular, frequent basis.

A word of caution is in order. Before managers become aware of the full range of activities for which they can supply recognition, they rely heavily on the more commonplace, nonwork-related items such as complimenting employees on their dress, their manners, and so forth. There are even many managers who believe that this is a way to supply positive impulses. This is largely an illusion. The employees may sense the manager's desire to be friendly, but since his or her remarks are unrelated to work, they are misdirected. Friendly gestures rarely, if ever, have an impact on the desire to achieve or on performance, except possibly in an emergency when the friendly managers can call on a store of good will.

A serious misunderstanding is possible here. Creating a warm atmosphere in which people will respond favorably in crisis situations because they "like" the manager or "like" the organization for which they work is far different from creating an environment in which internal generators are developed that make people strive, without external stimulation, for better performance. Real motivation needs more, much more, than a friendly approach.

Managers who embark on a program of providing recognition should attempt to gain the support of any supervisors or managers who report to them, and in turn support them, so these will gradually develop their own recognition programs. For most managers it is easier when a small group jointly embarks on a program, even though it requires some additional expenditure of time for sharing information and ideas. The additional time is generally outweighed by the benefits of mutual support that come from such joint activity.

Since continuity depends so heavily on variety, it is not only necessary to use all media and forms which are currently acceptable in the environment but also to take steps which will assure favorable reception for all others. There obviously is a problem here. People clearly seek recognition, but the forms and the media which have been used by most organizations have been inadequate to satisfy this need. Instead they often have contributed to the impression that the organization is not really interested in the psychological needs of its employees. There is considerable evidence that people respond very favorably to commendations and to awards when they feel that these are deserved and are given sincerely, with no ulterior motives.

In some organizations, for example, it would be rather difficult to give certificates or the like for performance. In all probability, these would raise eyebrows and possibly be received with cynical remarks. Yet trophies and plaques for minor accomplishments in bowling, golfing, or baseball are displayed proudly. There is a contradiction here that is striking: signs of recognition for achievement at work are often hidden or visible only in the study or private room, while those for performance in sports and other social activities are in the office or on the mantlepiece. All this is symptomatic of the climate that has been created by insincere and carelessly given awards in the past.

Obviously, the failure of management to develop comprehensive recognition programs has greatly contributed to the mixed feelings which recognition awards bring. Instead of developing a climate of appropriate recognition, many organizations attempt to use the yearning of employees for sincere appreciation to patch up some operation problem. For example, several employees may receive awards for good work during one brief time period because management is at the moment supporting the organization's "quality awareness program." In general, such awards are not likely to help create a positive atmosphere for recognition, particularly if the program is dropped a year later. Unfortunately, whenever there is a problem for which employee cooperation is needed, many organizations set up a program to resolve it; and when the problem has been solved, the program is quickly forgotten.

Selection criteria and standards also have helped to lower the esteem in which recognition awards are held. When there are only very few awards, the feeling of favoritism is widespread; at the other extreme, some companies have hurt the working environment by giving out awards too lavishly. Still others have done damage by taking themselves too seriously when presenting awards; the ceremonies are elaborate, the speeches flowery, and the occasions are rare—no wonder employees are not "turned on."

All in all, the approach which most organizations take to giving recognition is not only haphazard but also ill-coordinated and poorly planned. The result is that employees are apathetic and frequently cynical when an organization launches a recognition program. The solution to this apparent dilemma is not an easy one. It takes patience and perseverance and an understanding of all the sources, media, and forms that can be applied to help with the task.

BALANCING RECOGNITION OF SMALL AND LARGE CONTRIBUTORS

Recognition is usually given to outstanding contributors, but those employees whose contributions are average rather than exceptional also need recognition if they are to find the highest level of work motivation of which they are capable. Most managers find it fairly easy to commend exceptional employees and to send positive impulses their way. They may not recognize, however, that the real climate within a unit is created not by the few outstanding employees who are already highly motivated, but by the average or slightly below average employees who are even more in need of positive impulses to increase their desire to achieve and to excel. And since these employees are much more numerous than the outstanding ones, the task of giving them an adequate number of positive impulses in appropriate forms is extremely important even though it is often fairly difficult. Since average employees rarely contribute anything that is outstanding or attracts attention, considerable thought is required to sort out media that can be appropriately applied and to find ways to send positive impulses frequently enough to achieve the desired impact.

Another complication lies in the fact that many forms of media are not appropriate in most organizational climates. Given the need for positive impulses to be tailored to the individual employee's personality, a medium must be able to carry a variety of different messages well:

- To the ambitious employee, it should say, "We achieved what we did because *you* were with us and because you helped show the way."
- To the socially conscious, it should say, "We achieved what we did because we are such an excellent group, and your being here helps to make this group what it is."
- To the security oriented, it should signal that they are indeed secure and they can look forward to considerable stability.
- To the meek, submissive, and fearful it should say that they are doing fine; they merely need to continue the way they are going and they will be all right.

It is important to remember that in order to create a climate in which *most media* will be accepted by employees, it is necessary that *all* employees receive regular positive feedback so that their negative impulses are adequately balanced with the positive ones. The sincerity and variety of media are important. Without sincerity and adequate variety, any recognition program appears mechanistic, superficial, even false.

At the risk of being repetitious it should be stressed again that positive impulses are not intended to supplant negative feedback or corrective information which must be given to an employee in order to avert a specific problem in the future. Probably the most difficult task in supplying positive impulses to the average or below-average employee is the selection of activities and attributes for which recognition can be provided. This requires careful thought and discussion. Brainstorming can be used where joint lists are prepared from which each manager can draw ideas that fit his or her own style and which can be used comfortably and naturally.

PROVIDING RECOGNITION

Recognizing Opportunities

A manager who seriously wishes to increase the frequency and forms of positive feedback must develop the ability to recognize when and how positive impulses can be given. This is not easy, especially when most impulses are to be provided for less than outstanding or exceptional performance.

A manager's awareness of activities suitable for recognition improves with practice. Managers can train themselves in many ways to become more perceptive in recognizing opportunities, but one of the most effective ways is to concentrate on one type of activity at a time. For example, a manager could observe two or three staff members when they work with others, when they speak to others, when they prepare work for their subordinates, when they respond to instructions, when they make friendly remarks, etc. Observing a limited number of such activities will help a manager sharpen perceptiveness. The more limited the study of an activity, the more detailed the manager's observation can be and the greater the gain in enhanced awareness. In fact, a manager may discover much about subordinates that may otherwise escape his or her attention, things that may open up communications and ultimately result in an improved working relationship and more effective work.

Developing Good Habits

Habits spring naturally from routines. Just as compulsive smoking starts with voluntary smoking of a few cigarettes a day, so do desirable habits such as gaining control of food intake or doing daily exercises begin with the discipline of regular, daily performance. After a period of time, the body or the mind somehow "accepts" the activity as a necessary part of life and soon it takes little or no effort at all.

The same is true of providing recognition. Less effort is required as opportunities are recognized more readily and as the manager acquires better command over a wide variety of media and forms. The experienced speaker knows many anecdotes and stories which can be used to enliven a talk; the successful salesman has good "openers" and convincing responses to common objections which seem to come without effort; and the experienced interviewer knows what questions to ask without having to give them a great deal of thought. Similarly, the manager who is skilled in providing recognition has strong habits which stem from regular attention. To further strengthen routines, such a manager is likely to review once a week what has been done during the preceding week so no one has been overlooked and so that a wide range of media and sources has been used.

Appropriate habits are the key to continuity and to the gradual expansion of media. The manager who develops the three habits of (a) reviewing employee performance, (b) searching for additional media and forms of recognition and, (c) reviewing his or her own progress will succeed in continuously improving the climate which forms the basis of real motivation.

An Example of One Form of Recognition

Some media are used extensively by managers; others are rarely if ever used and have been abandoned in some organizations as unworkable. For example, pins, certificates, plaques, trophies, and other tangible evidence of work-related recognition which carry no significant monetary value are not in wide use. An important reason for the failure to take advantage of these devices possibly is the memory of misuse in the past. Another reason is management's lack of understanding of how these media can be used creatively so that they will spur the desire for achievement. Take certificates, for instance. Many organizations have certificates which are not viewed favorably by employees. The climate is such that employees do not display any they have received—they possibly even discard them. Thus, in many organizations, certificates are not awarded because management believes that employees would not value them.

Since certificates are a major medium for recognition, establishing their social acceptability is highly desirable. A plan to gain full acceptance of certificates is likely to be successful, however, only if it does not stand by itself. A manager who shows people in many ways that their efforts are appreciated is not likely to encounter any difficulties. Certificates awarded in a positive environment are cherished by recipients. Social obstacles and concern about the views of others are problems for the recipient of a certificate only when awards are perceived as insincere, mere "window dressing" by a manager indifferent to the needs of employees.

If the attitude toward certificates is one of apathy or if cynicism is likely, the introduction of certificates requires a gradual, carefully planned approach. First of all, certificates should not be given until employees are clearly aware that more people are being recognized for their work and that more forms of recognition are being used. Once the decision has been made to use certificates, then employees, or at least supervisors and group leaders, should be involved as much as possible in the selection of activities for which the awards will be given. It is, of course, essential that everyone be aware that certificates will not only be given to the *most* deserving employees but also to others who have contributed their best efforts, even if these efforts did not result in spectacular achievements. All those administering the program should be aware that the purpose of the certificates is to express the organization's and the manager's appreciation for reliable as well as for superior performance.

Any new certificate award program should be light-hearted and informal. It should mix serious topics with a large portion of humorous ones. The environment for the presentation, however, should not be too casual; and, as much as possible, managers from higher eche-lons in the organization should be present at awards. It is advisable to explain that certificates will be presented at *regular* intervals. The in-terval should be fairly long, however, to avoid debasing the value of the awards. A very small number of certificates may be presented quarterly, or a slightly larger number semiannually. No person should receive more than one award, or at most two, in any year, and 10 to 25 percent of the people should receive something each year.

Appendix D

The Effective Organization:
Morale vs. Discipline*

Today, radical; tomorrow, taken for granted. On a modest scale, that truism may apply to the hypothesis presented here—an approach to organizational effectiveness that, at least on first view, appears to be at considerable variance with popular theories on the development of organizations. Some of the conclusions on which the hypothesis is based have gradually emerged during discussions with managers in many seminars, but much work still needs to be done to corroborate and refine them, and many changes will undoubtedly be made before a definitive new theory will take clear shape. There are, however, strong indications that these investigations will lead to significant insights and new guidelines for managerial decisions.

Since much of the validity of the concepts involved hinges on clear definitions of the terms discipline, morale, and productivity, their meanings should be reviewed:

Discipline. It is, of course, not very fashionable these days to speak of discipline. To many people the word conjures up visions of overly tight controls, even of harsh punishment for those who do not abide by the rules of an authority that sometimes, or even frequently, trespasses on the rights of the individual. It is therefore somewhat perilous to use it when describing a complex system of leadership patterns, even if such a system fully endorses job-enrichment concepts, appropriate and extensive participation in decision making, and other sound behavioral science principles. The problem exists even if the system's goal is improved perception of the organizational climate, coupled with sound judgment in implementing constructive policies that will lead to greater accomplishment as well as to enhanced personal satisfactions.

Still, no other word so aptly describes the necessary range of meanings: voluntary commitment to organizational goals, voluntary subordination of personal interests, enforced adherence to rules, and a close relationship to morale.

*Erwin Rausch. *The Effective Organization: Morale vs. Discipline*, MANAGEMENT REVIEW, June 1971. Copyright © 1971 by the American Management, Inc. Reprinted by permission.

It is for these reasons that "discipline" is used here to describe an atmosphere in which there is substantial adherence to the rules of the organization or a strong commitment to them. This acceptance of the environment and of the organization's goals and objectives can stem from a personal, self-generated willingness to oblige, implying a recognition by individuals that their self-interest is thus furthered, or it can stem from the knowledge that adherence to rules is a requirement for sustained and successful membership in the organization.

The other meaning of the word discipline, which imparts some feeling of undesirable restrictions, or even punishment, implies that one cannot discipline oneself or someone else without creating a measure of unpleasantness. The reader is asked to ignore this negative connotation, and instead to go along with the general view of an organization with good discipline, as one that can muster its resources more effectively toward the accomplishment of its goals than one with less of this quality.

Morale. This word describes a general feeling of satisfaction, an atmosphere in which people are in harmony with their surroundings and pleased to be a part of the organization.

Productivity is used here in the broad sense of competent, well-organized effort directed toward the organization's goals. A highly productive organization or organizational unit is one that performs as effectively as possible within the constraints that the environment or higher echelons impose upon it. It need not forge rapidly ahead to be considered productive; indeed, under difficult circumstances it can be considered productive if it fights a valiant or even losing battle.

A MORALE-DISCIPLINE CONTINUUM

Before detailed examination of the model that is the basis of the hypothesis, a brief description is in order. The diagram [in Figure D.1], the morale-discipline continuum (MDC), depicts all combinations of discipline and morale for a specific organizational unit. The area within the parallelograms represents mixtures that allow the unit to function. Shaded areas I and II represent serious deficiencies in morale or discipline. In the first, morale is so low that the unit cannot exist, even for a very limited period of time. In the second shaded area, on the other hand, there is so little discipline that the people in the organization are unable to cooperate on the necessary tasks.

In any unit, the morale-discipline mix of the moment is influenced by many internal factors, such as the atmosphere of the larger organization of which the unit is a part, the quality of leadership in the unit, the attitudes of its members, and the ability of the unit's members to handle their tasks effectively. Where the organization finds itself at any particular time, with respect to its MDC, depends not only on these internal factors but also on favorable or unfavorable external conditions or events.

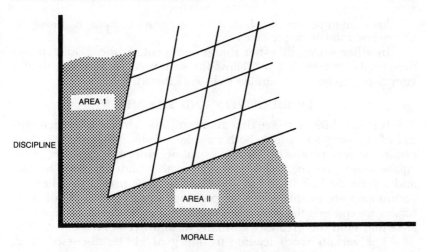

Figure D.1. The Morale-Discipline Continuum

It should be noted that with the horizontal and vertical axes respectively representing morale and discipline, the shape, location, and angles of the parallelogram graphically depict the fact that an organization, if it has any morale at all, must contain a certain amount of discipline, and that higher levels of morale carry with them at least some additional discipline. Similarly, in an organizational unit with even the smallest measure of discipline, some morale exists, and increases in discipline bring at least some small amount of morale.

It is interesting to speculate about the probable sources of discipline. It is highly probable that the further to the left an organization finds itself, the more likely it is that the largest share of the existing discipline is imposed by authority, while toward the right, much more is likely to be self-motivated. Higher morale, in other words, is consistent only with greater measure of personally generated discipline. At the same time, however, higher levels of morale can be achieved only with increasing influence of authority. The ideal situation would be represented by a point in the upper right corner, which represents the best possible combination of externally imposed and internally contributed subordination of personal interests and preferences.

One more concept that should be discussed as a preliminary concerns an aspect of decision making that is fundamental to any conclusion that can possibly be drawn from MDC—the reversibility principle. This principle may be stated, in general terms, as follows:

If a choice is to be made from two or more alternatives and if it is impossible, with the existing available information, to determine which one is preferable with respect to the facts of the situation and the intangibles that need to be considered, then the alternative that can most easily be reversed should be preferred.

In other words, all other things being equal, one should choose the specific course that will allow for easiest correction if it should later prove to be less desirable than anticipated.

PRODUCTIVITY AND THE MDC

It is not difficult to see that an organization in the lower-left corner of the diagram, where both morale and discipline are very low, cannot be very productive or successful, if, indeed, it can exist at all. At the other extreme, the organization with a high degree of morale and a great deal of discipline is likely to be most productive. Few organizations are in this fortunate position, so the questions for most managers concern the daily decisions and the choice of management style that hold the greatest possibility of improvement.

The various roads leading to that goal will be discussed later; first, the other areas in the MDC and their implications for productivity should be considered. An organization in the lower-right corner of the parallelogram is, by definition, one with very high morale but with a minimum amount of discipline. The diverse interests of its members pose a constant threat to the organization, and stability is difficult to achieve. Initially, morale can be very high as a result of an outstanding goal, uniting the group in commitment to it, but this is not likely to last very long, as differences in personal needs and opinions about direction begin to create dissension.

With little discipline, it is quite difficult for an organization to harness and direct the resources of its members toward a common goal. Furthermore, since the small amount of discipline that the high morale level induces is based almost exclusively on willingness to subordinate individual preferences, the organization is in jeopardy when various courses of action are under consideration. The decision-making process is extremely complex, requiring consideration of many opinions, and often frustrating to the individual because majority opinions usually dominate, or less-than-optimum choices are made in politically necessary compromises. These solutions may mean strong dissatisfactions among individuals, which combine to reduce the morale of the whole organizational unit. As a result, it cannot sustain its lower-right corner position very long. It must either accept more central direction to increase discipline, or slip further to the left, where it becomes increasingly less productive.

On the other hand, the high discipline-low morale organization in the upper-left corner of the continuum can be very productive, particularly during periods of stress. Its achievements can even temporarily exceed those of the organization with strong morale and discipline. However, it, too, is quite unstable, since it depends almost exclusively on the strength and technical competence of its leadership. Unless held together by its effectiveness in coping with an emergency, it will have very high turnover, taxing the ability of the strongest leader to see that all the rules are adhered to.

Discipline under these conditions must often be maintained by punitive measures, and this leads to desertions; the more competent members leave first and their loss reduces productivity, resulting in increased demands by the leadership on those who remain. This, in turn, brings opposition and leads to polarization. Inevitably, the organizational unit must then adopt policies designed to improve morale, even at the expense of productivity and effectiveness, or slip down toward lower discipline without compensating increases in morale.

Notwithstanding all these difficulties, however, the upper-left positions in the MDC are generally more productive than those in the lower-right areas.

EFFECT OF REVERSIBILITY

It is probably safe to assume that all managers are attempting to pursue strategies that lead toward the upper-right corner area of the MDC. In the case of most decisions, however, it is not possible to assess accurately whether the particular alternative will point straight for this target or will deviate from it either up or down. It is even quite likely that none of the possible options are exactly on course. For instance, in [Figure D.2] below, alternative C (or decision vector C) points roughly in the most desirable direction. Still, as a rule, in both routine decisions and the more important and more carefully ana-

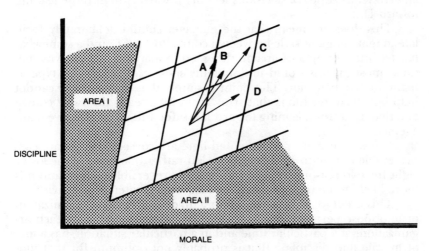

Figure D.2. The Morale-Discipline Continuum–Decision Vectors

lyzed ones, the manager cannot be sure whether that is indeed vector C and not vector B or even A or D that is more accurately on course.

Here is an example: Operator Smith asks permission to take some time off in the afternoon for personal reasons. Because of the situation at that particular time a very friendly denial of the request, coupled with a detailed explanation of why the refusal is necessary, may be closer to vector C than granting the request and pointing out that such privileges can be approved only if they are made very rarely. Yet, at another time, in the same circumstances, the second alternative might be more appropriate.

Sometimes it is quite apparent that one is preferable but often both appear to be equally desirable or undesirable; actually, no matter how well-balanced they may seem, one is more likely to lead to improvement in performance of the organizational unit than the other.

Applying the reversibility principle may show the difference fairly clearly. Most managers will agree that if they were to change their style for a limited period of time toward slightly tighter discipline, by granting fewer privileges or by asking for stricter observance of rules, some dissatisfaction among subordinates would result. Whether it is deliberate or unintentional, such a change in the "normal" behavior of the manager would not go unnoticed, but the members of the organization would probably think little of it if the manager soon resumed the usual leadership pattern. When the situation is reversed, the reaction is different. Privileges once granted to an employee are very difficult to cancel. If a manager drifts into looser patterns, it is not easy to return to the previous, more restrictive style.

The implication then is that it would generally be easier to correct an erroneous series of decisions leading toward A than those leading toward D.

This does not mean that the manager should deliberately vacillate in management style between a course toward C and a somewhat harder line during a campaign designed to increase productivity, because most groups would undoubtedly sense and resent this type of manipulative behavior. The point is simply that the manager cannot help but make decisions that stray from the ideally desirable course and that, therefore, leaning toward B is safer and more effective management.

If the basic concepts presented here are correct, then, it appears preferable to lean toward the upper left rather than toward the lower right for two reasons. It is the more easily reversible course, and it is more likely to be the approach that leads to greater productivity.

This is not to advocate tightening up discipline in an organization or to oppose permissiveness per se. The point is simply that each organization, at a particular time and in a particular situation, has a mix of morale and discipline that is probably not optimum for that moment. The organization that can develop its people in such a way that they can recognize more clearly what this mix is and help them improve it throughout the changing situation will, in the long run, be healthier for it.

A word of caution: Keep in mind that there is a subtle line between a gradual but deliberate attempt to manipulate an organization into a tighter discipline pattern to force increased output and a sincere policy of searching for the optimum mix of morale and discipline—the point at which the overwhelming portion of commitment to the organization's goals is voluntarily contributed.

IMPLICATIONS OF MDC

Effective motivation requires the leader of an organization unit to maintain a delicate balance of appropriate management styles for the variety of situations that must be faced. It could be highly unrewarding to train supervisors or managers in the application of the MDC unless they have first proven themselves capable of sensing changes in climate of their organizational units and applying appropriately participative styles to the varying demands of different situations.

As the various aspects of the MDC hypothesis are tested in the field, the findings will shed more light on the effects of changes in management style in any direction, but particularly with respect to insistence on reasonable rules that have been mutually arrived at or that were authoritatively imposed. Managers recognize, of course, that they should strive to increase not only awareness of their own styles at the moment but also their knowledge of the impact of all their decisions on the *direction* in which they are moving, especially with respect to the effect on esprit de corps. In the final analysis an accurate sense of direction is even more important than a clear view of the realities of the moment. As a guide to action, to the daily decisions a manager must make, perception of the nuances of the MDC should prove to be most useful.

Index

About the Author

Erwin Rausch is President of Didactic Systems, Inc., Cranford, New Jersey, a management training and development firm which distributes the widely used *Catalog of Ideas for Action Oriented Training/Communicating*. Before starting his own firm, he served for almost 20 years as Vice President of the Wing Company, a division of Aero-Flow Dynamics, Inc., and as Director of Manufacturing for the Bogen-Presto Division of Lear Siegler Corporation.

Mr. Rausch is originator of the didactic simulation/game technique; editor of the text *Management in the Fire Service*, which applies his views on human resource management to fire departments; and co-author of numerous training materials, including the series *Handling Conflict in Management*, over 50,000 copies of which have been used. For 15 years, he has taught evening undergraduate and graduate courses at Rutgers University, Kean College of New Jersey, and Fairleigh Dickinson.

He is a panel member of the American Arbitration Association, and has been a member of the American Management Association's Manufacturing Planning Council and its Advisory Committee for Education and Training Conferences. He holds a B.M.E. from Cooper Union, an M.S.I.E. from Columbia University, and an M.A. from New York University.

Date Due

M.